YOU MIGHT BE FROM BRITISH COLUMBIA IF...

Dan Murphy

MacIntyre Purcell Publishing Inc.
194 Hospital Rd.
Lunenburg, Nova Scotia
B0J 2C0
(902) 640-3350

www.macintyrepurcell.com
info@macintyrepurcell.com

Printed and bound in Canada by Marquis.

Design and layout: Channel Communications

Library and Archives Canada Cataloguing in Publication

Murphy, Dan, 1951-, author You might be from British Columbia if... / Daniel Murphy.

ISBN 978-1-927097-88-5 (pbk.)

1. British Columbia--Social life and customs--Caricatures and cartoons.
2. Canadian wit and humor, Pictorial. 3. Comic books, strips, etc. I. Title.

FC3811.3.M87 2015 971.1 C2015-903116-8

MacIntyre Purcell Publishing Inc. would like to acknowledge the financial support of the Government of Canada through Department of Canadian Heritage (Canada Book Fund) and the Nova Scotia Department of Tourism, Culture and Heritage.

FSC
www.fsc.org
MIX
Paper from responsible sources
FSC® C103567

FOREWORD

Every editorial cartoonist is familiar with a particular ritual. First, you get out a blank piece of paper and stare into the vellum void. Feeling a whiff of inspiration, you begin to blacken the paper with doodles. You then sit back and survey the results. Dissatisfied, you crumple it up into a ball and throw it at the wastebasket. Repeat until published.

In the effort to open a satirical Stargate in their Earthbound brainpans, the average working cartoonist can, in the space of an afternoon, whittle a stack of paper into an SPCA station's worth of cat-friendly playthings.

It's well known that Washington, Oregon, and California can fit into British Columbia with room to spare. The province would be even bigger If you could flatten out its mountainous topography. You could say B.C. is like an enormous crumpled paper retrieved from a wastebasket and half-heartedly flattened out, retaining its wrinkles and ridges. The Rockies over here, the Coast Mountains over there, Jimmy Pattison's Fortress of Solitude up there.

Some believe BC's immense scale, with all its boreal/temperate nooks and crannies, could conceal a viable breeding population of Sasquatches. But the place is plenty weird enough already without a resurgent Socred Party in the woods.

In any case, I can honestly say that after previewing the cartoons in this collection, I haven't come across a wrong note or a bad joke. Perhaps Dan Murphy whittled a Cathedral Grove's worth of paper into crumpled rejections in the process. Perhaps he rescued a few he initially doubted from the wastebasket; I haven't asked him. All I know, as a working editorial cartoonist, is that inspiration is a messy business, full of false starts, full stops, bathroom breaks, long walks, and discarded origami — even with a province as obligingly whacked as this one to work with.

Murphy's elegantly rendered whimsy, with its filagree of penwork, reminds of British writer G.K. Chesteron's explanation of how angels fly: "because they take themselves lightly."

I'm not saying the guy can perform a vertical takeoff and landing, or heal Nickelback. I'm just saying that to date no humourist has summed up this beautiful, baffling province with such an economy of line and wit, in one volume. If you catch every cryptic (and cryptid) reference in these cartoons, you will know for certain you are a true British Columbian, from your MEC-encased toes to your Lulelemon headband-branded 6th chakra.

— *Geoff Olson*

INTRODUCTION

Like a lot of people, I came to B.C. from somewhere else — and like some future upstanding citizens, my arrival was not overburdened with official sanction. One of my first jobs here, doing political cartoons for *The Western Voice*, introduced me to the politics of the province. And crewing for a military-vessel-turned-cruise-boat, ferrying hotshots, dignitaries, stags and salmon-obsessed Idaho plumbers from Indian Arm to Texada Island, gave me a sense of the province's beauty.

So I fast got an appreciation of B.C.'s astounding vistas, and its abounding rascals. This is a special, fascinating place — with a lot of kind, decent folks not averse to taking in a stray.

Thanks to Michael de Adder, Gerry Hummel, Roy Henry Vickers and Tofino's Eagle Aerie Gallery, the Musqueam First Nation, Chief Wayne Sparrow, Johnna Sparrow, Iran Seyed-Raeisy, Terry Hurdle, Terry Tang, James McNulty, Mordecai Briemberg, Frank and Jim Kouwenhoven, Chardon Labrie, John MacIntyre, Brent Mills, the Four Winds Brewing Company, Inez Cook, the Salmon n' Bannock Bistro, Geoff Olson, Pat Carney, Adrian Raeside, Brennan Robinson and Cait.

— Dan Murphy

YOU MIGHT BE FROM BRITISH COLUMBIA IF...

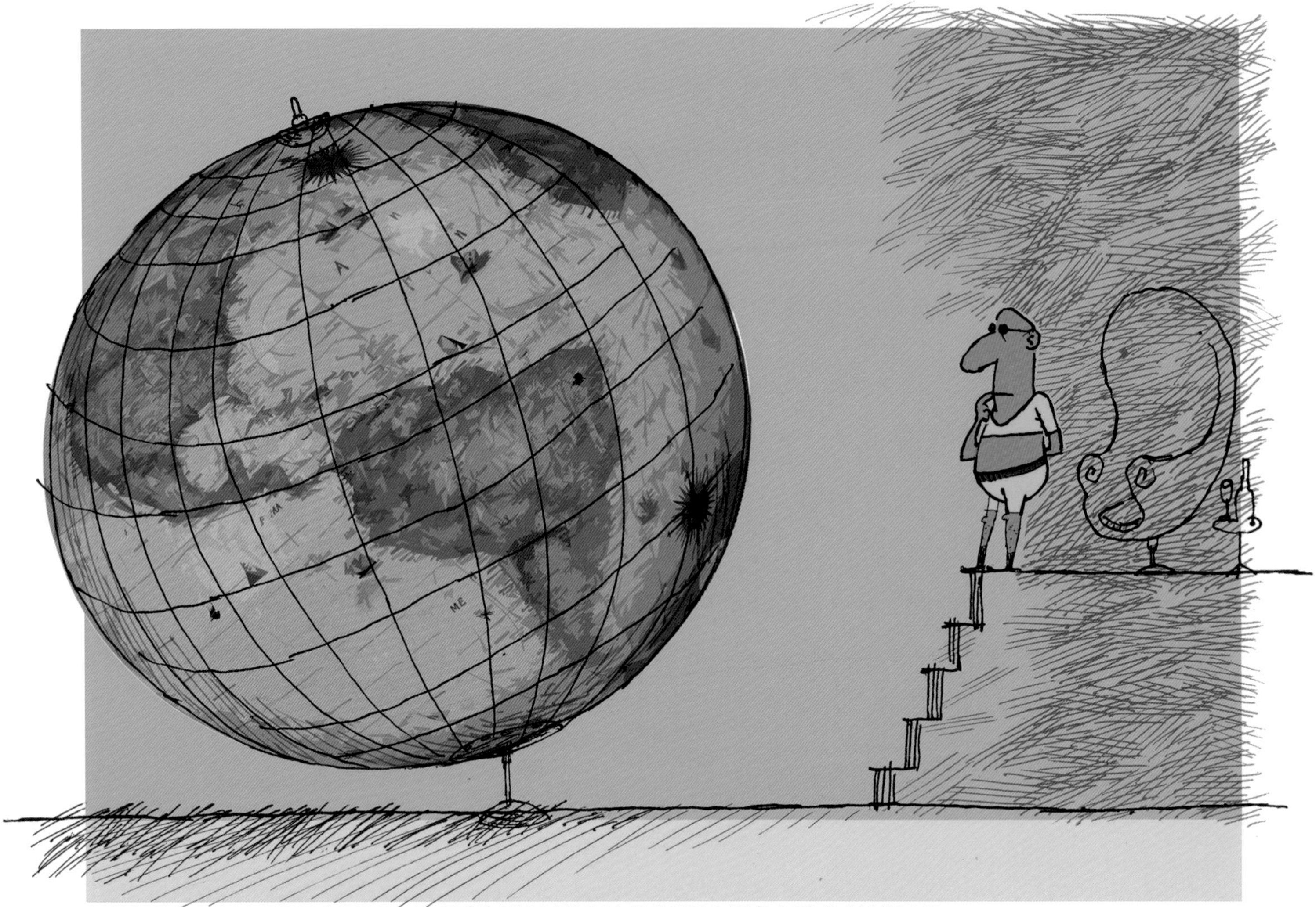

YOUR PLAN FOR WORLD DOMINATION INVOLVES YOGAWEAR

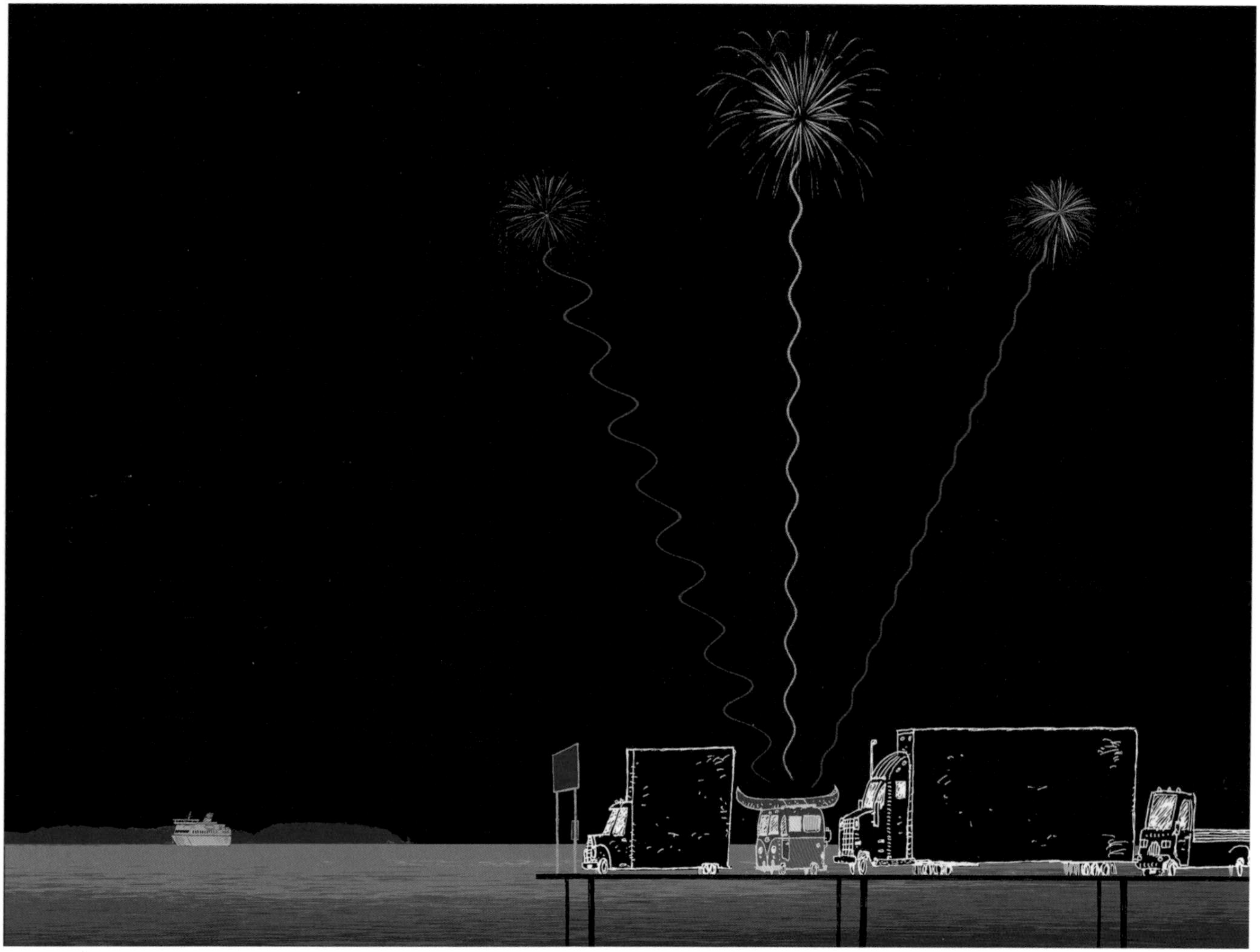

YOU WERE CONCEIVED DURING A THREE-SAILING WAIT

MICHAEL BUBLÉ WAS IN YOUR CHOIR

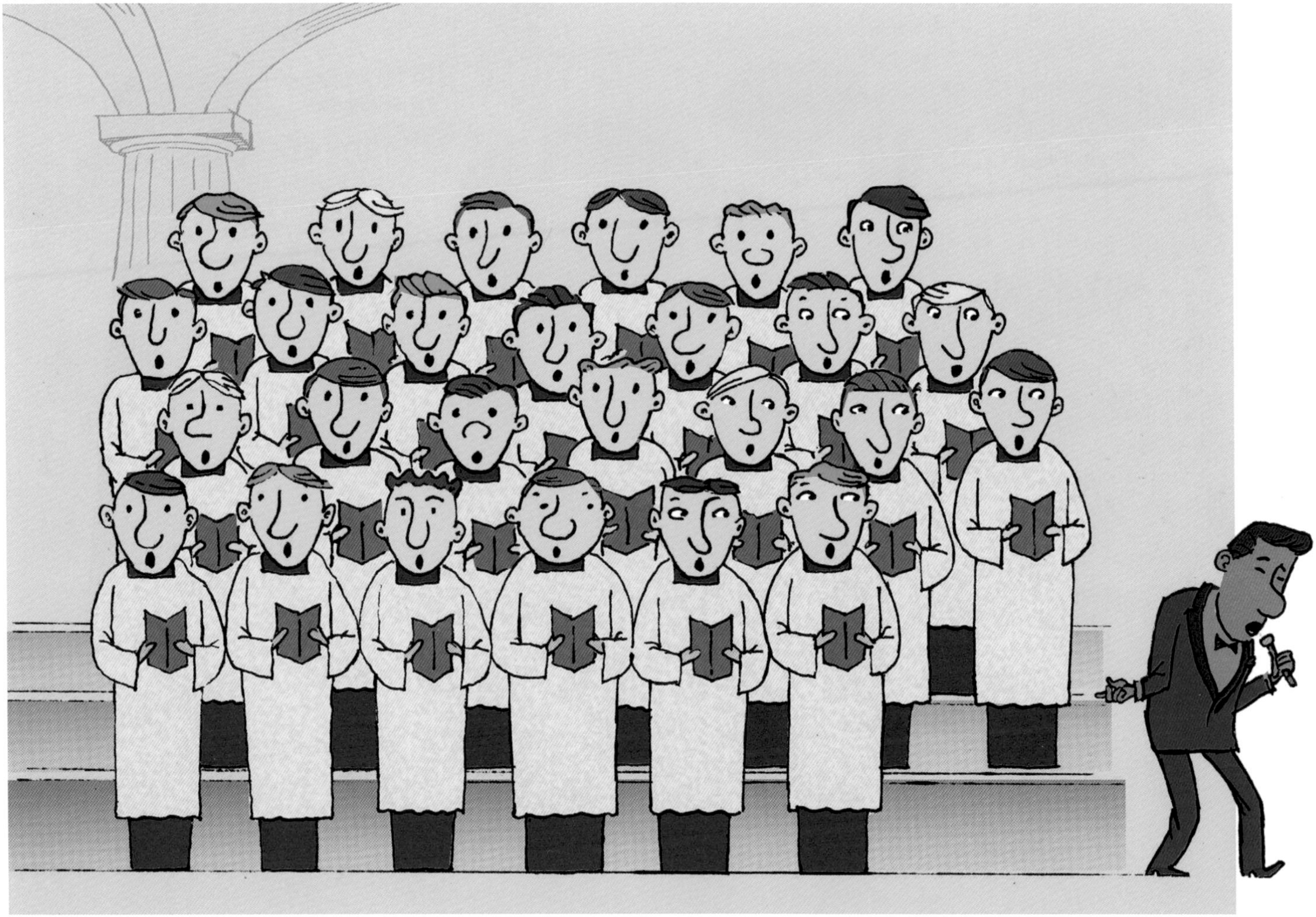

YOU HAVE OVER-INVESTED IN BURLS

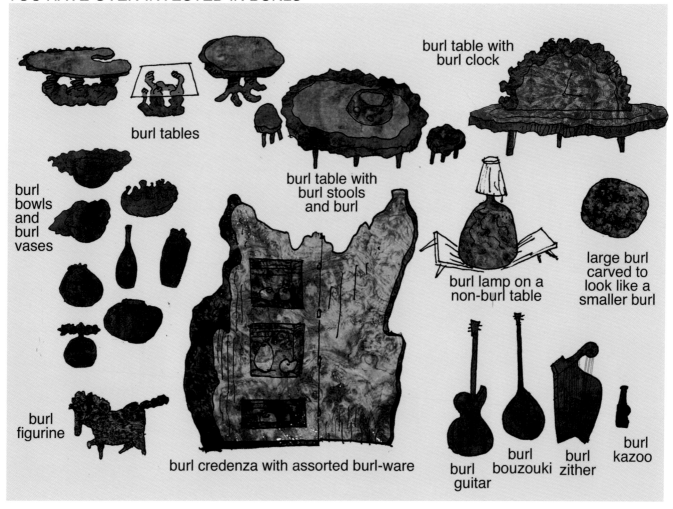

burl tables

burl table with burl clock

burl table with burl stools and burl

burl bowls and burl vases

large burl carved to look like a smaller burl

burl lamp on a non-burl table

burl figurine

burl credenza with assorted burl-ware

burl guitar

burl bouzouki

burl zither

burl kazoo

ONE OF YOUR NECK TATTOOS IS A NANAIMO BAR

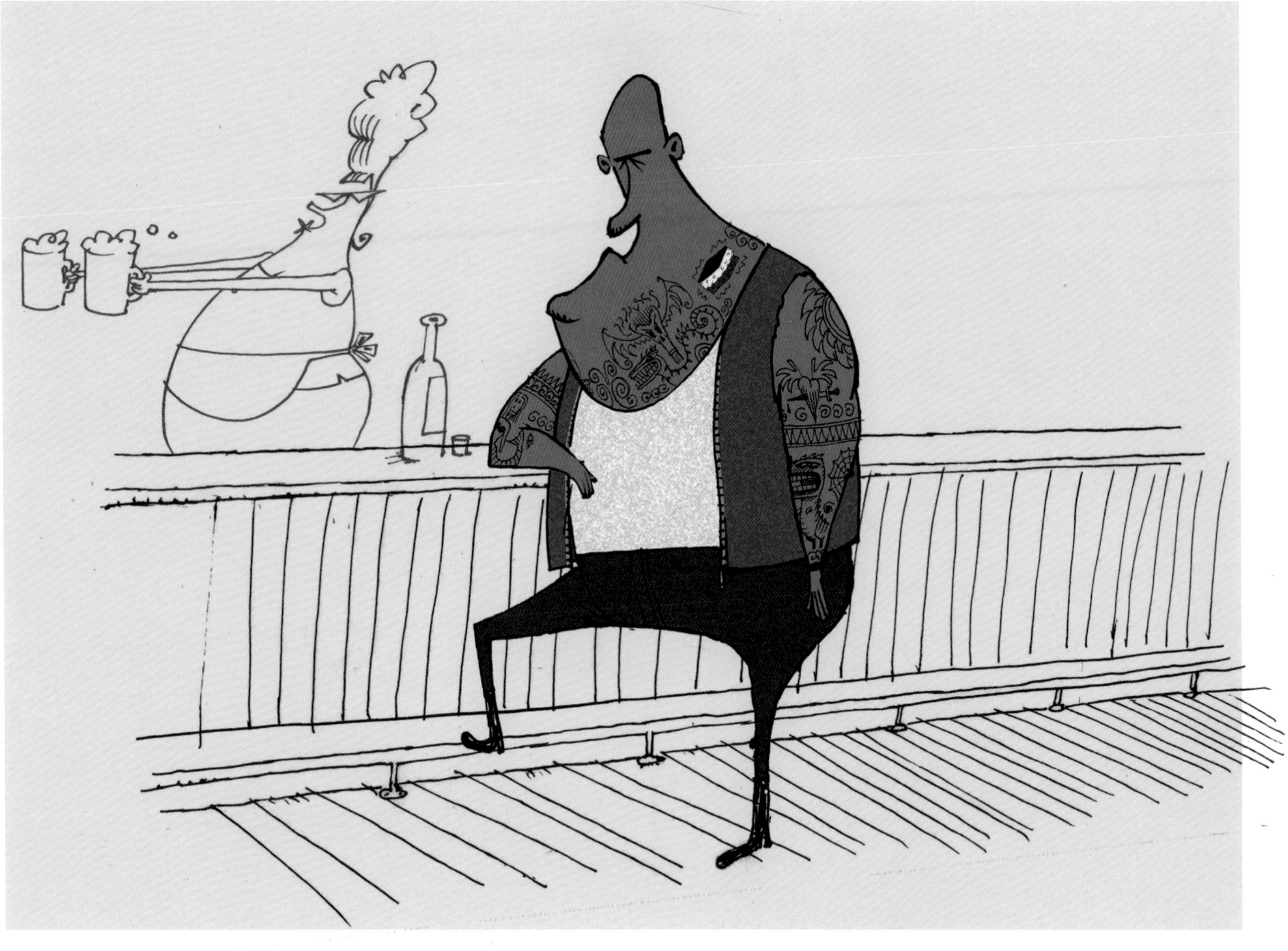

YOU BOUGHT THE BIKE TO WEAR THE OUTFIT

YOU'VE SET YOUR WATCH BY THE 9 O'CLOCK GUN

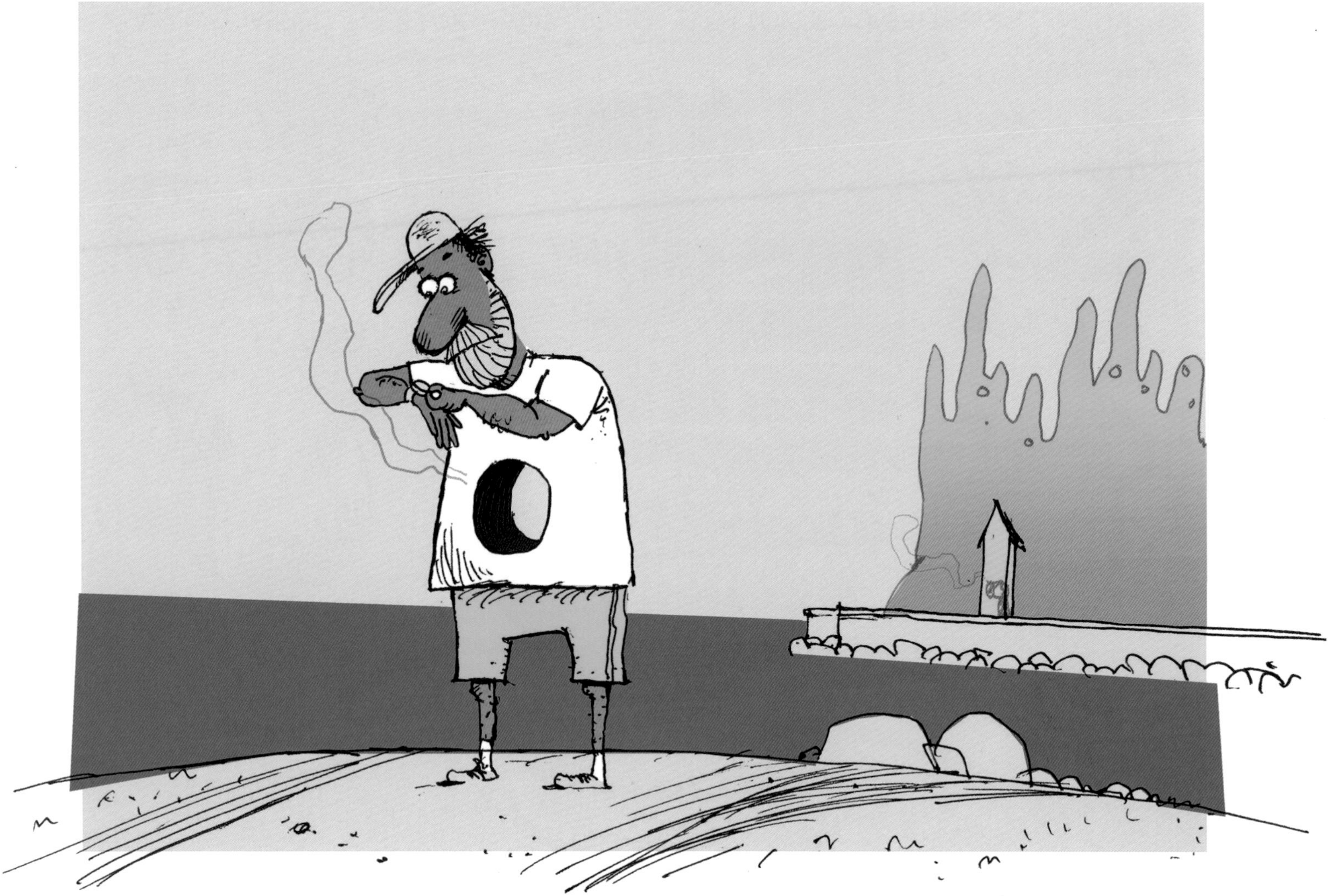

YOU KNOW THE PROVINCE'S MOTTO IS *"SPLENDOR WITHOUT DIMINISHMENT"*

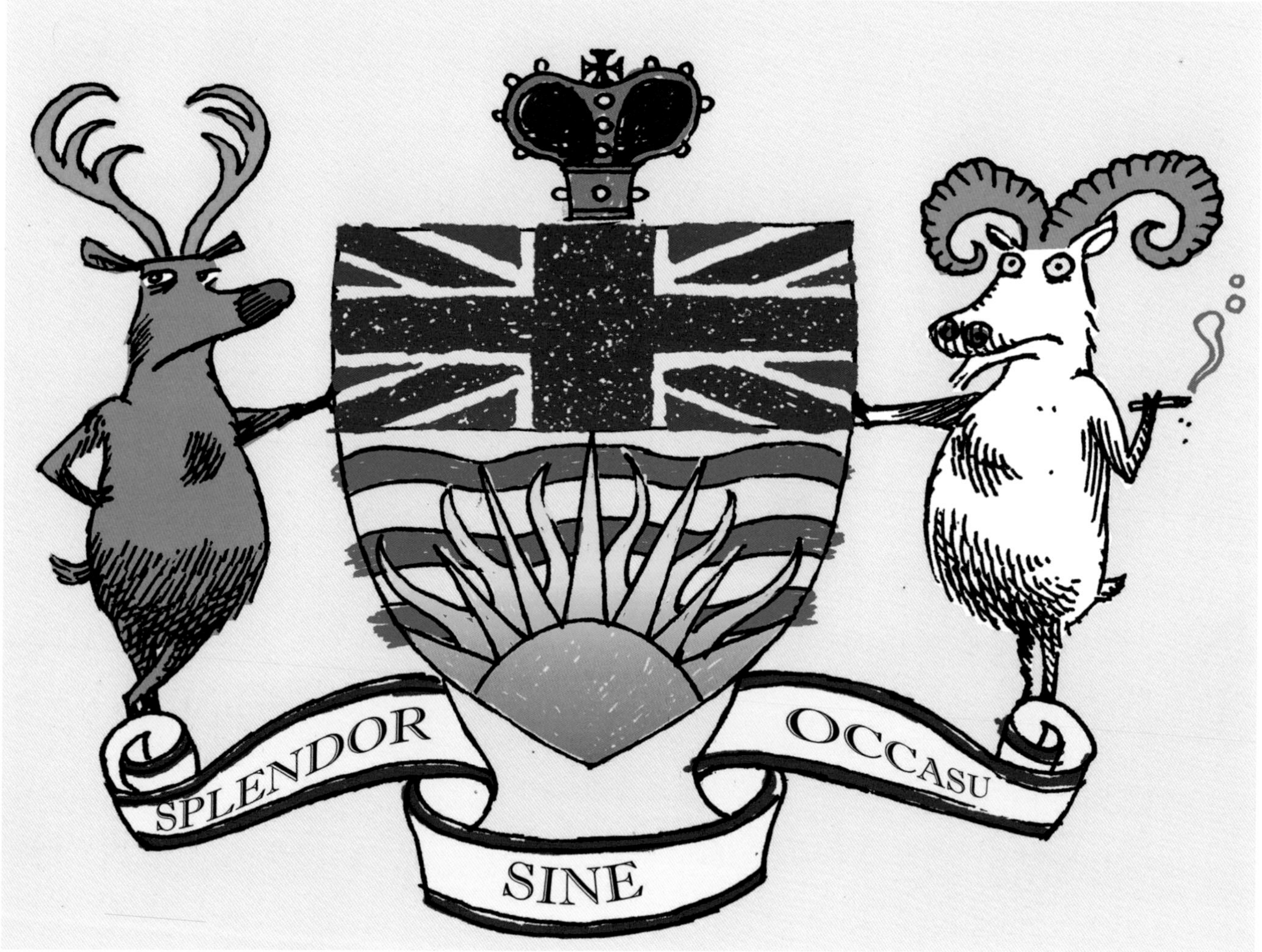
SPLENDOR
SINE
OCCASU

YOU ALSO KNOW SOME B.C. CITY MOTTOS

VANCOUVER

"SPLENDOR WITHOUT AFFORDABLE PARKING"

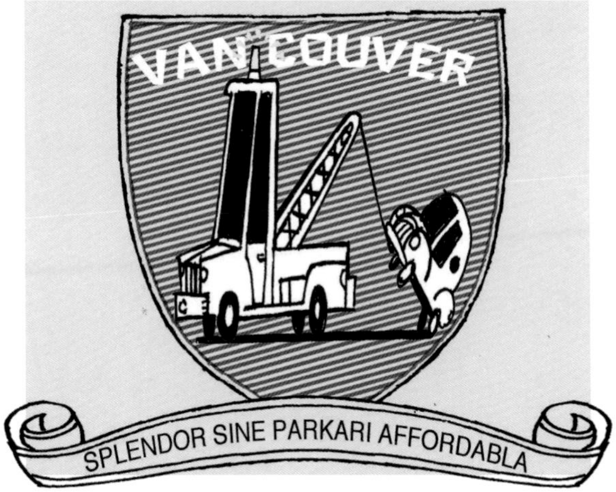
VANCOUVER
SPLENDOR SINE PARKARI AFFORDABLA

NELSON

"SPLENDOR WITHOUT THE HASSLE"

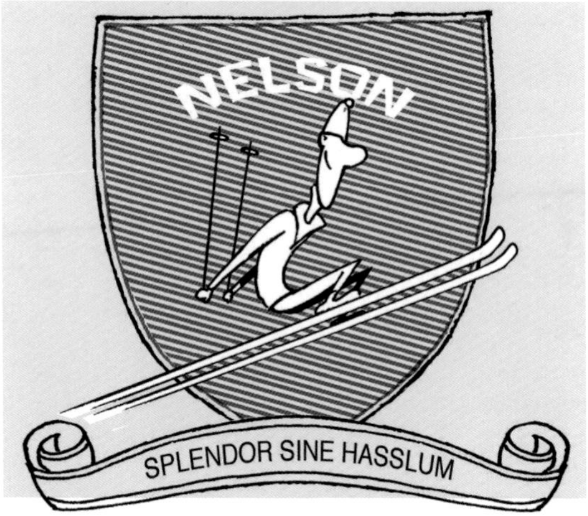
NELSON
SPLENDOR SINE HASSLUM

PRINCE RUPERT

"SPLENDOR AS SOON AS THE FOG CLEARS"

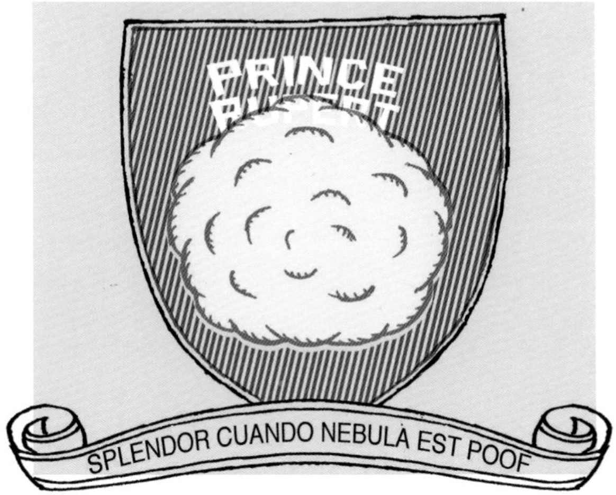
SPLENDOR CUANDO NEBULÀ EST POOF

WEST VANCOUVER

"NO SHOES, NO SHIRT -- NO SPLENDOR"

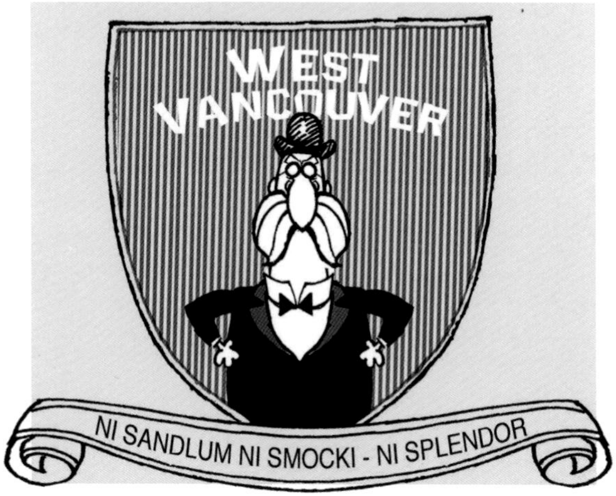
WEST VANCOUVER
NI SANDLUM NI SMOCKI - NI SPLENDOR

YOUR COFFEE DRINKS COFFEE

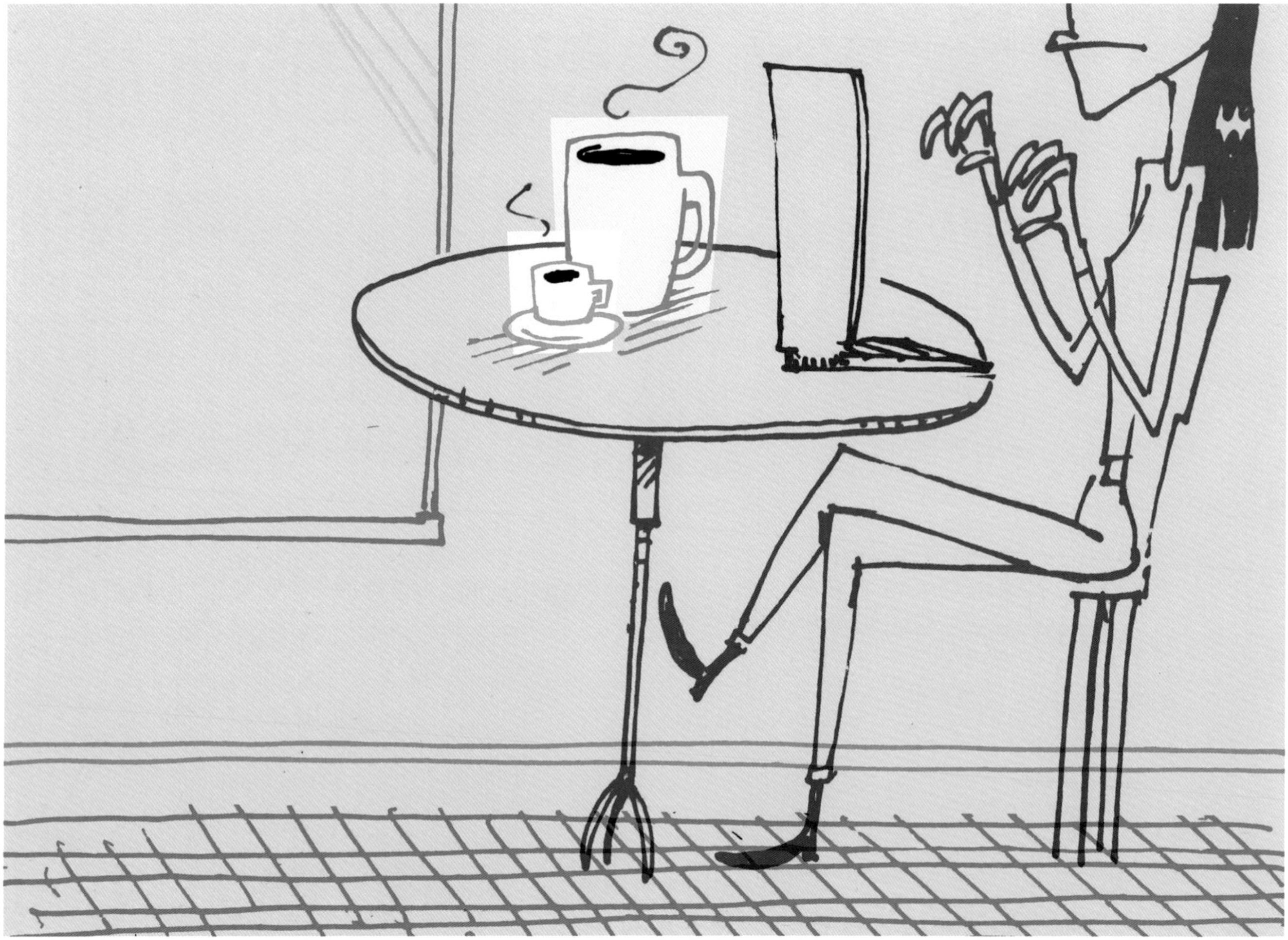

YOUR FAVOURITE RENAISSANCE ARTIST IS FROM SKIDEGATE

Charles Edenshaw

YOU BELIEVE IF ANYONE DESERVES A STATUE WITH AN ETERNAL FLAME, IT'S MARC EMERY

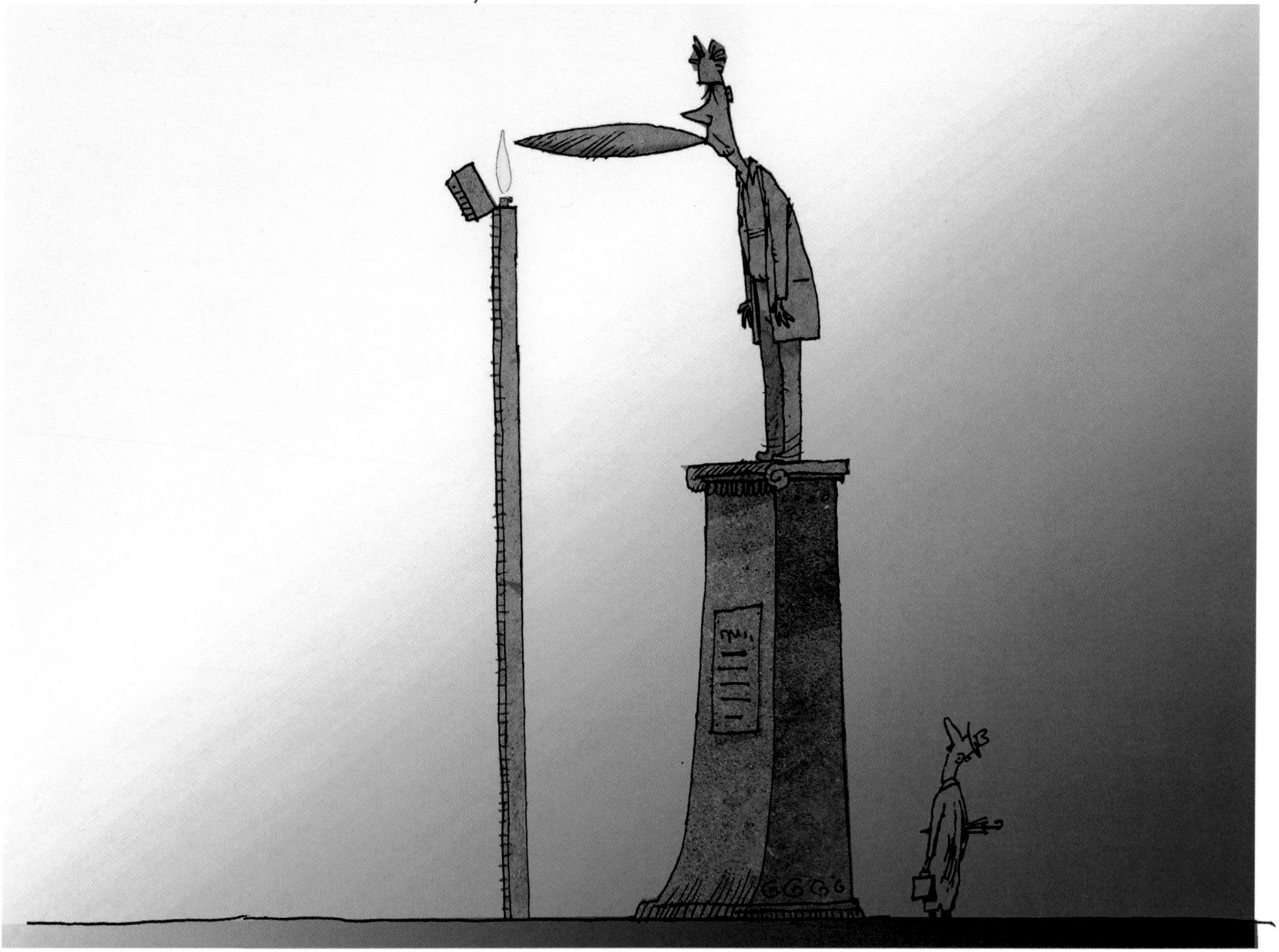

YOU DECIDED NOT TO DIE BEFORE THE CANUCKS WIN A STANLEY CUP

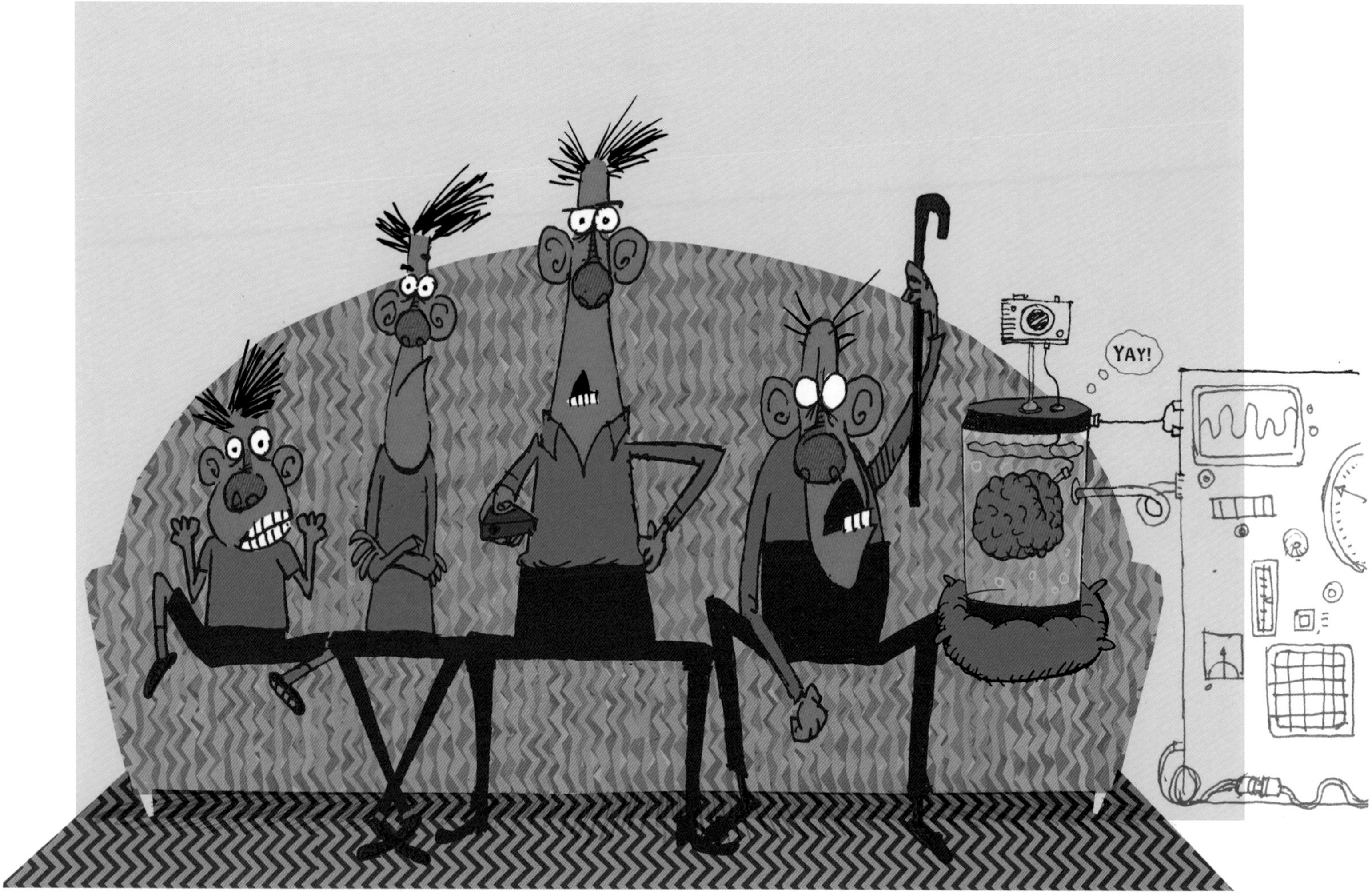
YAY!

YOU THINK A BRYAN ADAMS STATUE SHOULD WELCOME FOLKS TO NORTH VANCOUVER

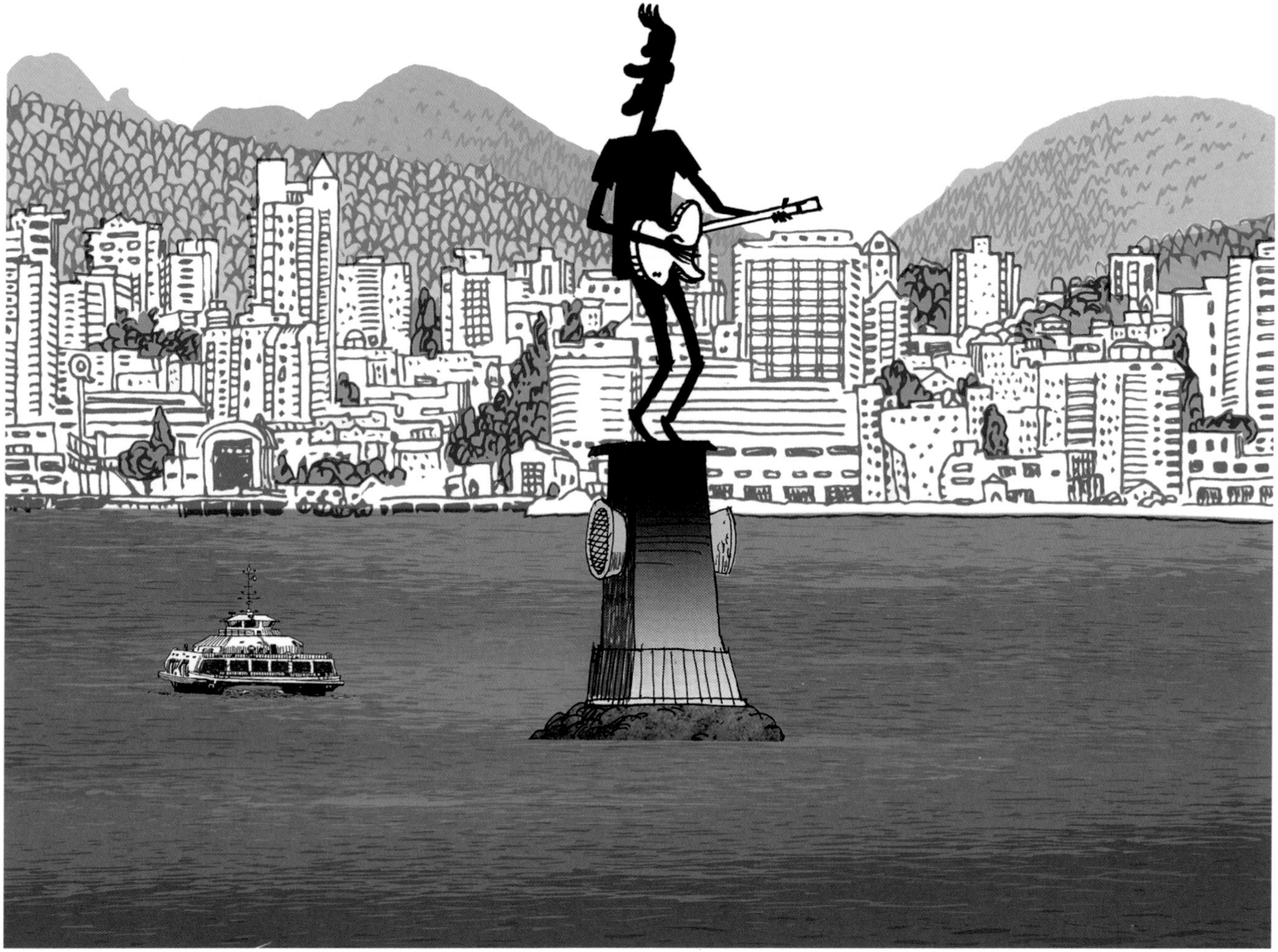

DITTO A BEN HEPPNER STATUE IN DAWSON CREEK

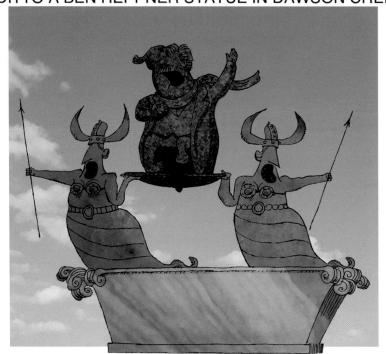

AND A DAVID FOSTER STATUE IN VICTORIA

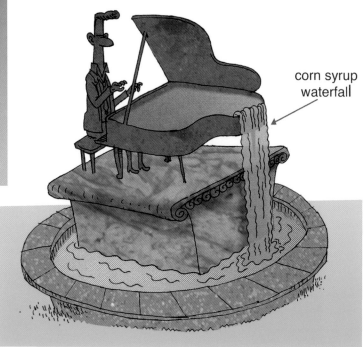

corn syrup waterfall

YOU ARE KNOWLEDGEABLE OF THE FACT THAT CARS IN THE LOWER MAINLAND ARE PROGRAMMED TO FAINT AT THE SIGHT OF A SNOWFLAKE

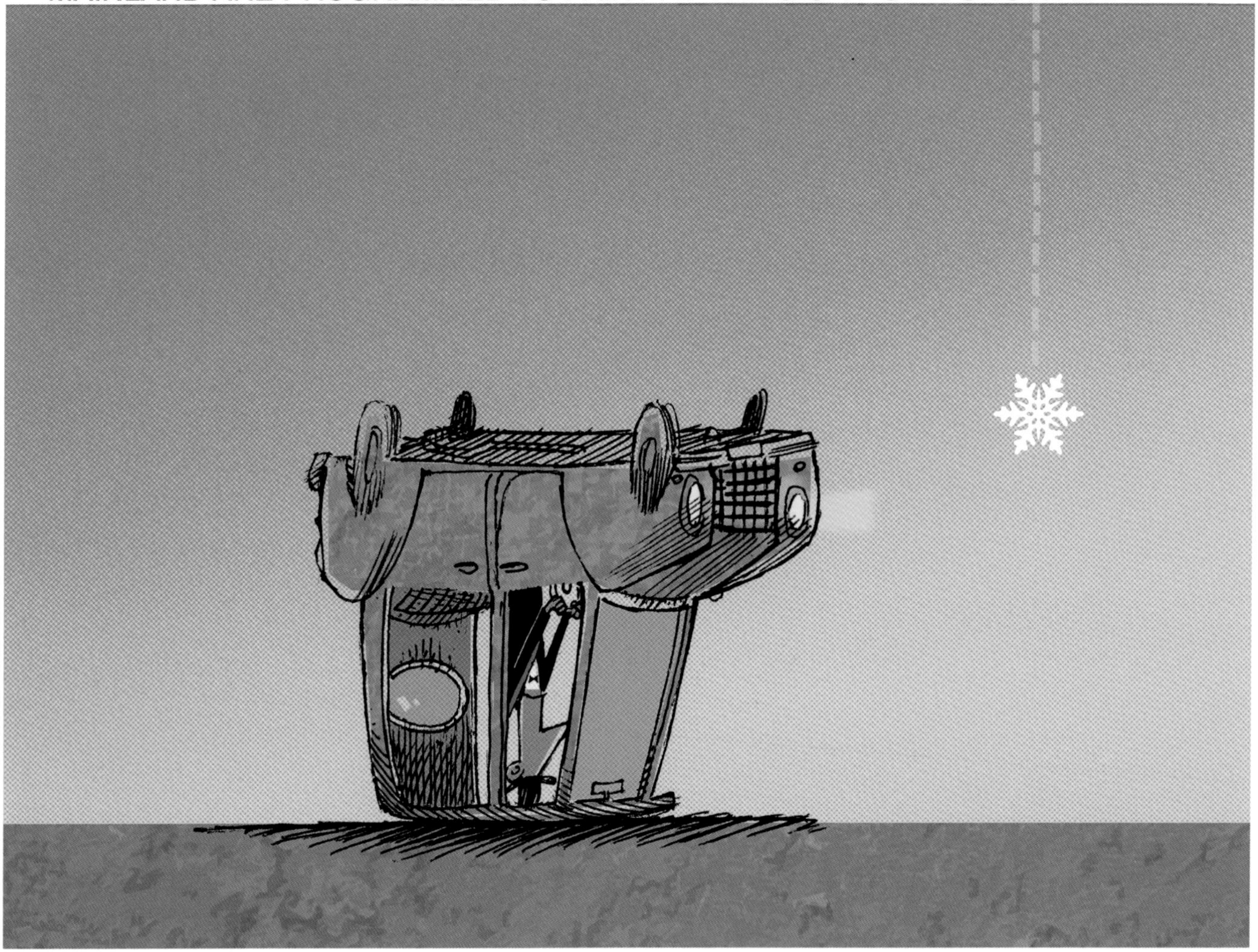

YOU'VE SAID IT WITH SOCKEYE

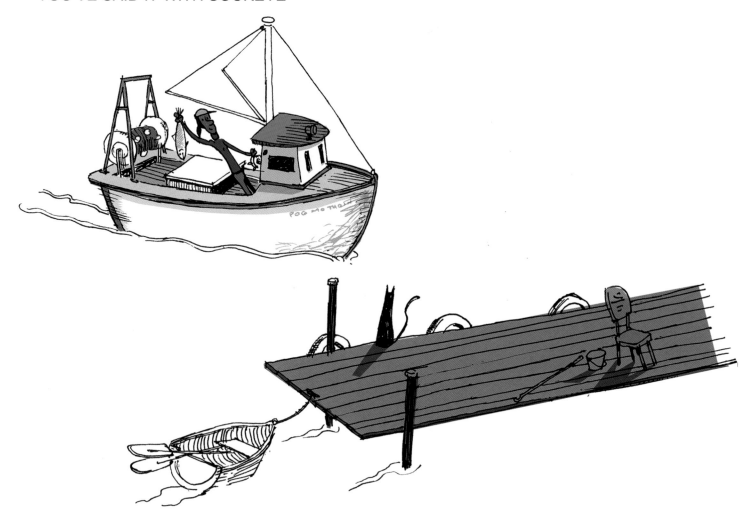

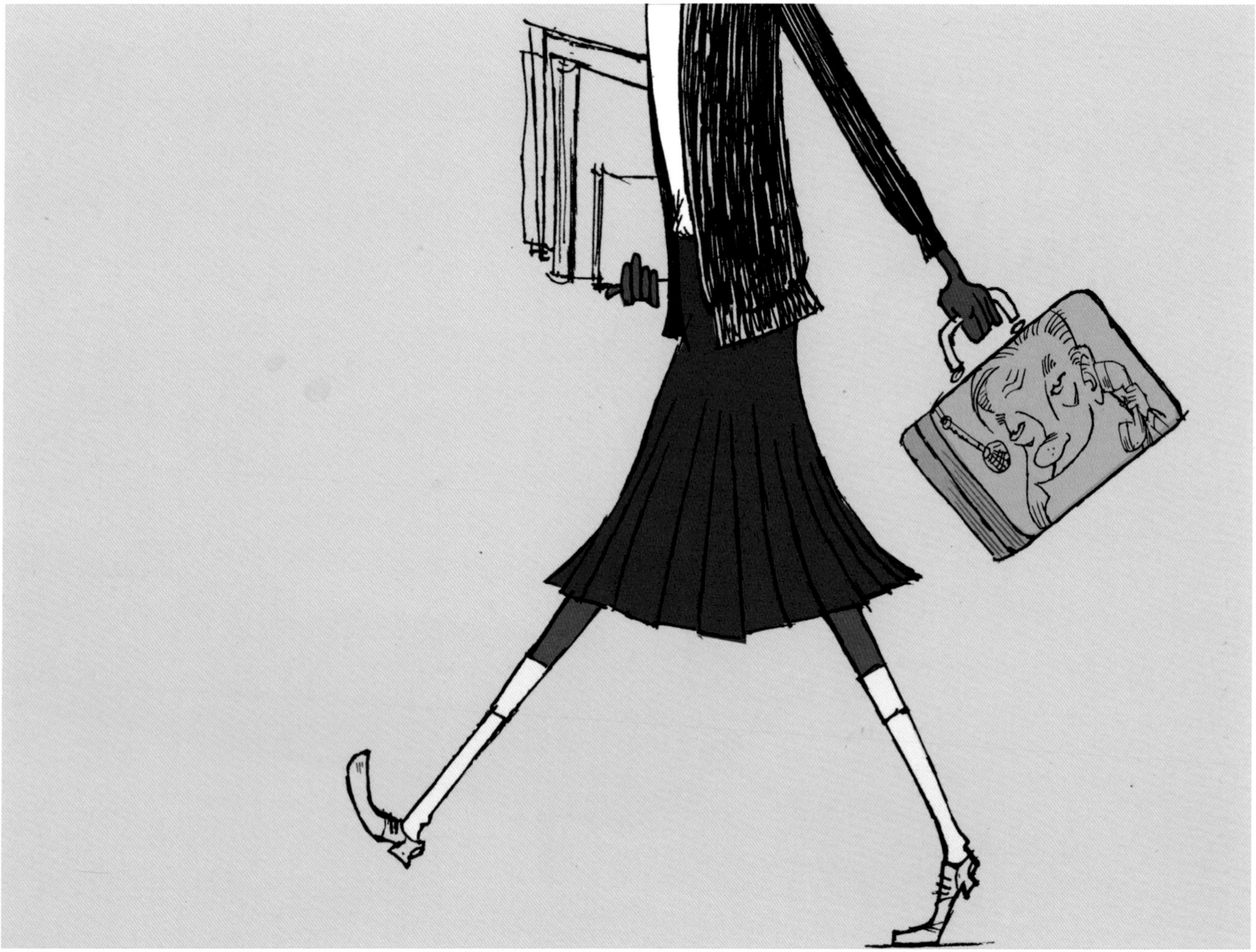

YOU HAD A JACK WEBSTER LUNCH PAIL

YOU REFER TO THE WINE-PRODUCING REGION OF PROVENCE AS —

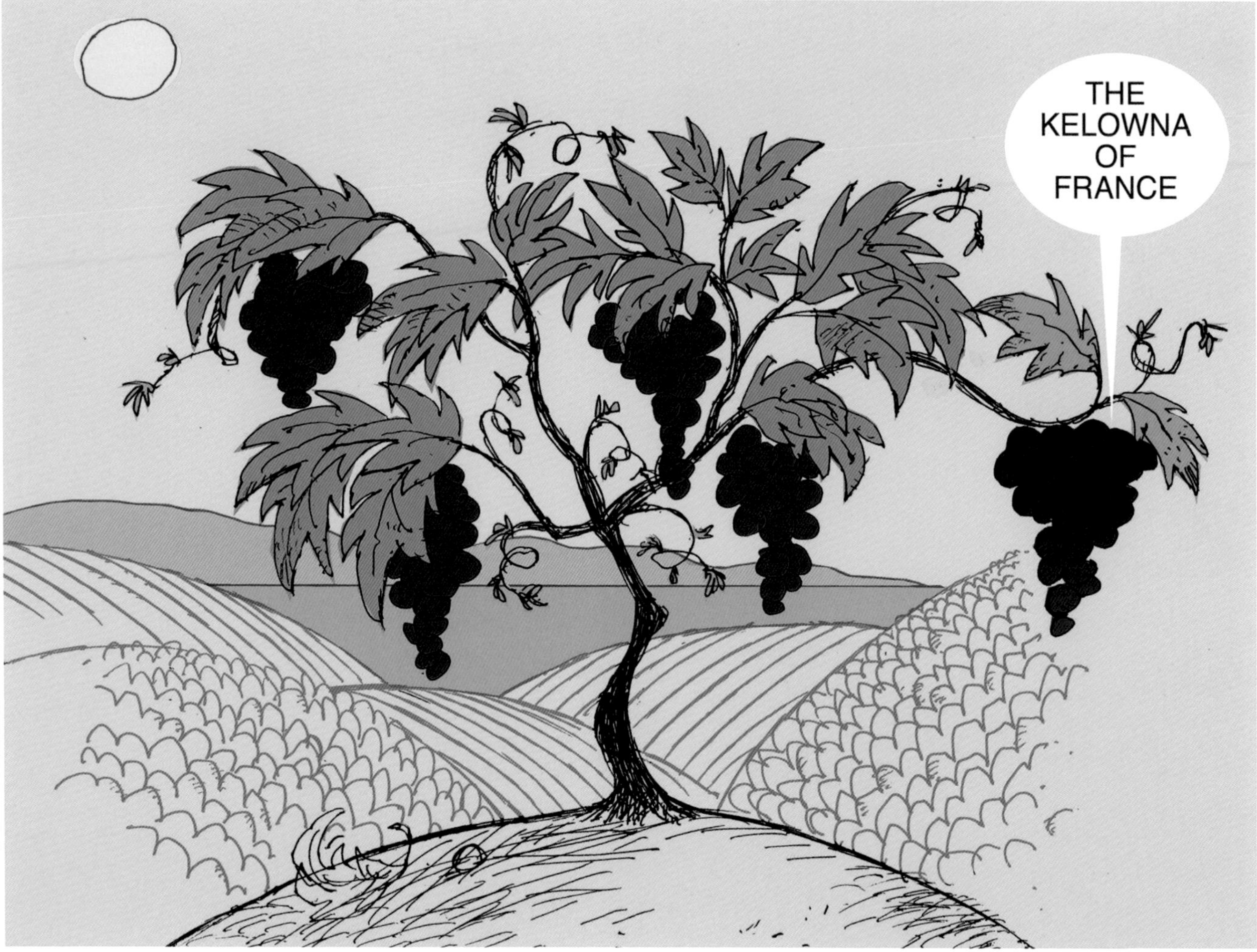
THE KELOWNA OF FRANCE

YOU'D LIKE TO SEE THAT CAPTAIN VANCOUVER STATUE ON THE LEGISLATURE REPLACED WITH ONE OF CHIEF DAN GEORGE

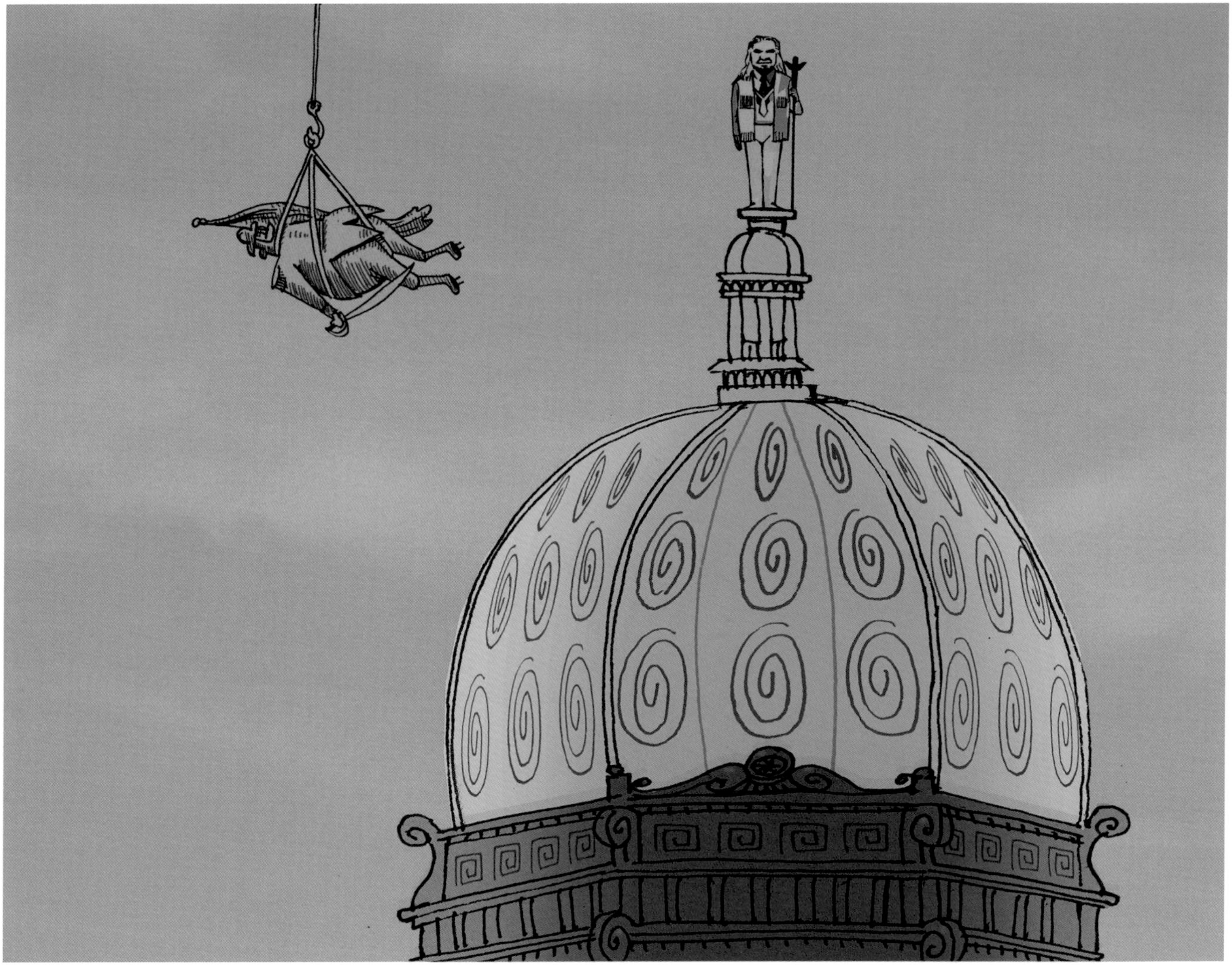

YOU NEVER EXPECTED TO SEE PRINCE GEORGE IN PRINCE GEORGE

OR FIND DESOLATION IN DESOLATION SOUND

AND YOU IMMEDIATELY SAW THE POINT OF POINT NO POINT

YOU'VE HAD THIS DREAM

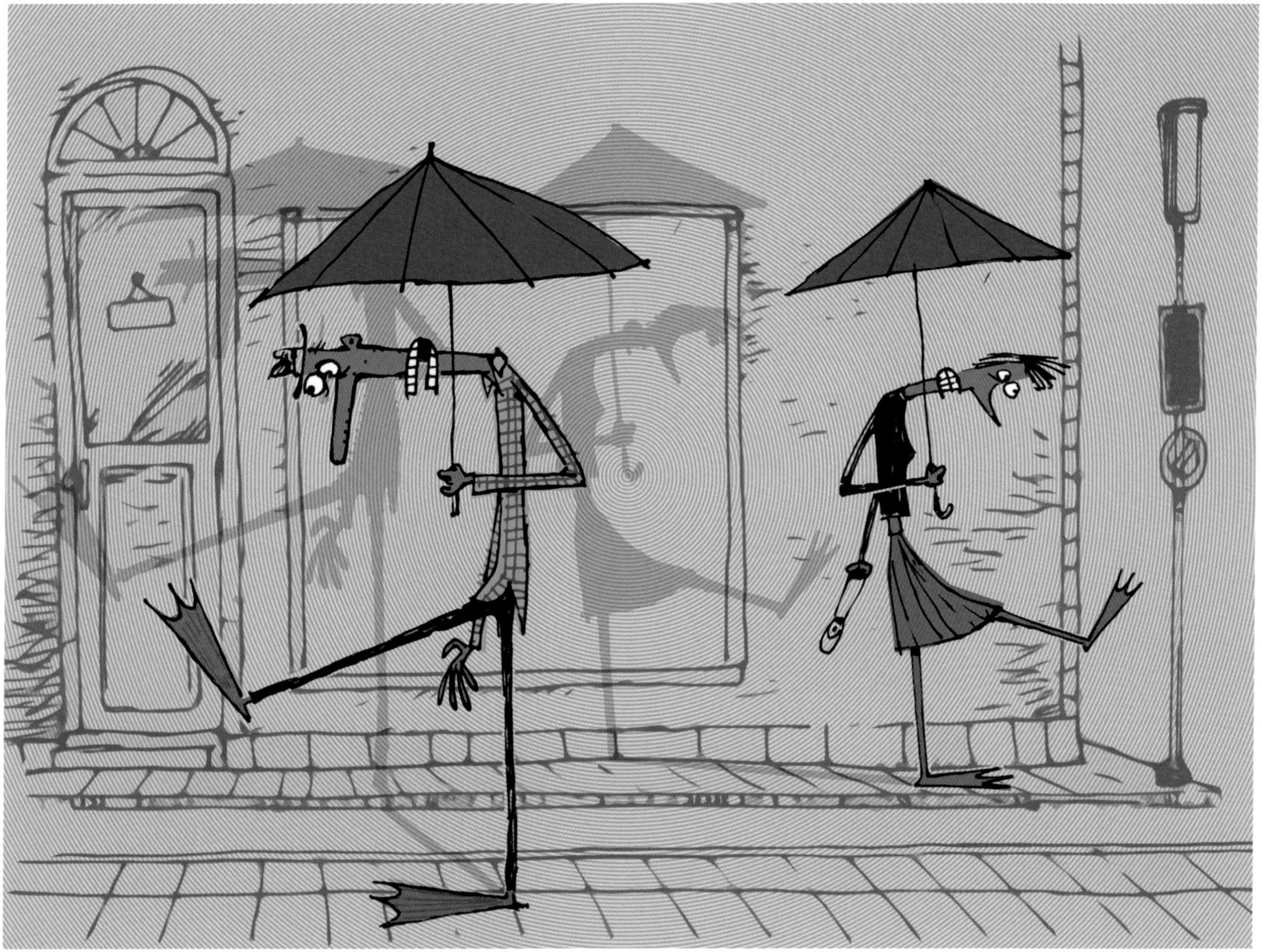

YOU CAN DRESS FOR ANY OCCASION — AS LONG AS THE OPTIONS ARE DRESS-CASUAL, CASUAL-CASUAL, OR WRECK-BEACH CASUAL

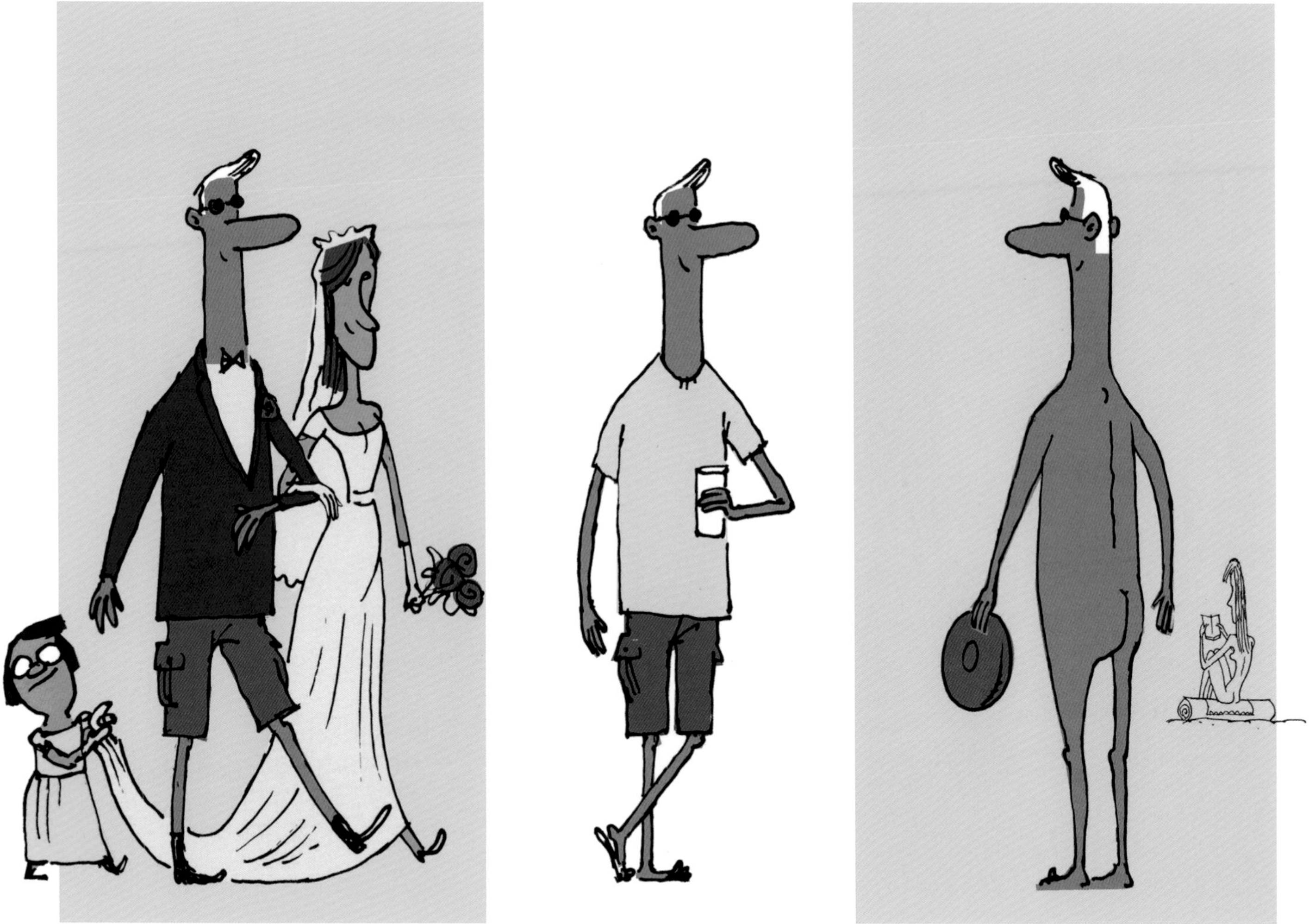

YOU MET YOUR LIFE PARTNER CHAINED TO EARTH-MOVING MACHINERY

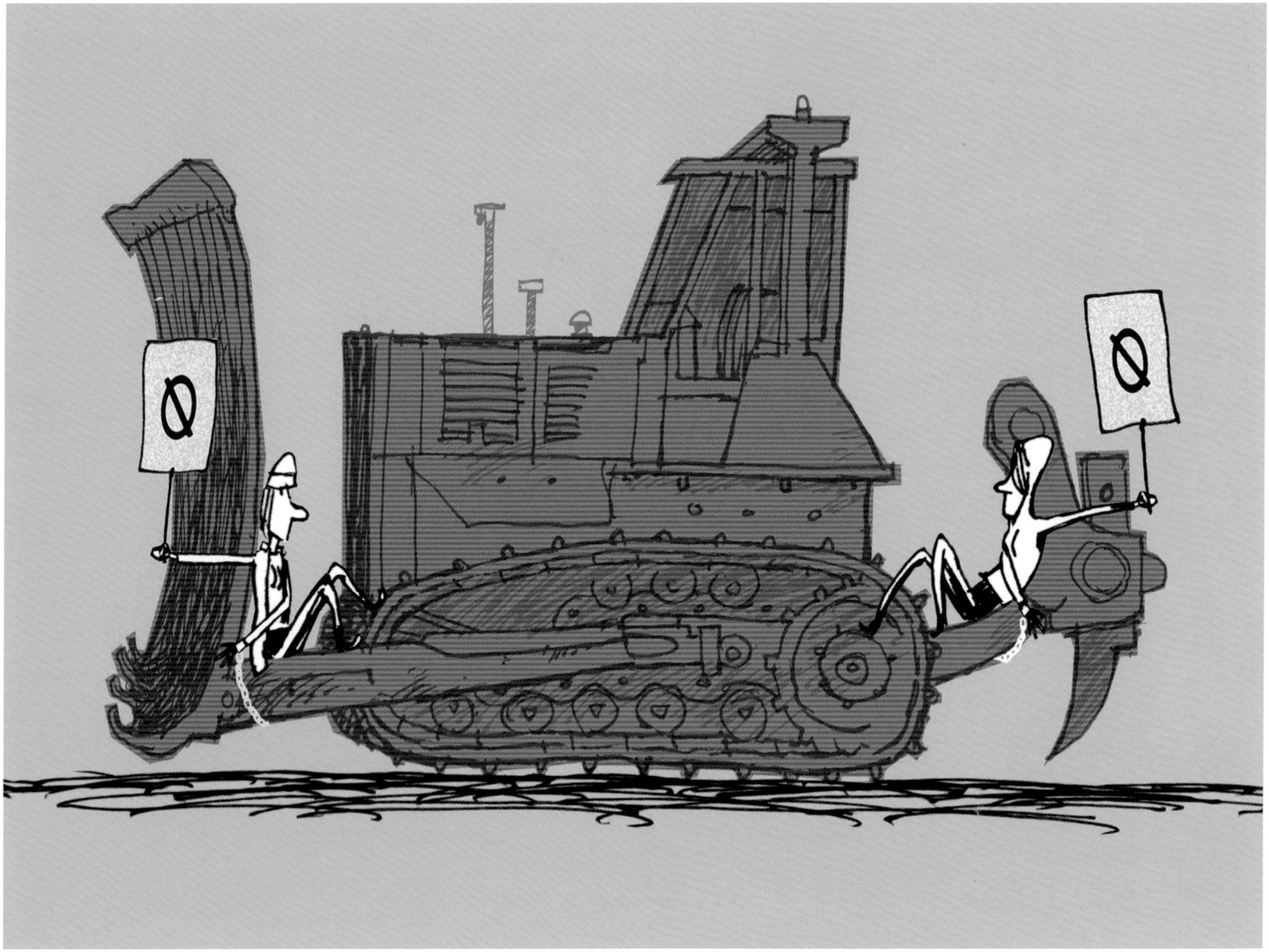

YOU'VE COME TO THE STARK REALIZATION THAT THERE CAN NEVER BE A TOP-40 BALLAD ABOUT THE ROMANCE AND GRANDEUR OF FERNIE THAT CONTAINS THE WORD "FERNIE"

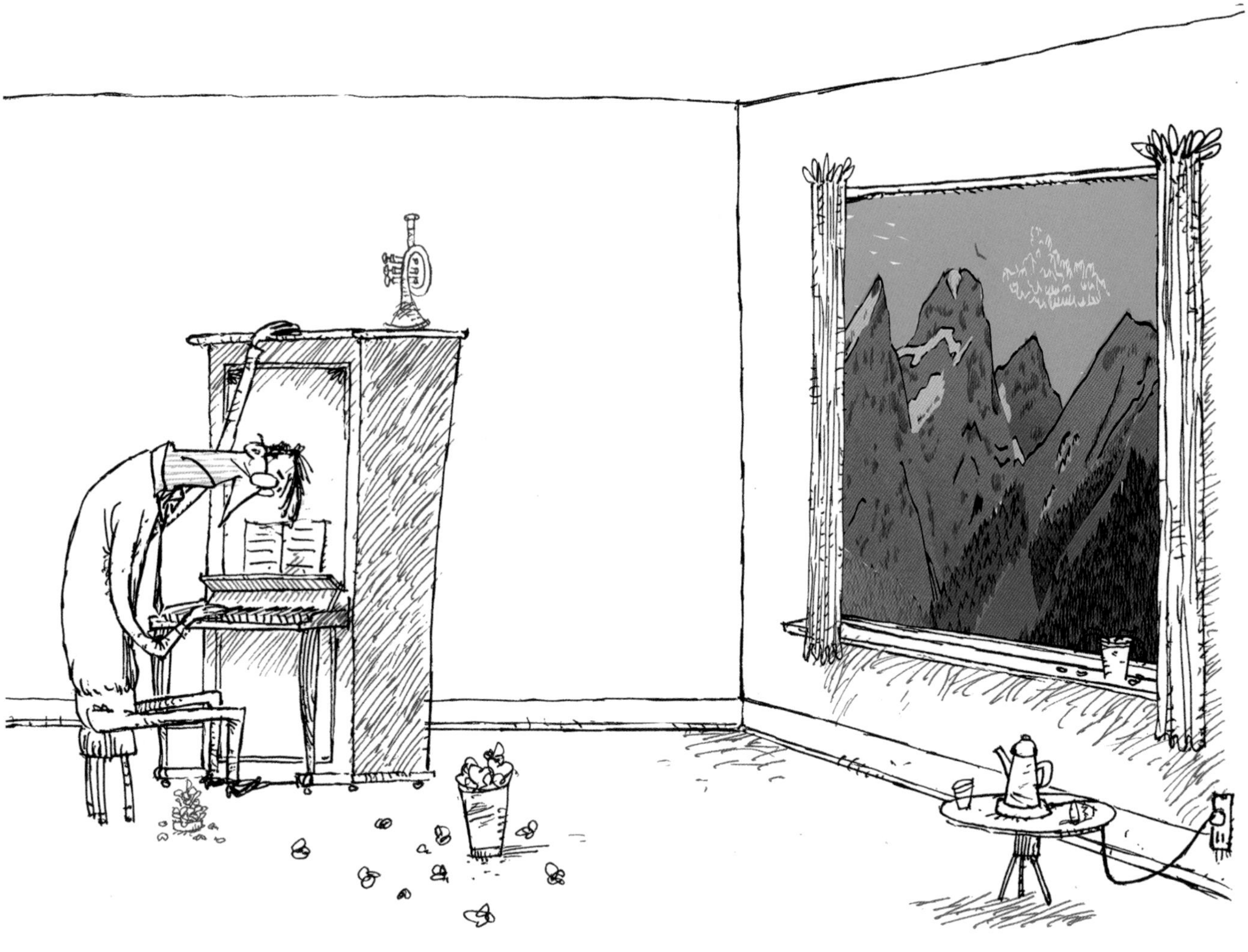

YOU'VE BEEN TO THE STATUE COMMEMORATING THE FOUR-MINUTE MILE IN VANCOUVER

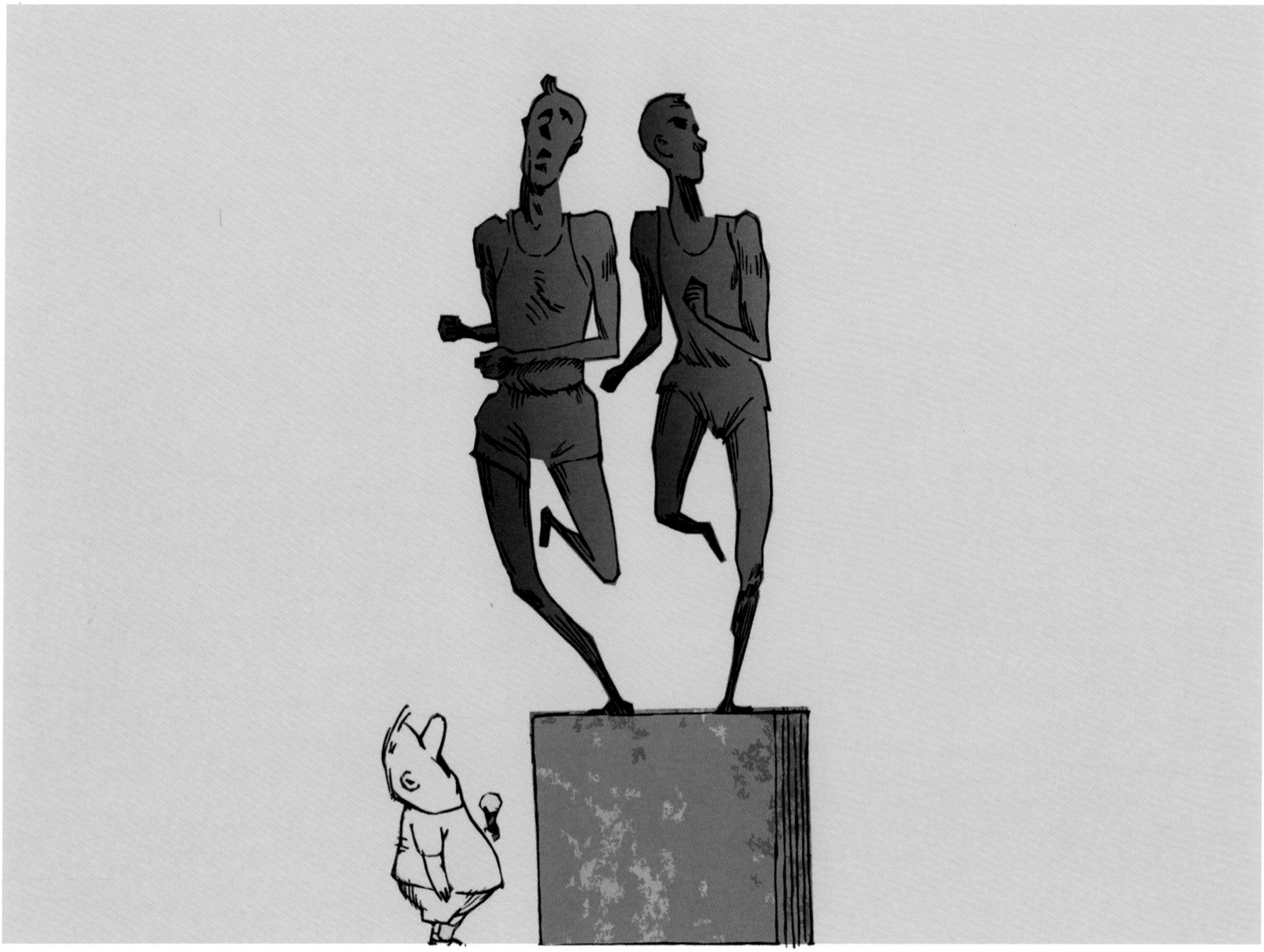

AND YOU'VE BEEN TO THE STATUE COMMEMORATING THE FOUR-MINUTE PRIME MINISTER, KIM CAMPBELL, IN PORT ALBERNI

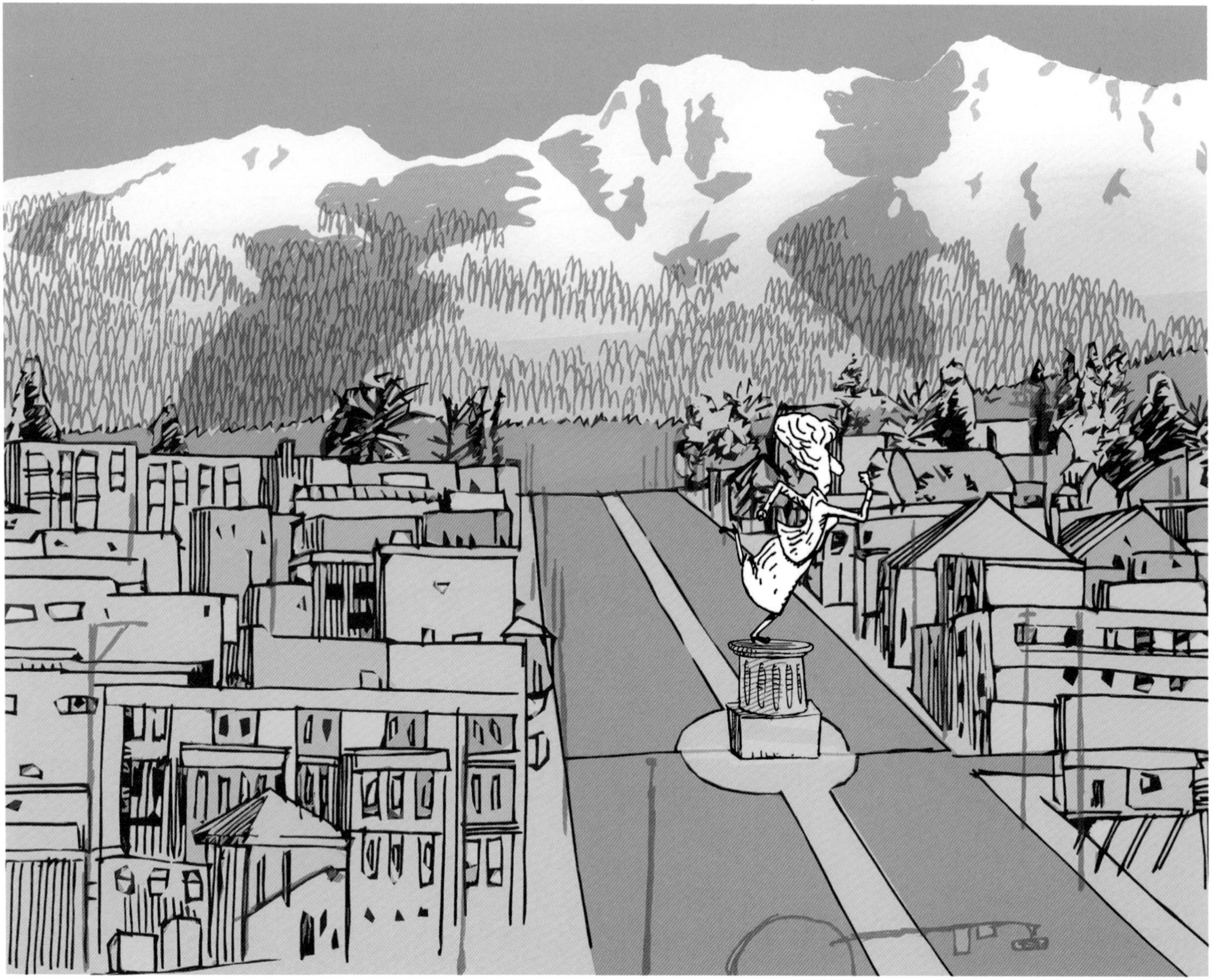

YOU KNOW A SALTSPRING ISLAND SHEEP WHEN YOU SEE ONE

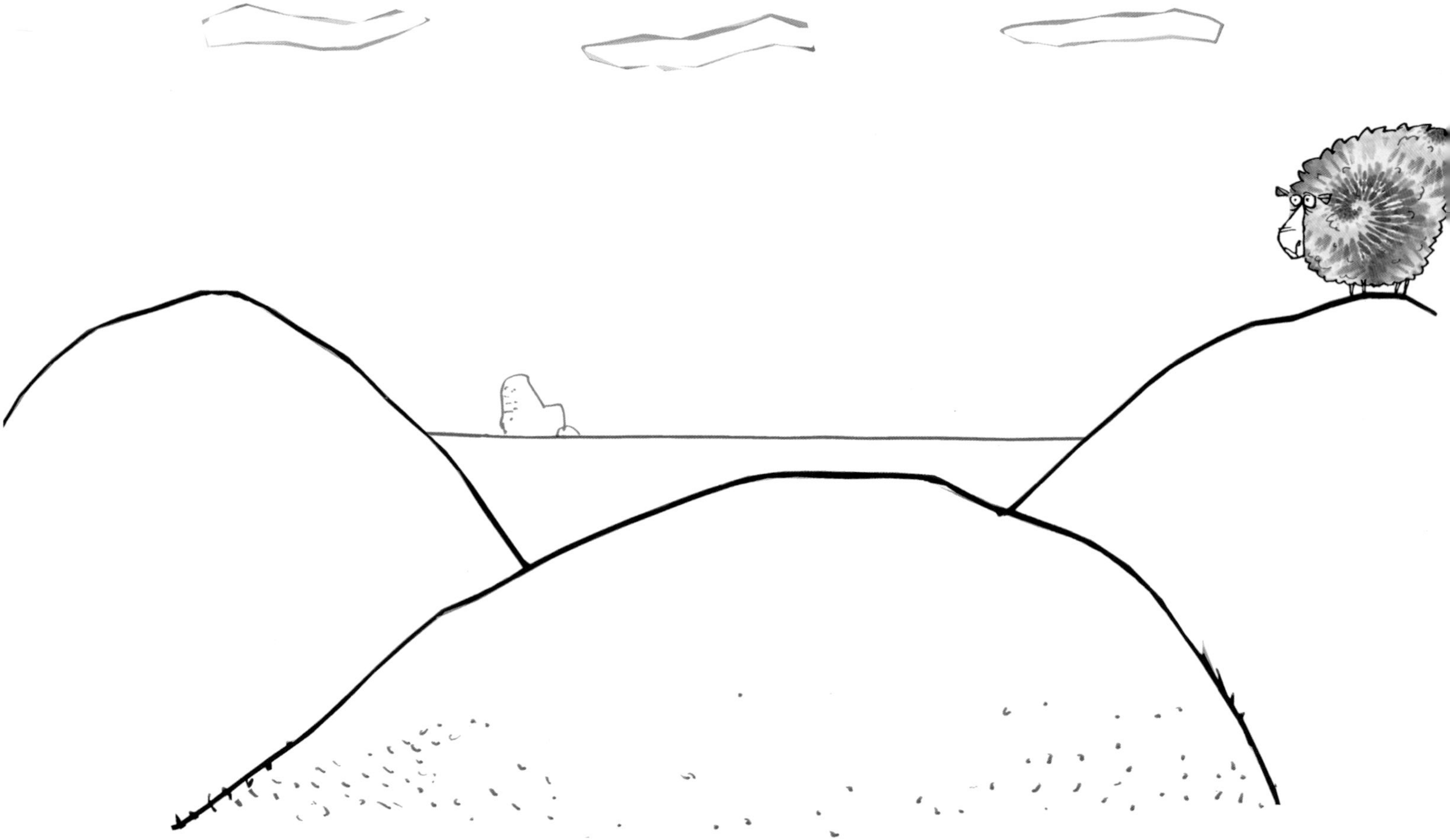

YOU WERE HAPPY WITH THIS PROVINCIAL SLOGAN

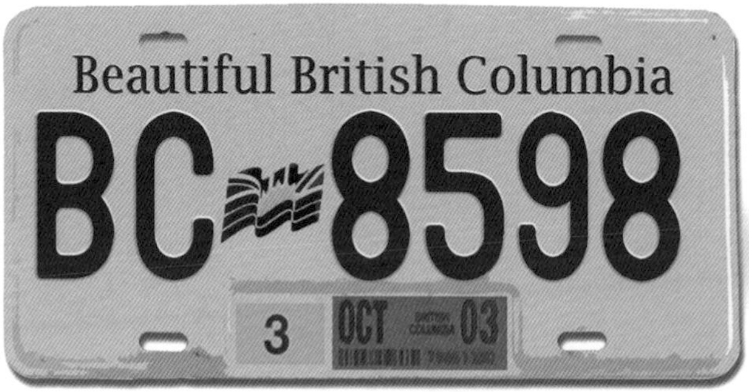
Beautiful British Columbia
BC 8598
3
OCT 03

EMBARRASSED BY THIS ONE

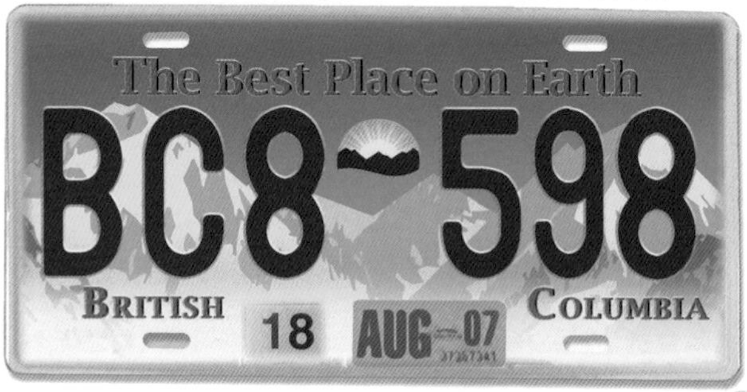
The Best Place on Earth
BC8 598
BRITISH
COLUMBIA
18
AUG 07

AND THINK THE NEW ONE IS PERFECT

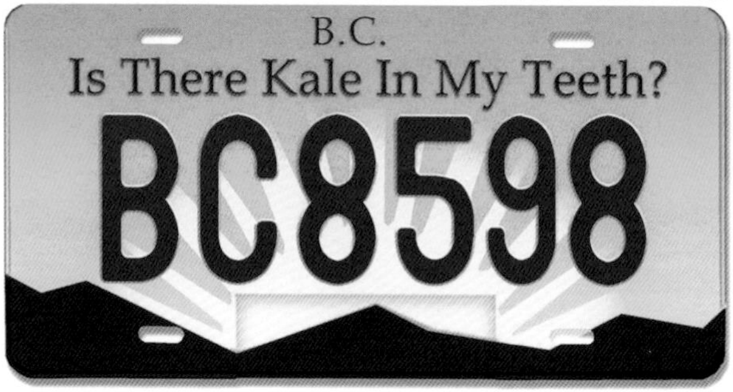
B.C.
Is There Kale In My Teeth?
BC8598

YOU KNOW THE PROVINCE'S OFFICIAL BEAR, BIRD AND FLOWER

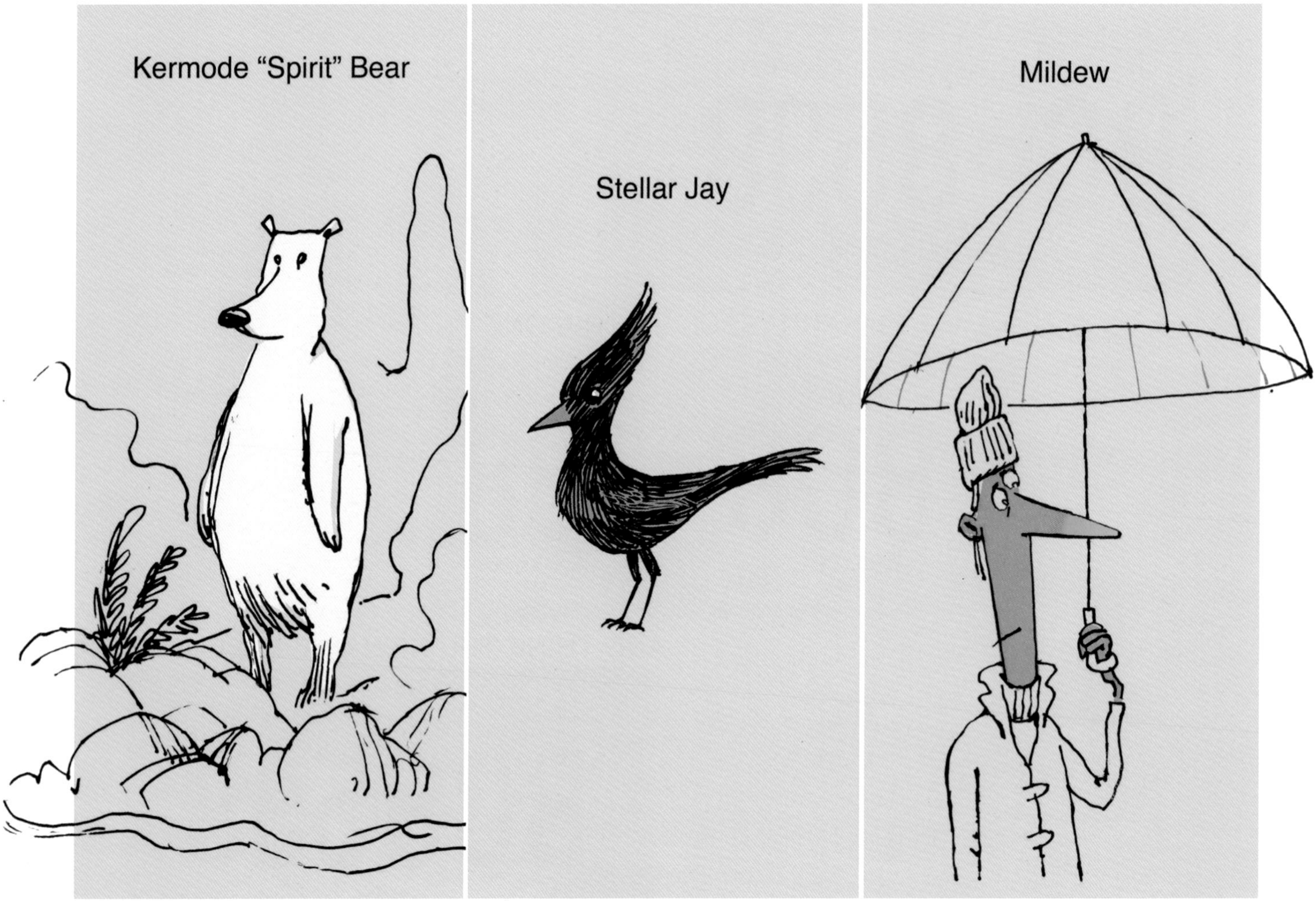
Kermode "Spirit" Bear
Stellar Jay
Mildew

AND YOU KNOW THE PROVINCE'S UNOFFICIAL OFFICIALS

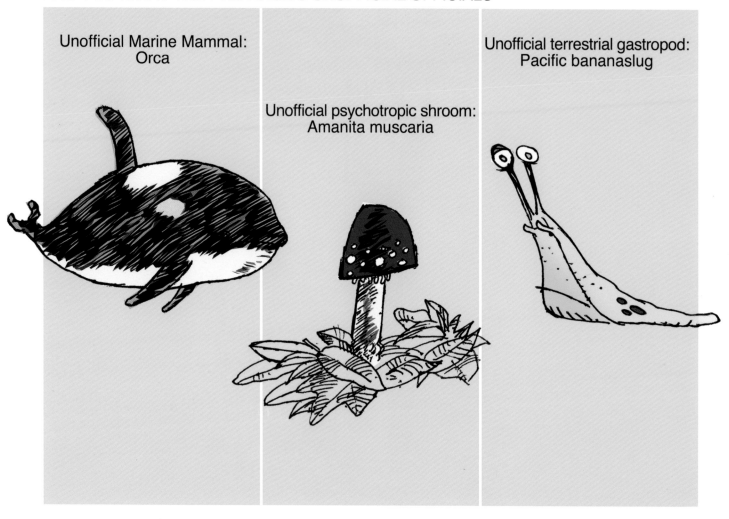

Unofficial Marine Mammal:
Orca

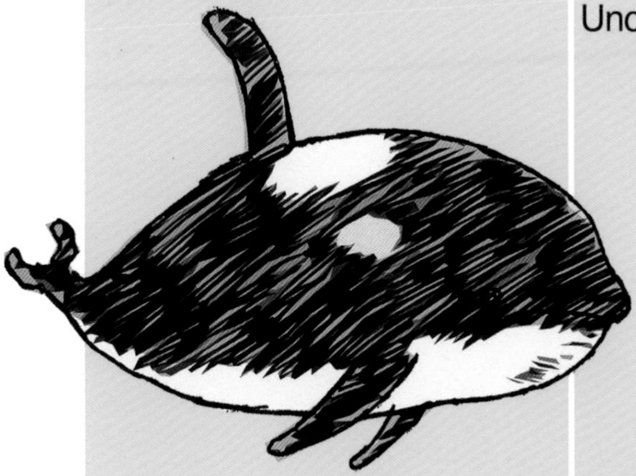

Unofficial psychotropic shroom:
Amanita muscaria

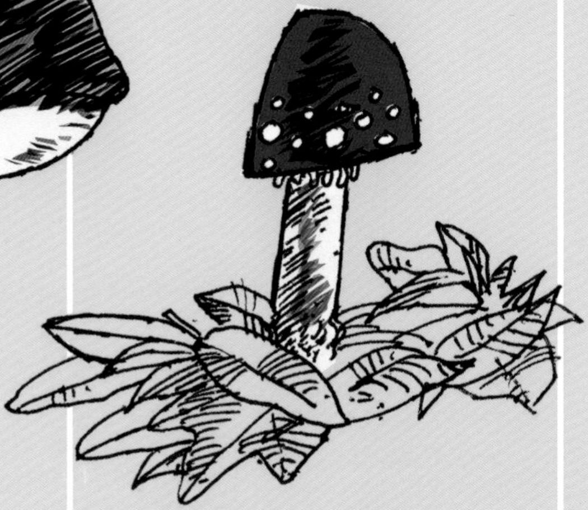

Unofficial terrestrial gastropod:
Pacific bananaslug

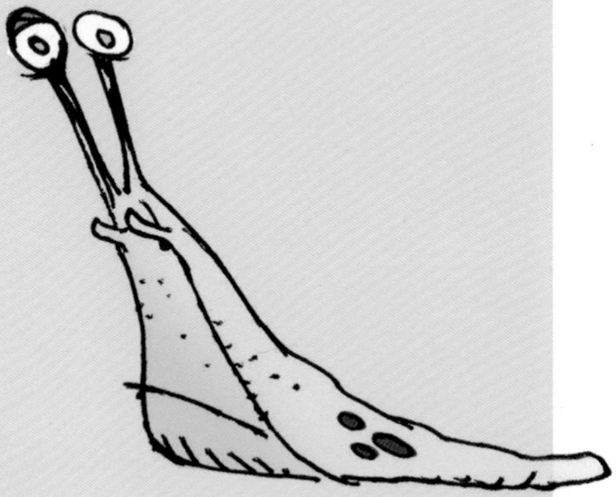

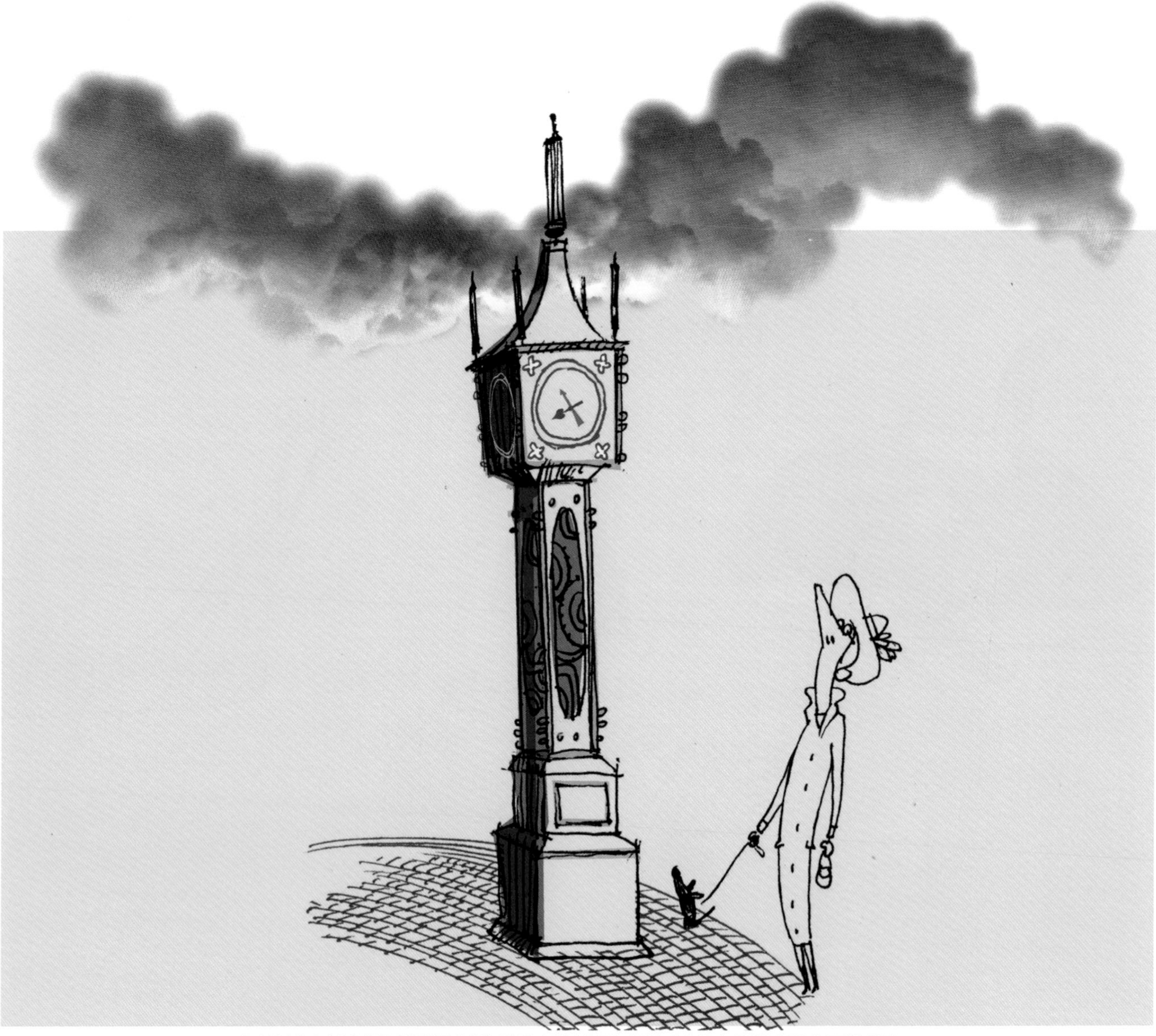

YOU HAVE DEDUCED THAT AT ANY GIVEN TIME
18 PER CENT OF THE STEAM CLOCK'S STEAM IS POT SMOKE

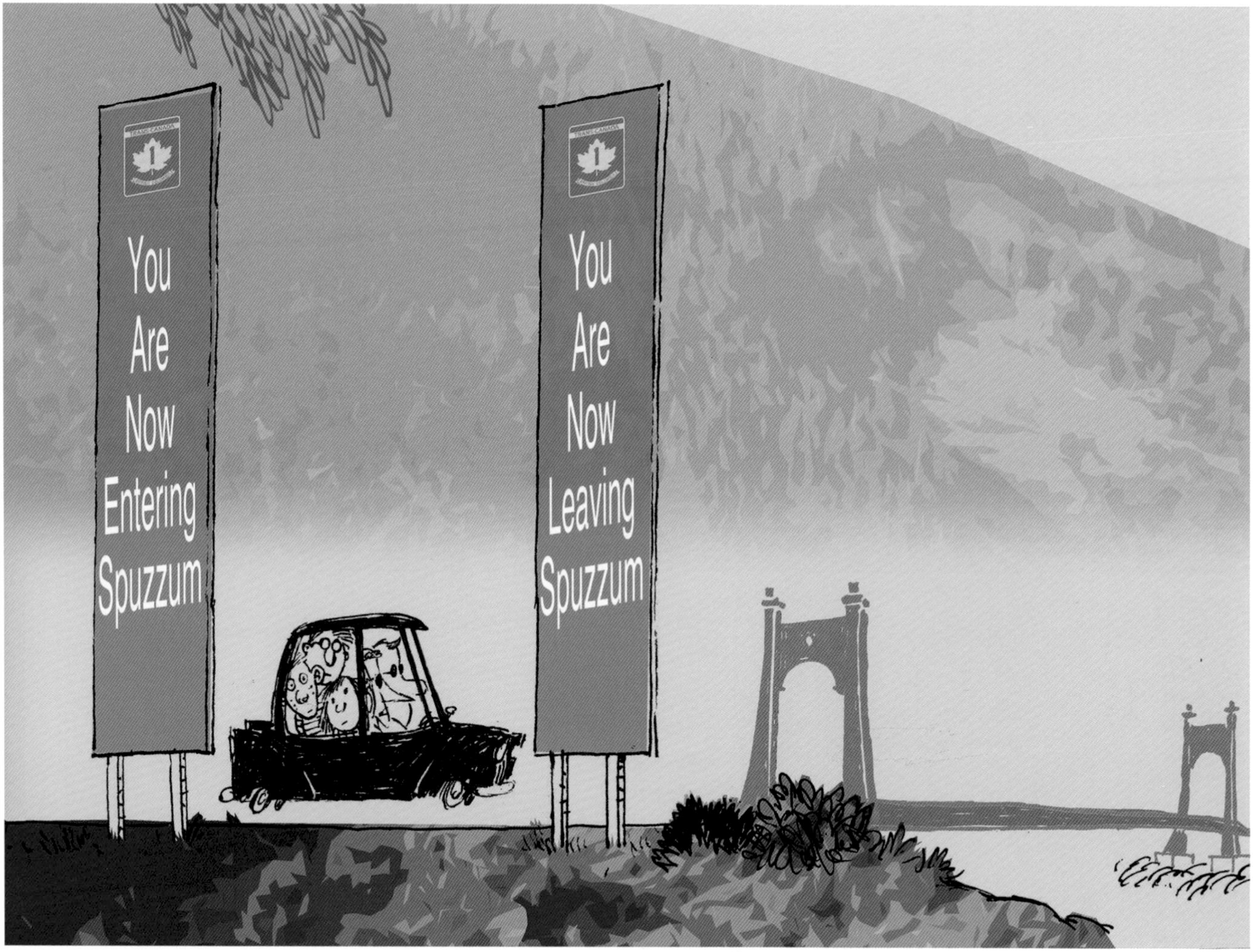
You
Are
Now
Entering
Spuzzum
You
Are
Now
Leaving
Spuzzum

YOU CHERISH THE SECONDS YOU HAVE SPENT IN SPUZZUM

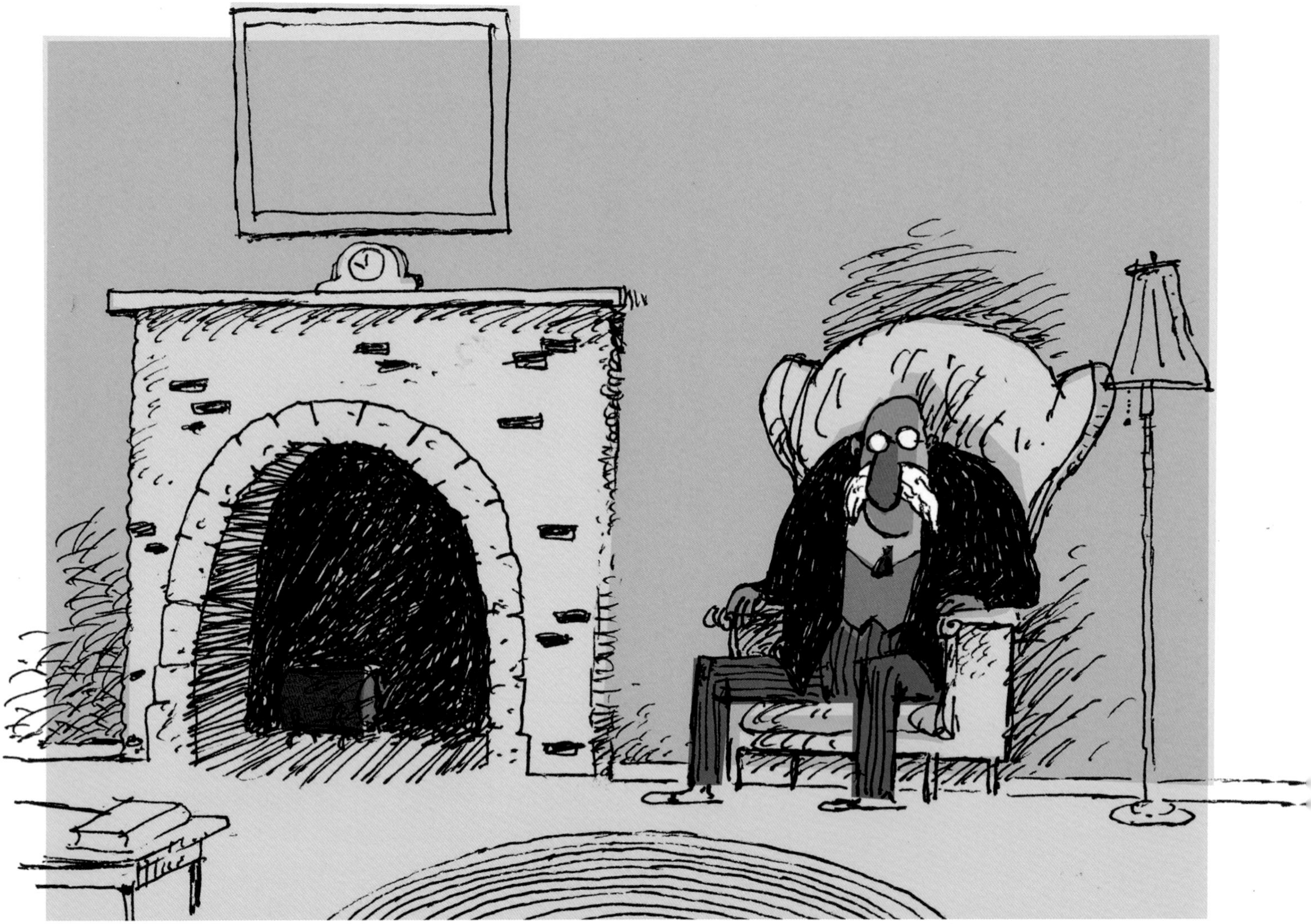

YOU ARE ALMOST THROUGH DIGESTING A SUNSHINE BREAKFAST FROM 1998

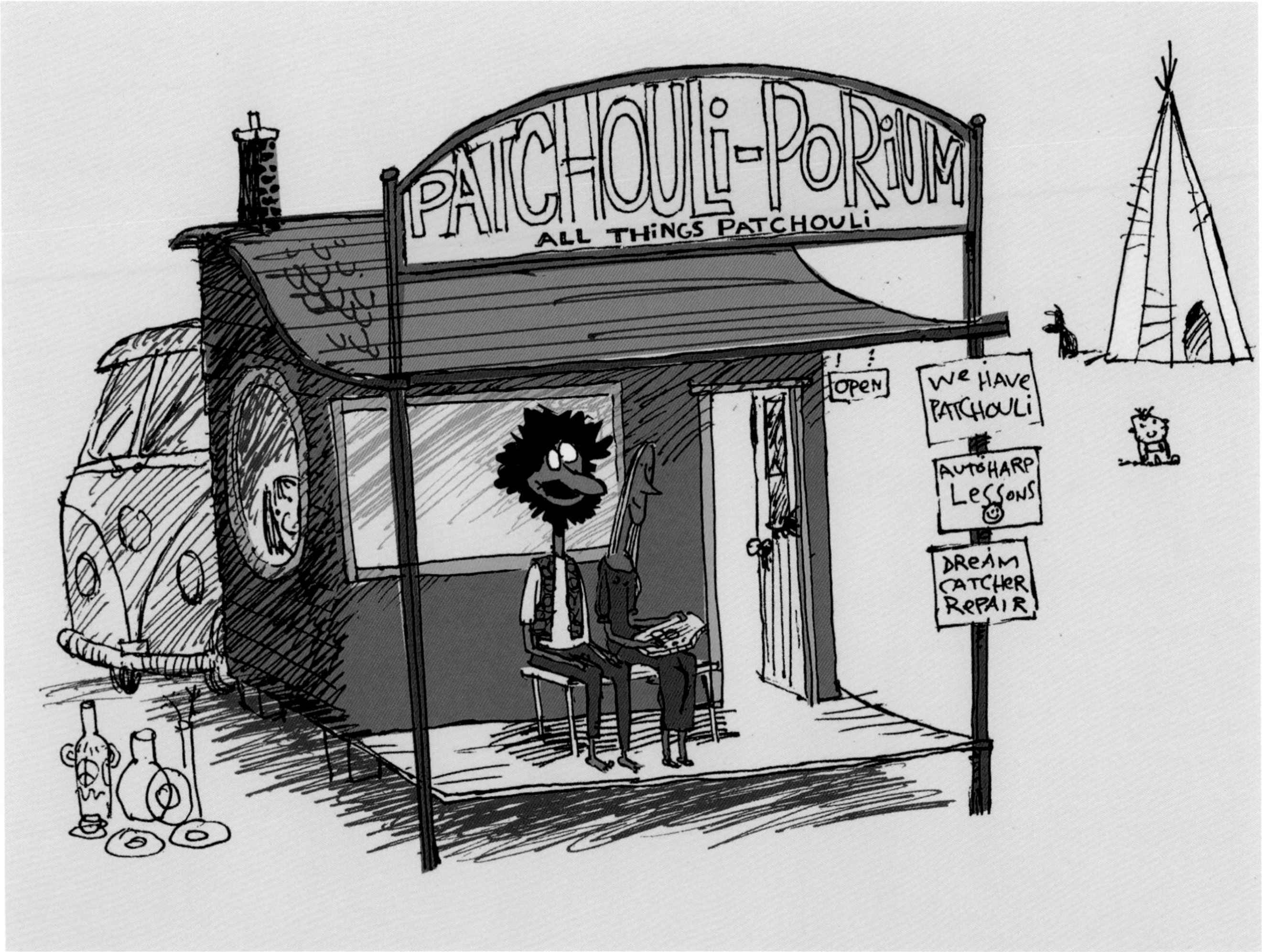
PATCHOULI-PORIUM
ALL THINGS PATCHOULI
OPEN
WE HAVE PATCHOULI
AUTOHARP LESSONS
DREAM CATCHER REPAIR
YOU BELIEVE IN TIME TRAVEL BECAUSE YOU'VE BEEN TO HORNBY ISLAND

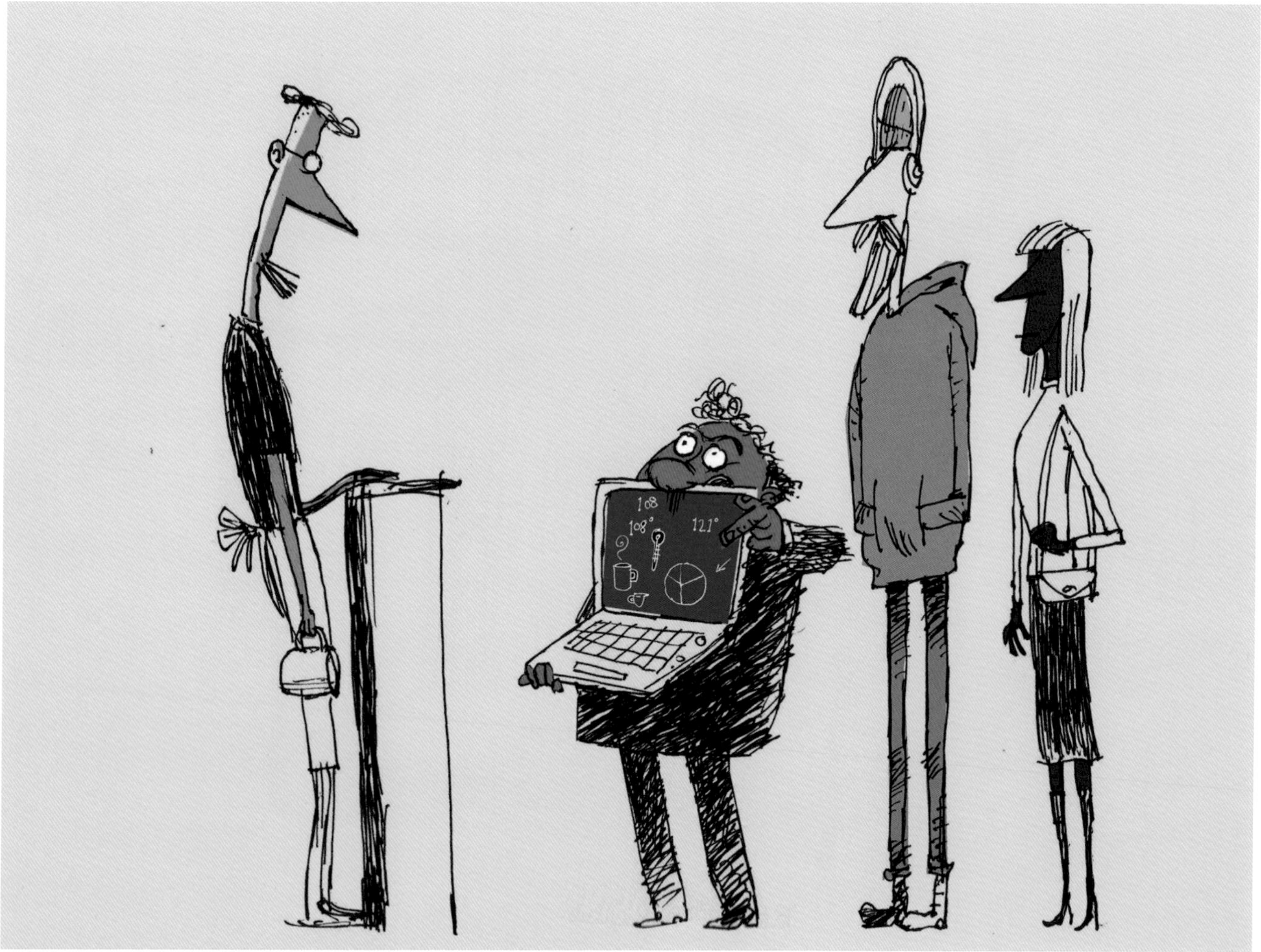

YOU ORDER COFFEE WITH A POWERPOINT

YOU LOVE THE SEDATE VILLAGE LIFE

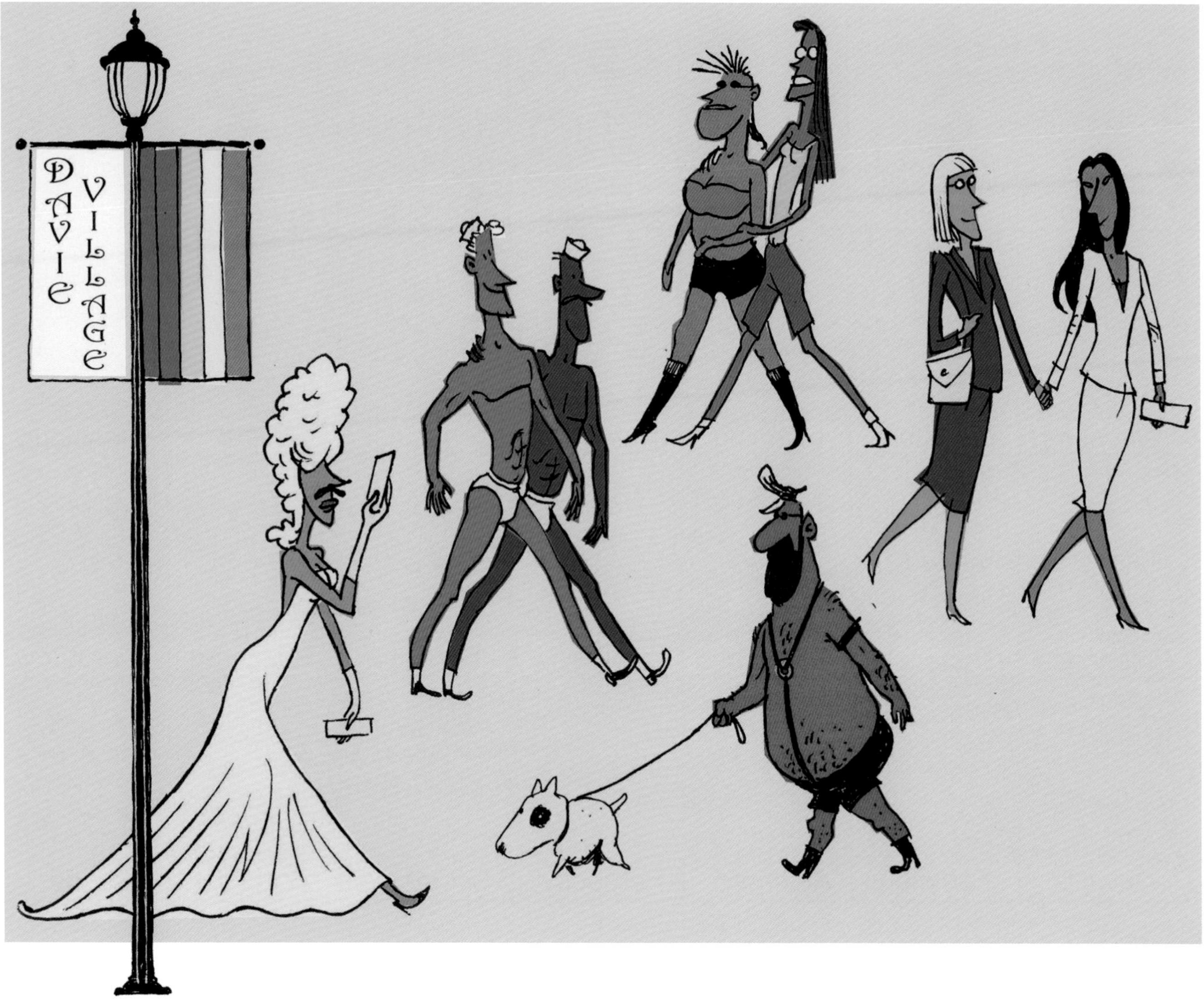
DAVIE
VILLAGE

YOU KNOW PRINCE RUPERT'S 28 KINDS OF FOG

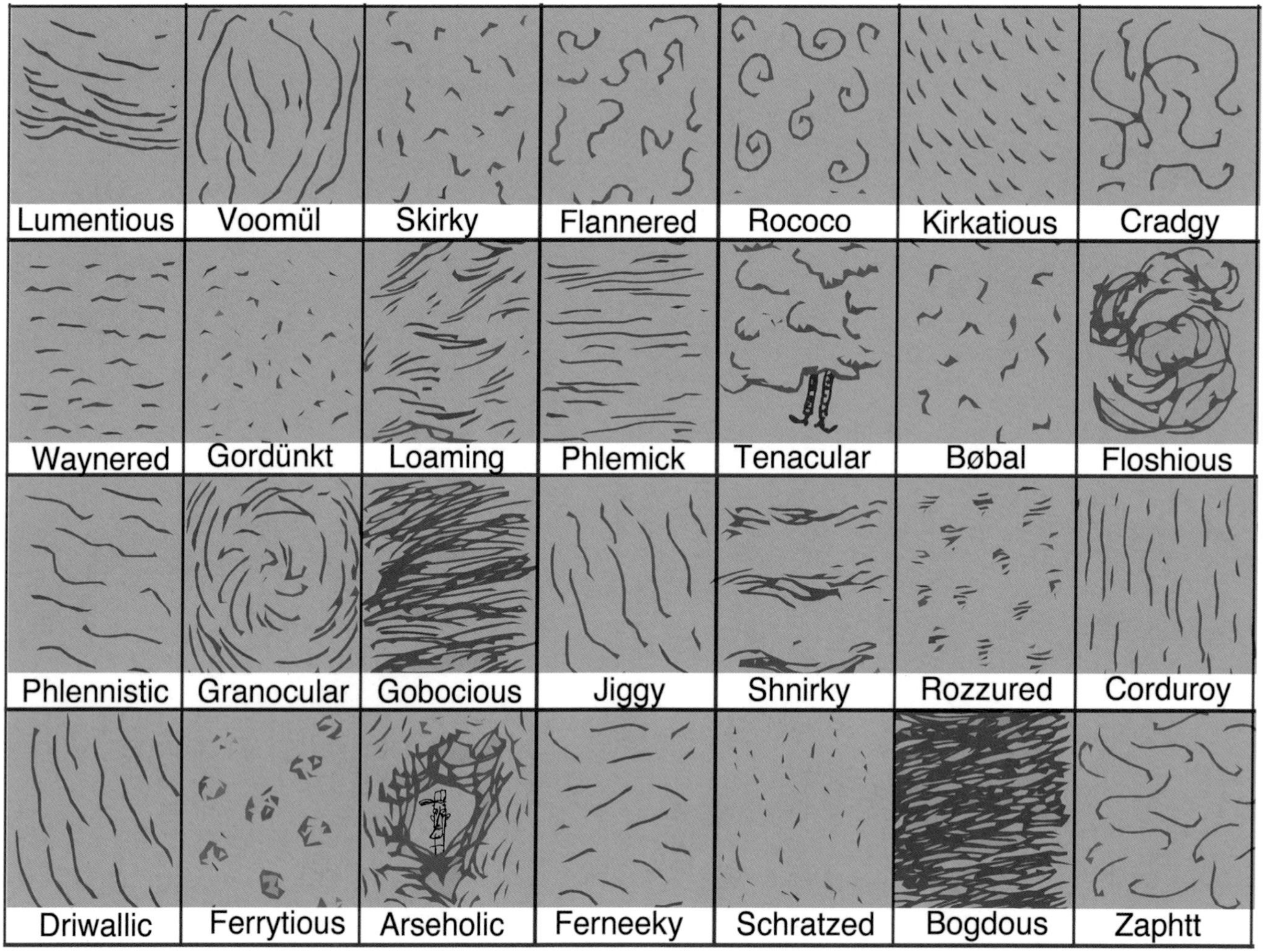

Lumentious	Voomül	Skirky	Flannered	Rococo	Kirkatious	Cradgy
Waynered	Gordünkt	Loaming	Phlemick	Tenacular	Bøbal	Floshious
Phlennistic	Granocular	Gobocious	Jiggy	Shnirky	Rozzured	Corduroy
Driwallic	Ferrytious	Arseholic	Ferneeky	Schratzed	Bogdous	Zaphtt

Lumentious	Voomül	Skirky	Flannered	Rococo	Kirkatious	Cradgy
Waynered	Gordünkt	Loaming	Phlemick	Tenacular	Bøbal	Floshious
Phlennistic	Granocular	Gobocious	Jiggy	Shnirky	Rozzured	Corduroy
Driwallic	Ferrytious	Arseholic	Ferneeky	Schratzed	Bogdous	Zaphtt

YOU'VE BEEN TO WHISTLER IN JULY

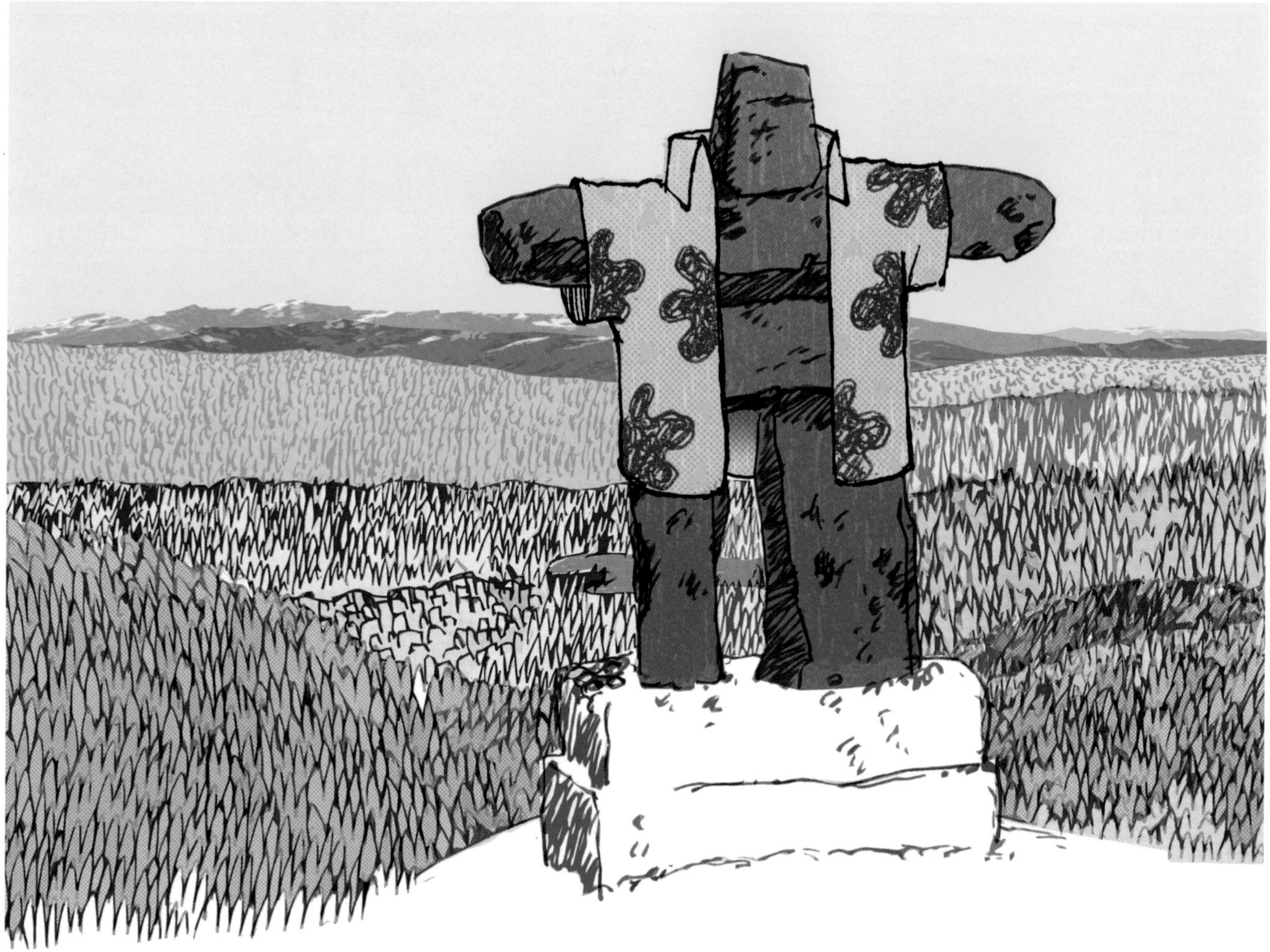

YOU'VE EVER WOKEN UP SCREAMING:

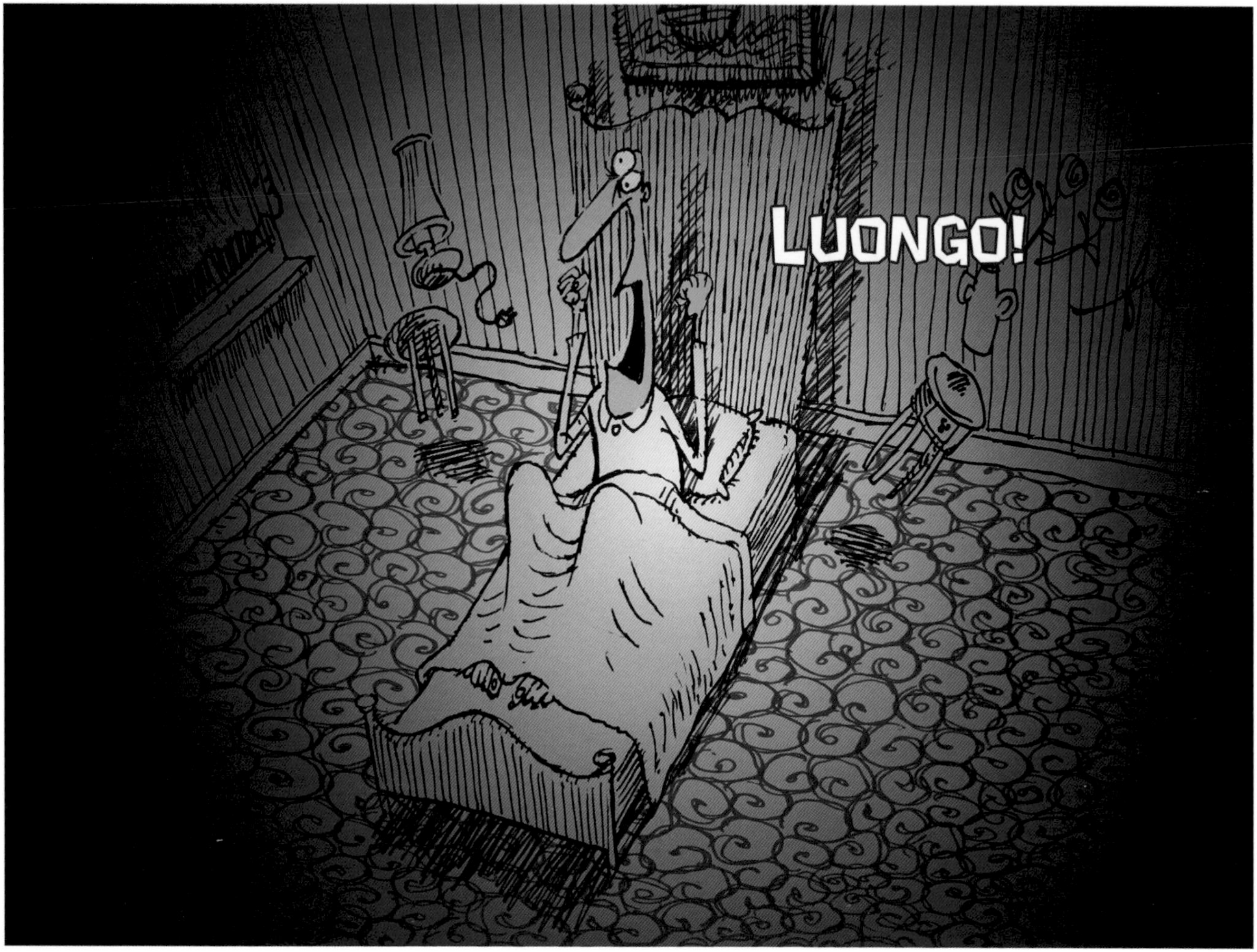
LUONGO!

YOU CONTINUE TO DERIVE ENJOYMENT FROM THE WHALE WATCHING INDUSTRY

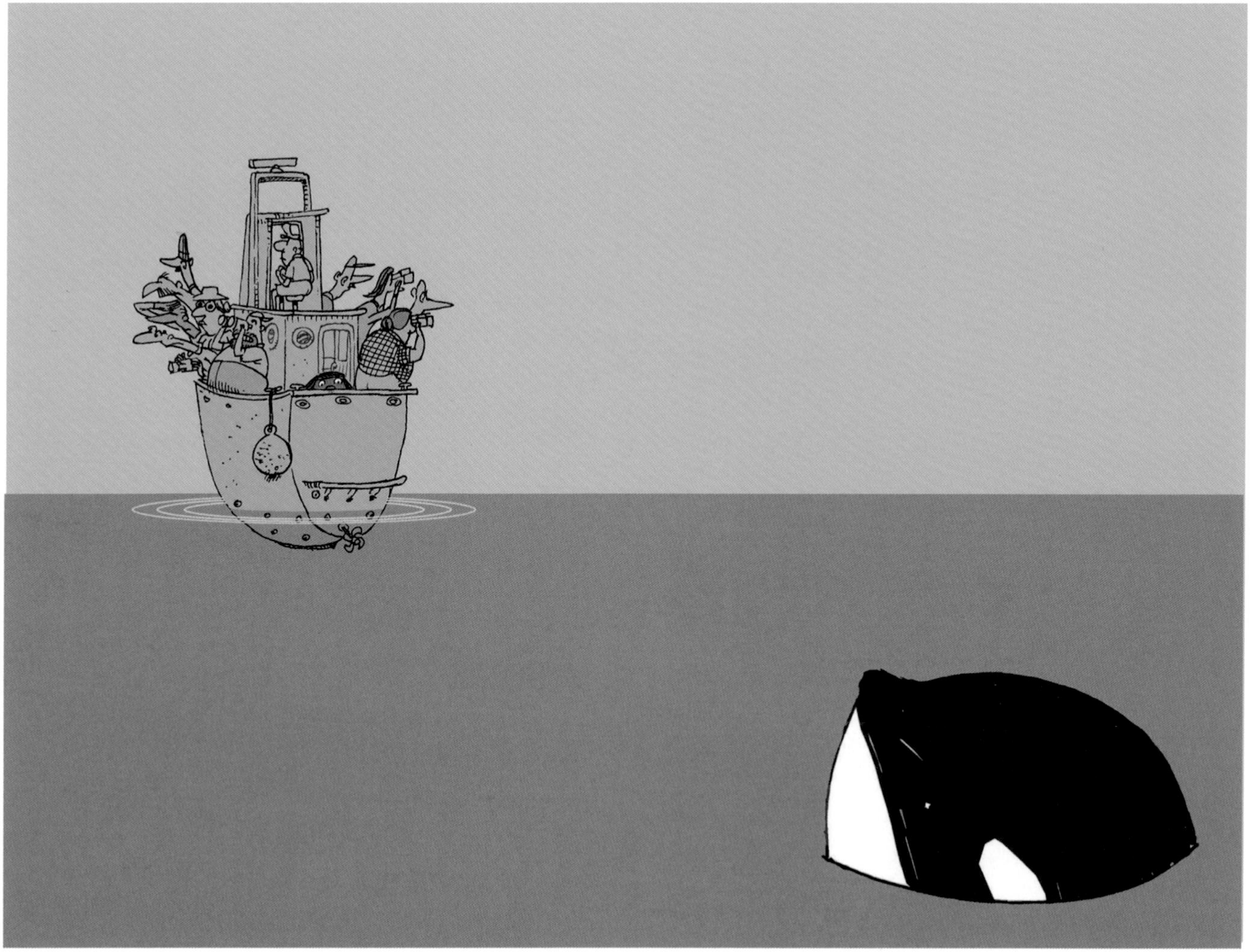

YOUR BIG QUESTION ABOUT VANCOUVER IS –

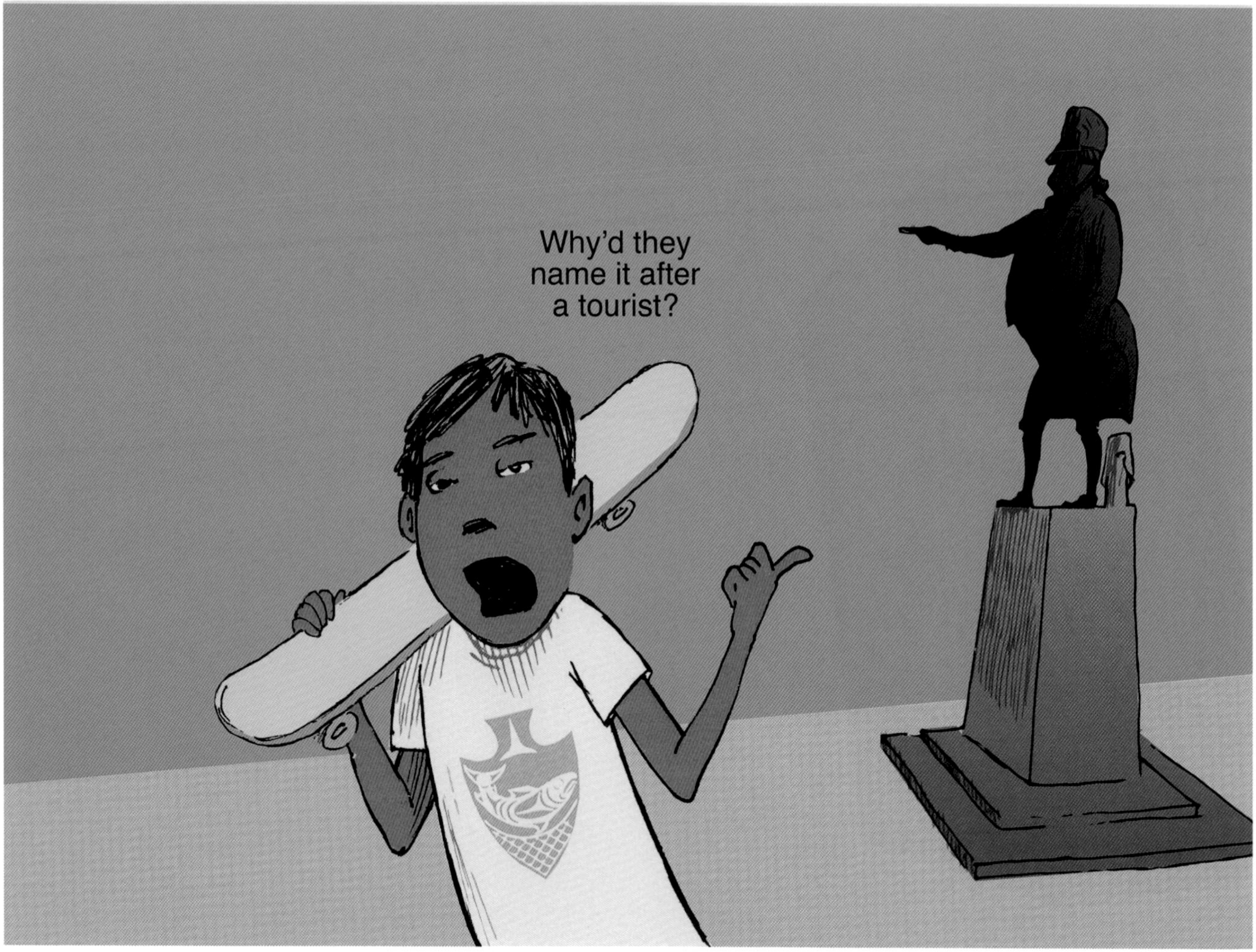
Why'd they name it after a tourist?

YOU KNOW YOU LOCAL WINES

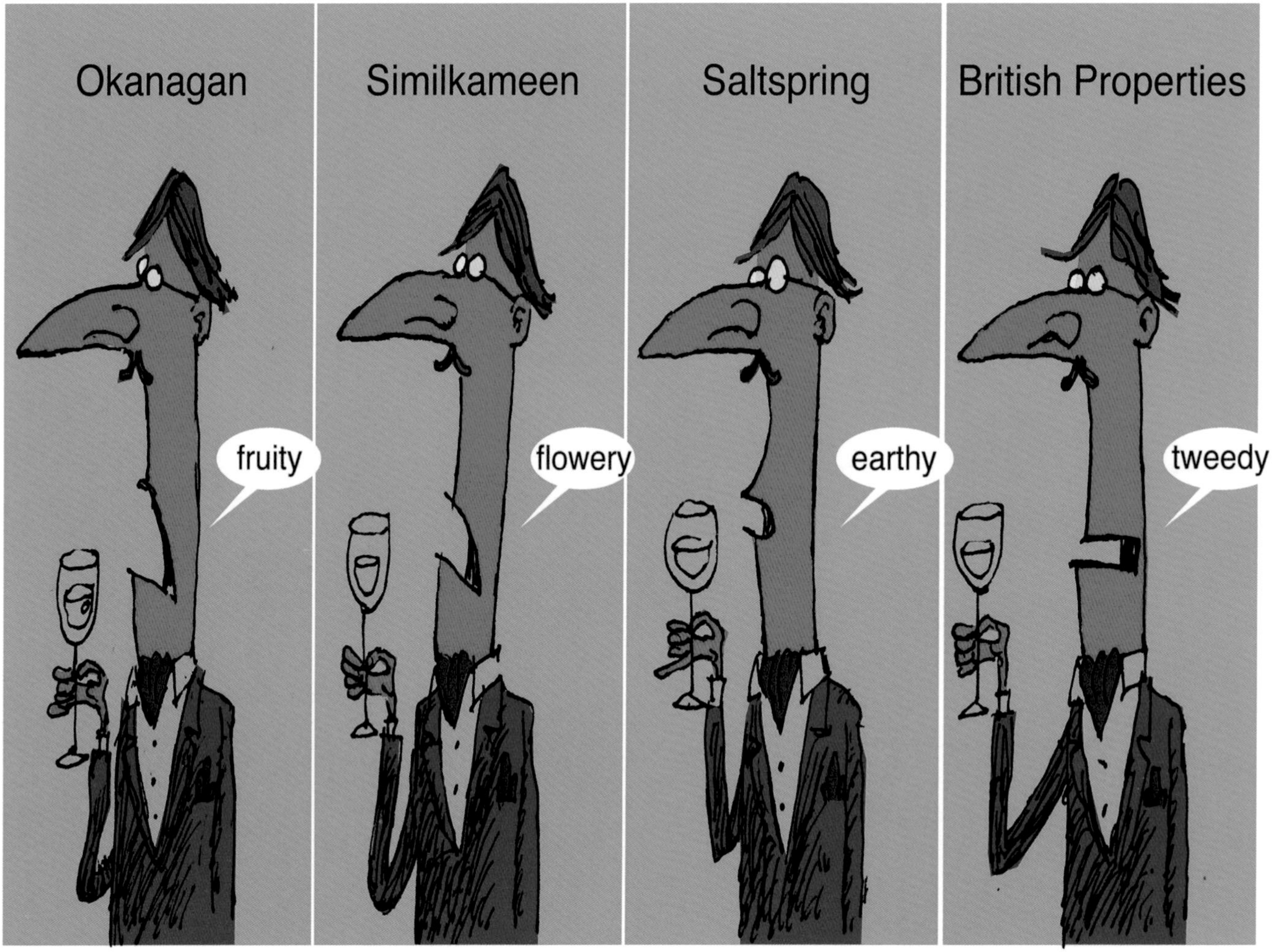
Okanagan
fruity
Similkameen
flowery
Saltspring
earthy
British Properties
tweedy

NO MATTER WHAT THE WEATHER'S LIKE, WHEN YOU CHRISTMAS SKYPE WITH EASTERNERS YOU SAY "BEEN KINDA WARM HERE..."

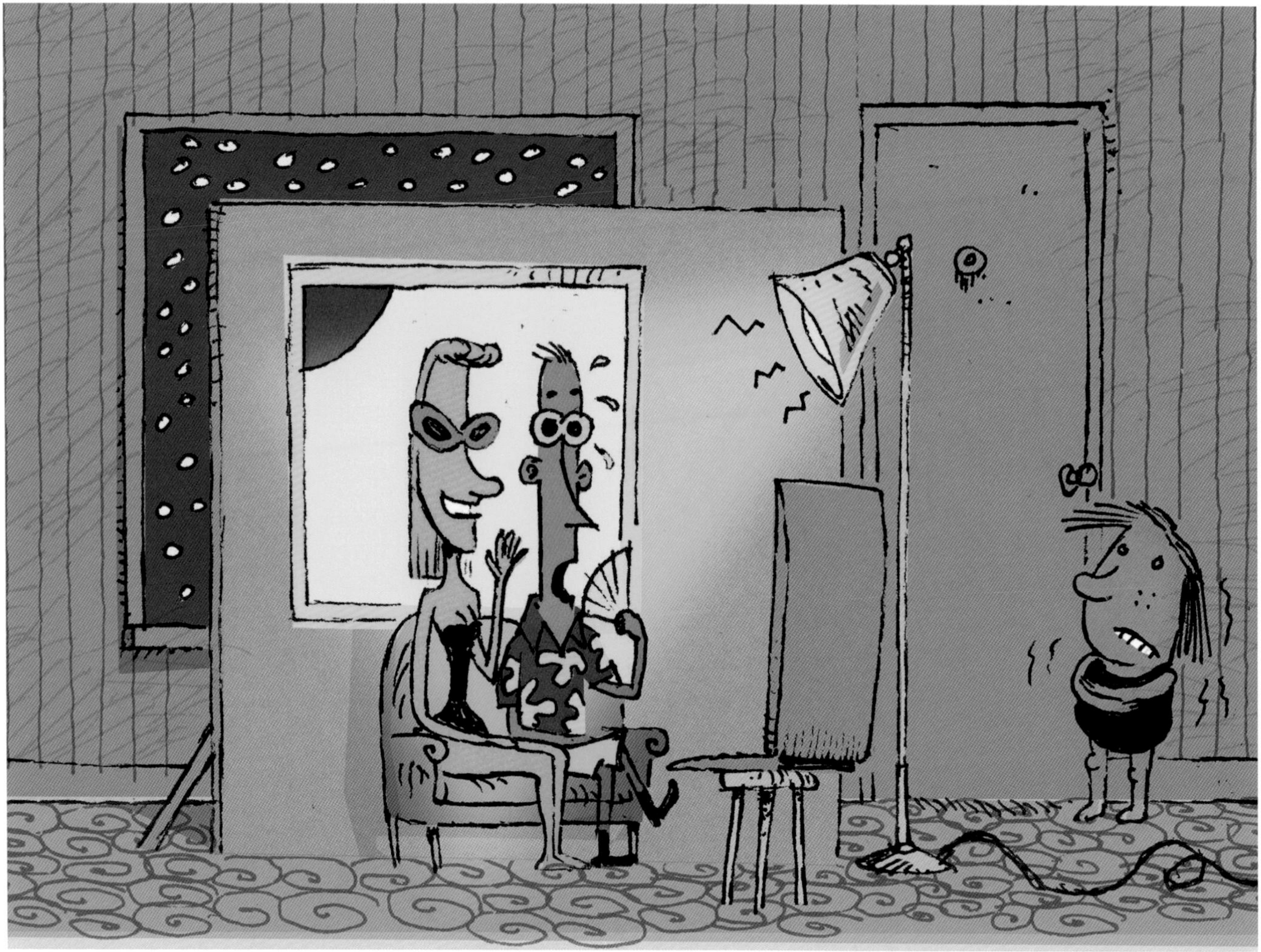

YOU DON'T MISS THE VANCOUVER STOCK EXCHANGE GANG,
BUT YOU DO MISS THEIR PARROTS

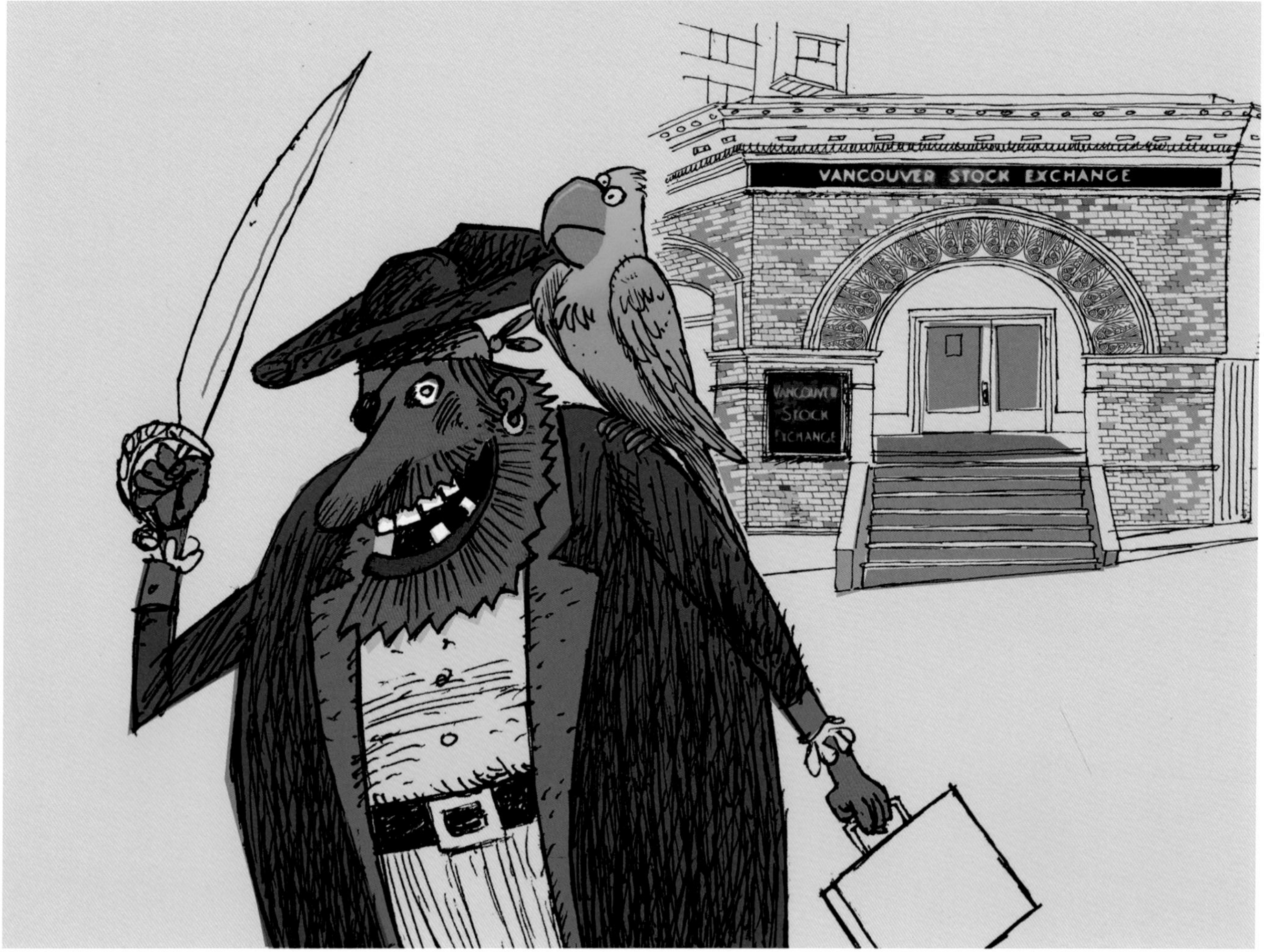

VANCOUVER STOCK EXCHANGE
VANCOUVER STOCK EXCHANGE

WHEN YOU FINALLY FIND THAT AFFORDABLE HOUSE LISTING . . .

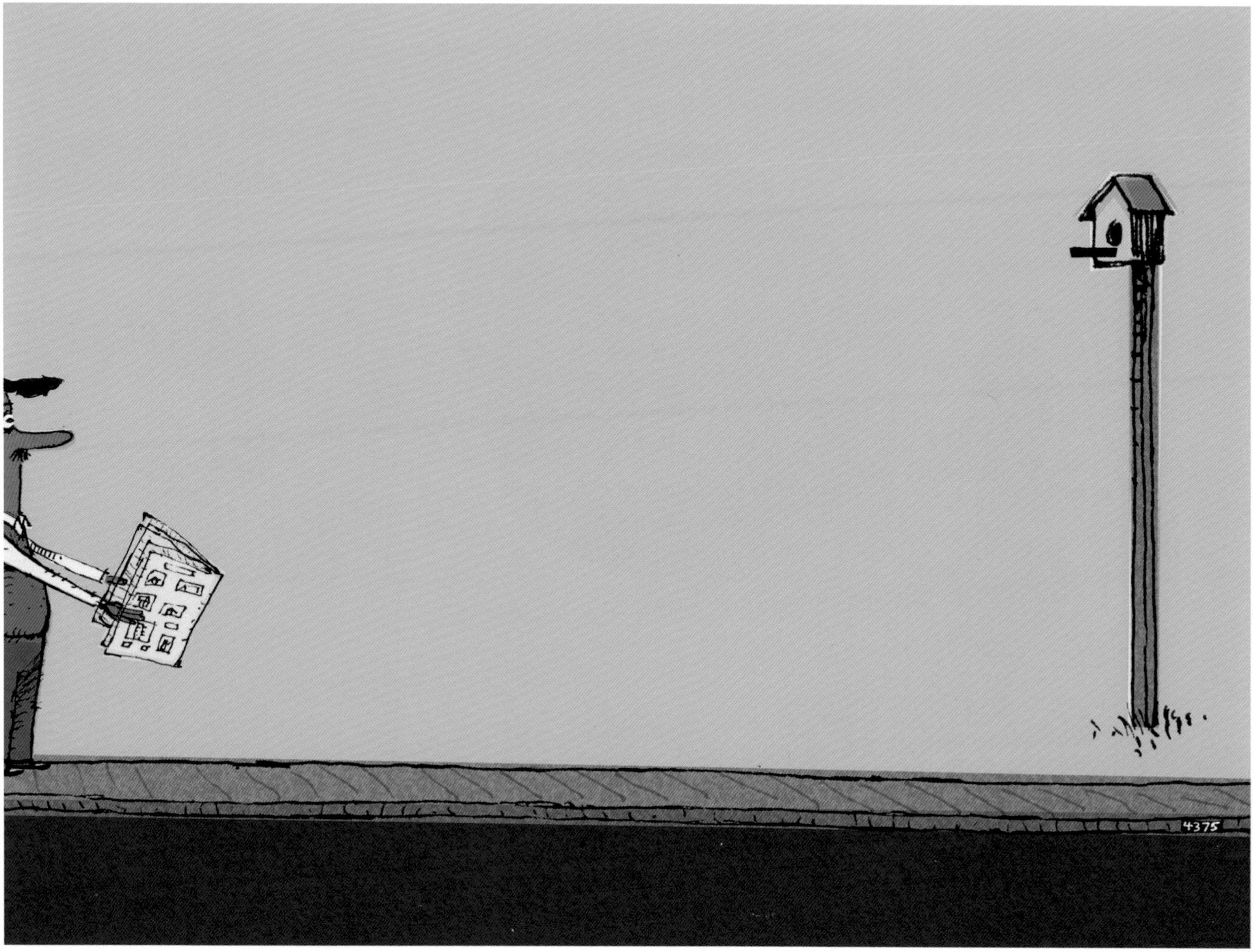
4375

YOU CELEBRATE B.C. DAY THE TRADITIONAL WAY: BY SHOPPING IN WASHINGTON

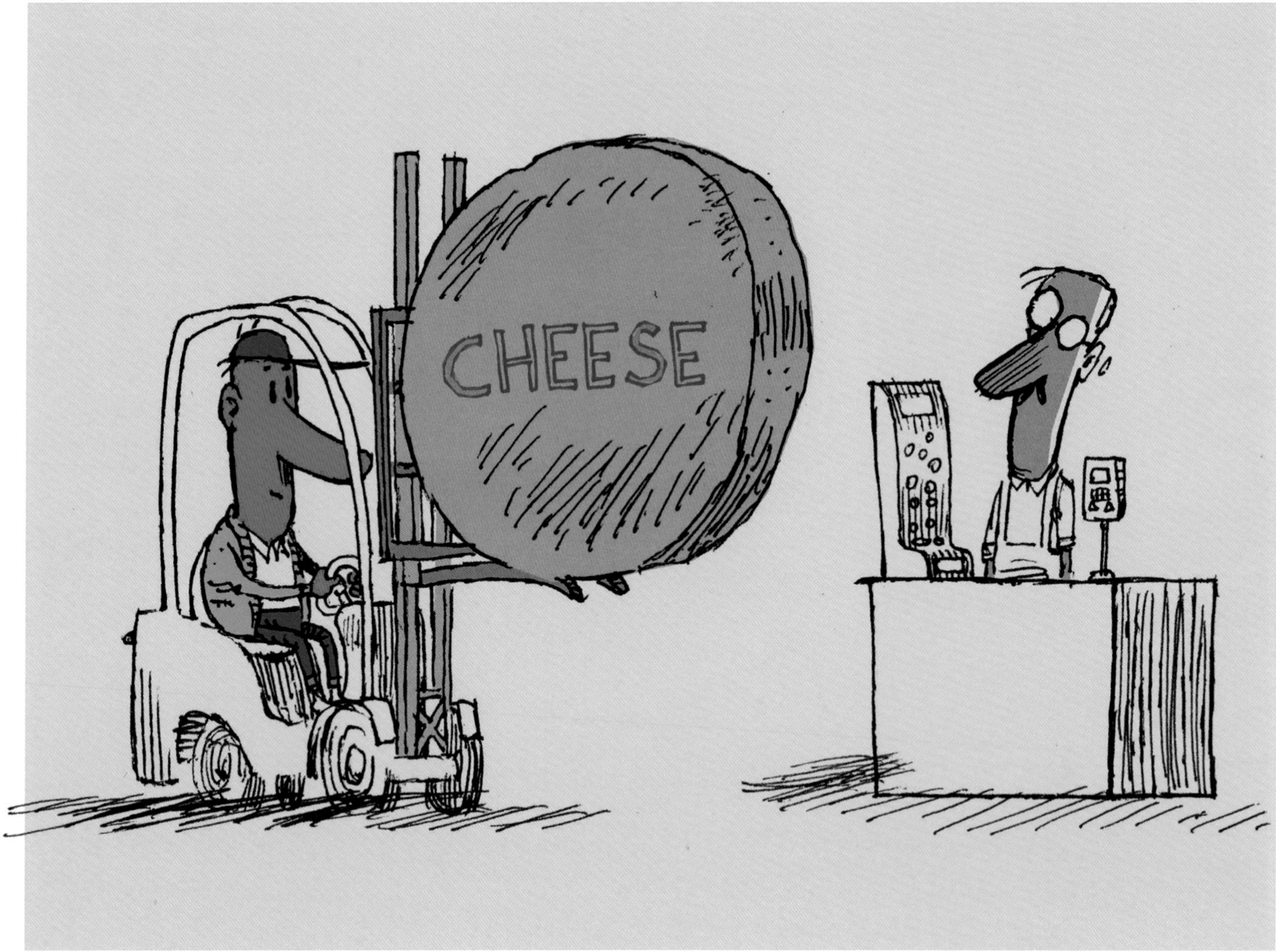
CHEESE

YOU'VE FOUND *MAYBE* THE WORLD'S BEST ORGANIC ALE — CERTAINLY THE WORLD'S *BEST-NAMED* ORGANIC ALE — IN SORRENTO

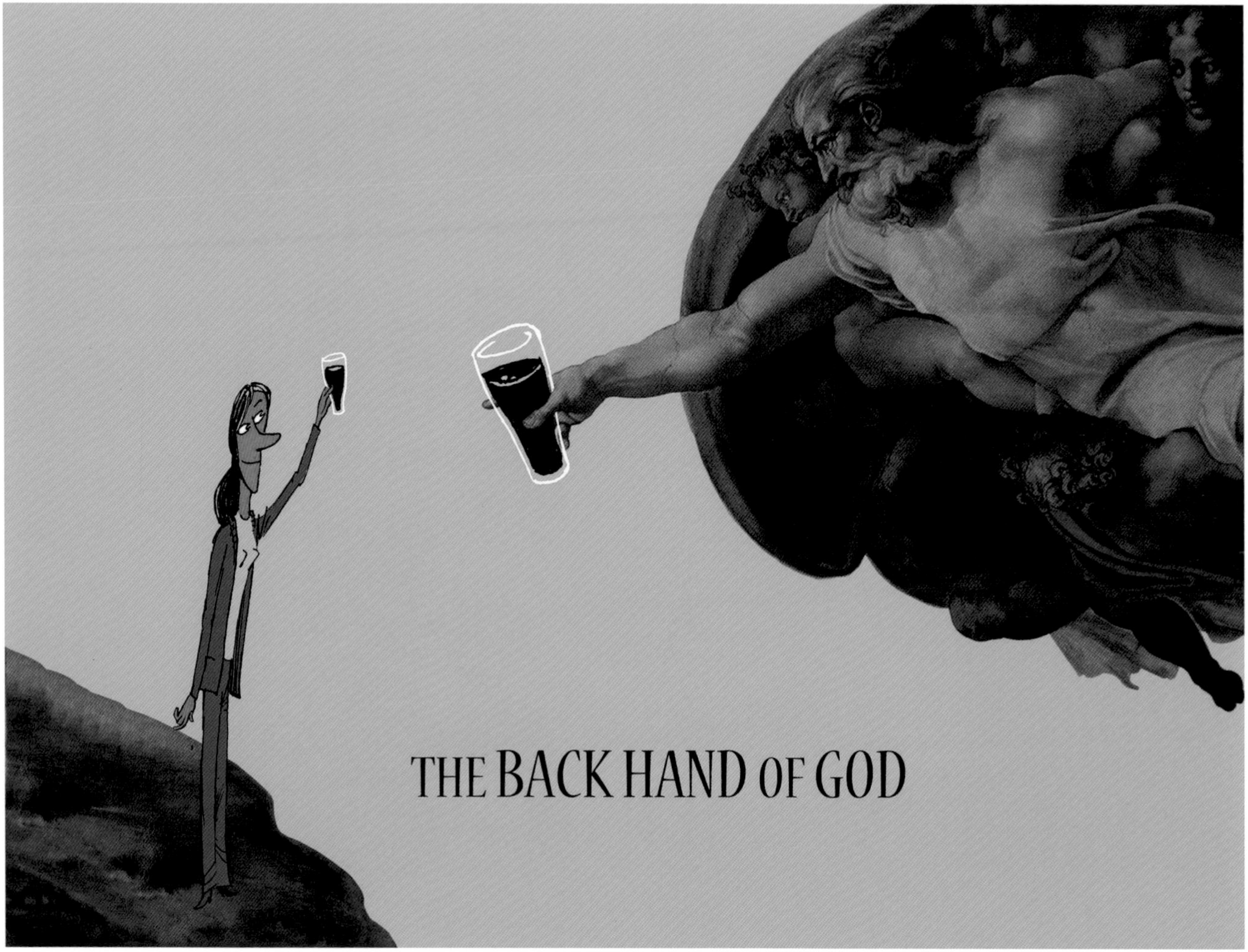
THE BACK HAND OF GOD

YOU HAVE, AT A TIME OF HEIGHTENED EMOTION, CALLED YOUR BELOVED BY THE NAME OF A NOW DEFUNCT PRINCE-GEORGE-BREWED STUBBY-BOTTLED MALT LIQUOR

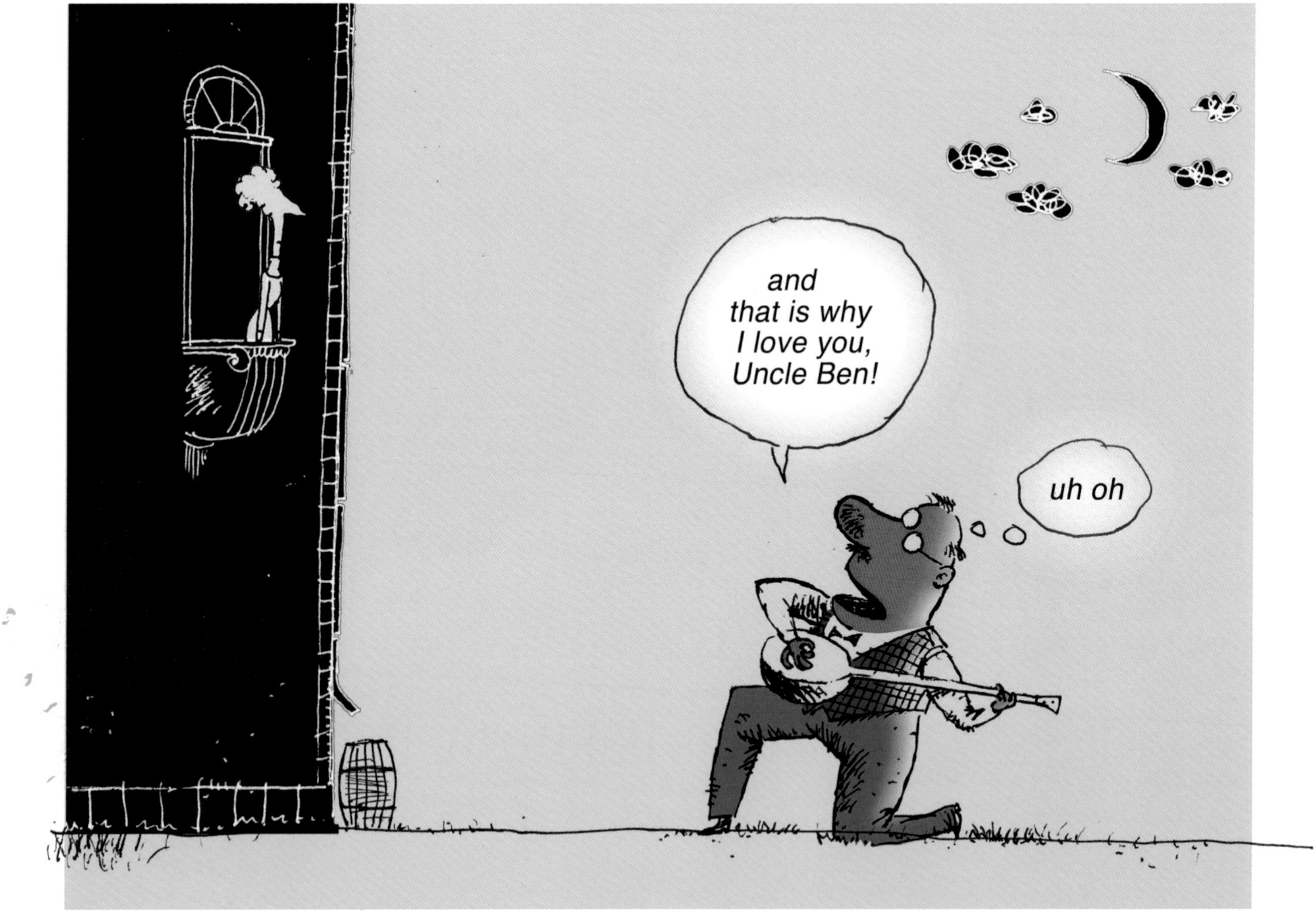

and that is why I love you, Uncle Ben!
uh oh

YOU KNOW WHAT THE NAME OF LADNER'S SIGNATURE PARFUM WOULD BE

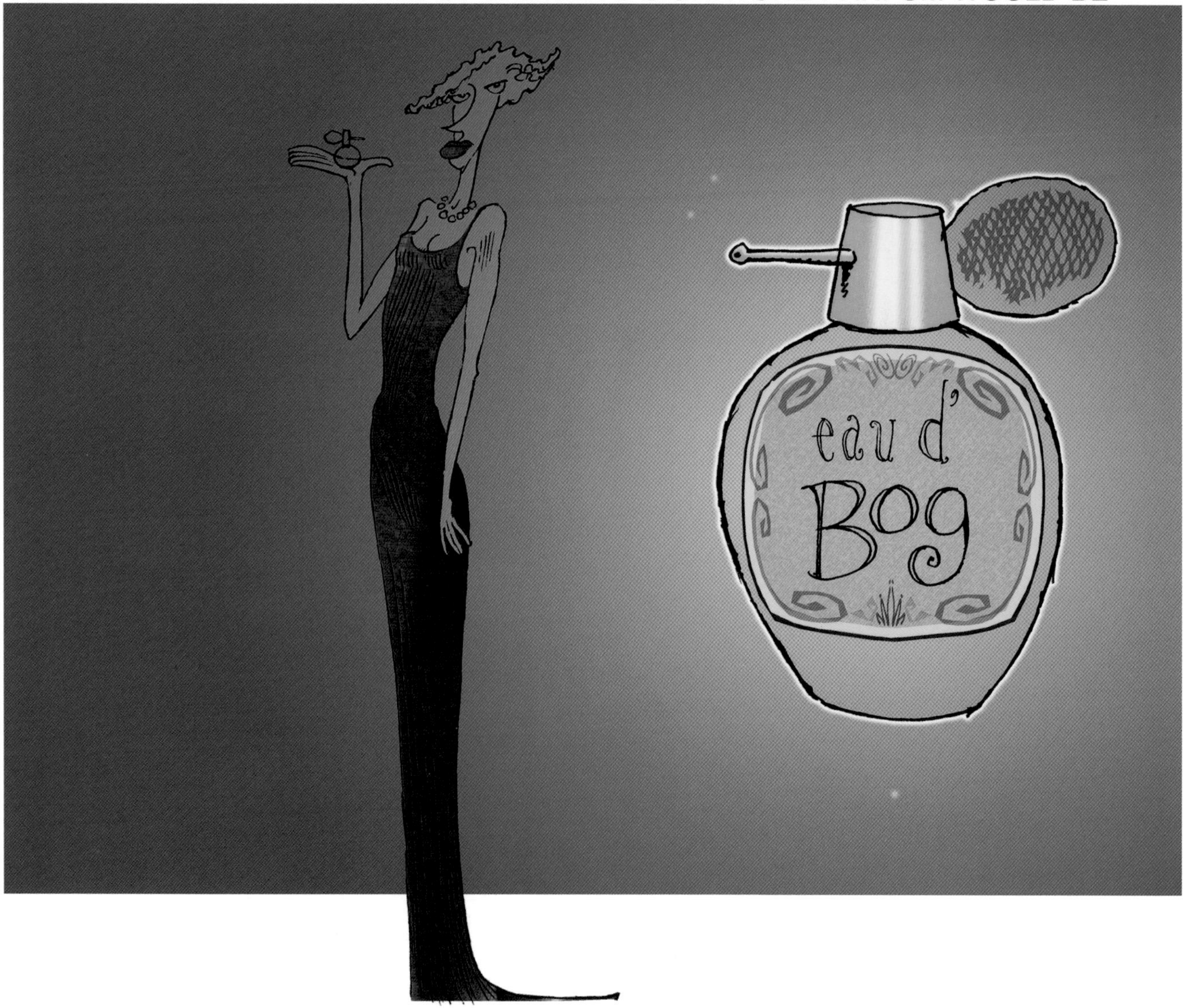
eau d'
Bog

YOUR CAR IS FESTOONED WITH CANUCKS FLAGS

AND YOUR
CASKET
WILL BE TOO

YOU'VE CONCLUDED SCARY CAMPFIRE STORIES WITH:
"AND THAT'S THE TALE OF GLEN CLARK'S FAST FERRIES"

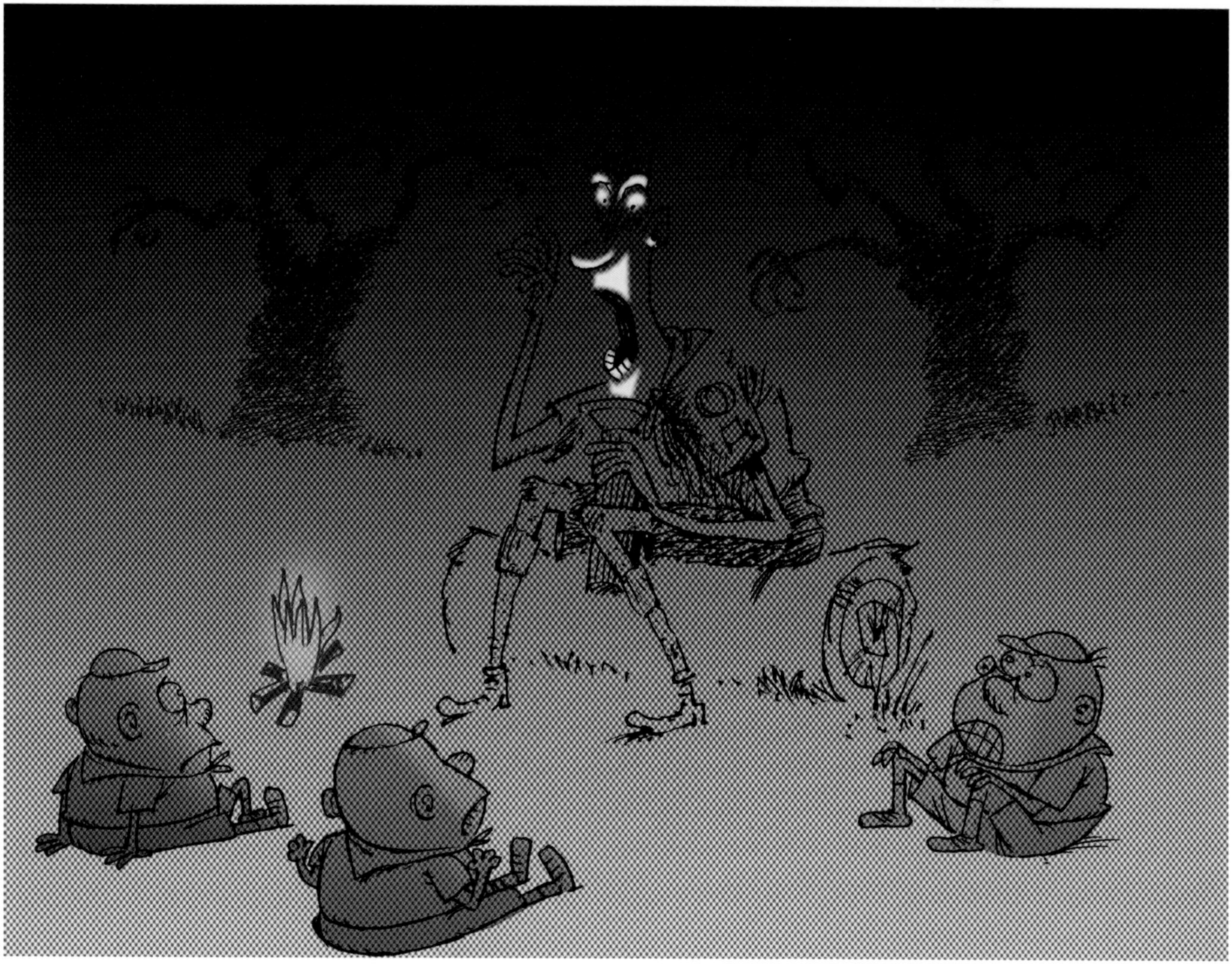

IT'S WHERE YOU LEARNED THAT YOU LOVE HIGHLAND DANCE MUSIC

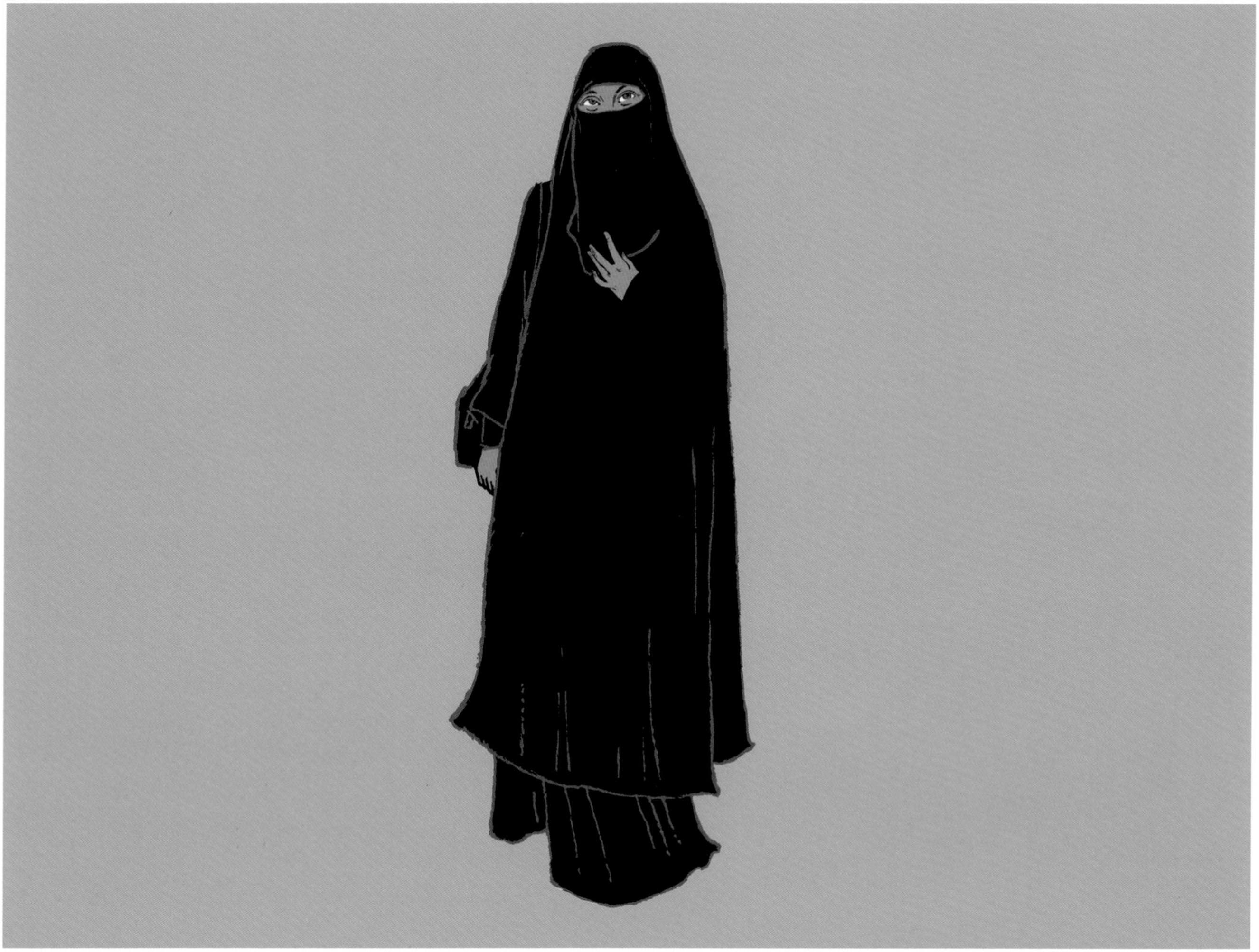

YOU CAN SPEAK KITIMAT WITHOUT A TRANSLATOR

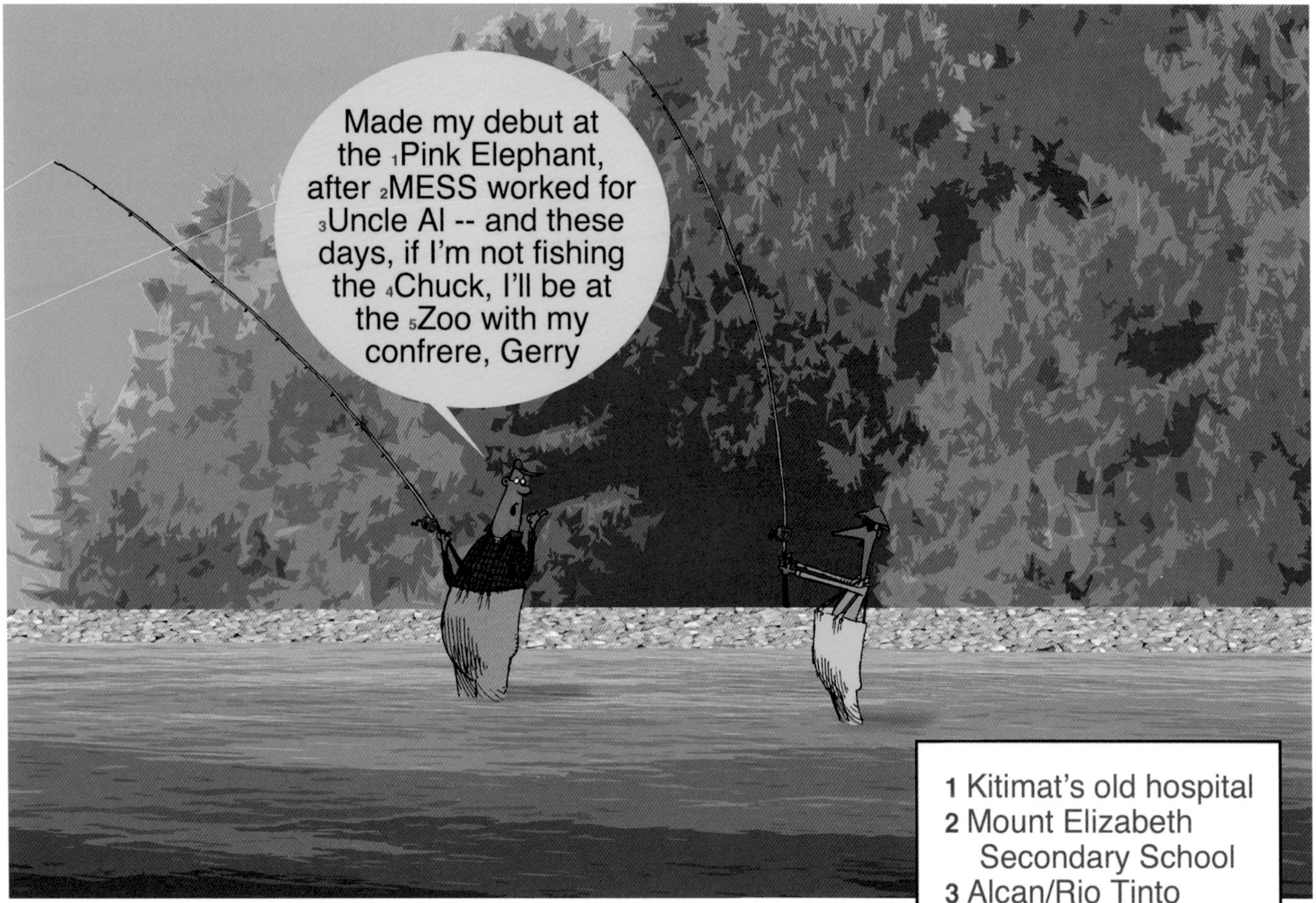
Made my debut at the [1]Pink Elephant, after [2]MESS worked for [3]Uncle Al -- and these days, if I'm not fishing the [4]Chuck, I'll be at the [5]Zoo with my confrere, Gerry

1 Kitimat's old hospital
2 Mount Elizabeth Secondary School
3 Alcan/Rio Tinto
4 Douglas Channel
5 Kitimat Hotel Pub

YOU'VE EXCHANGED CRUISE-SHIP-TO-CRUISE-SHIP COURTESIES IN ENGLISH BAY

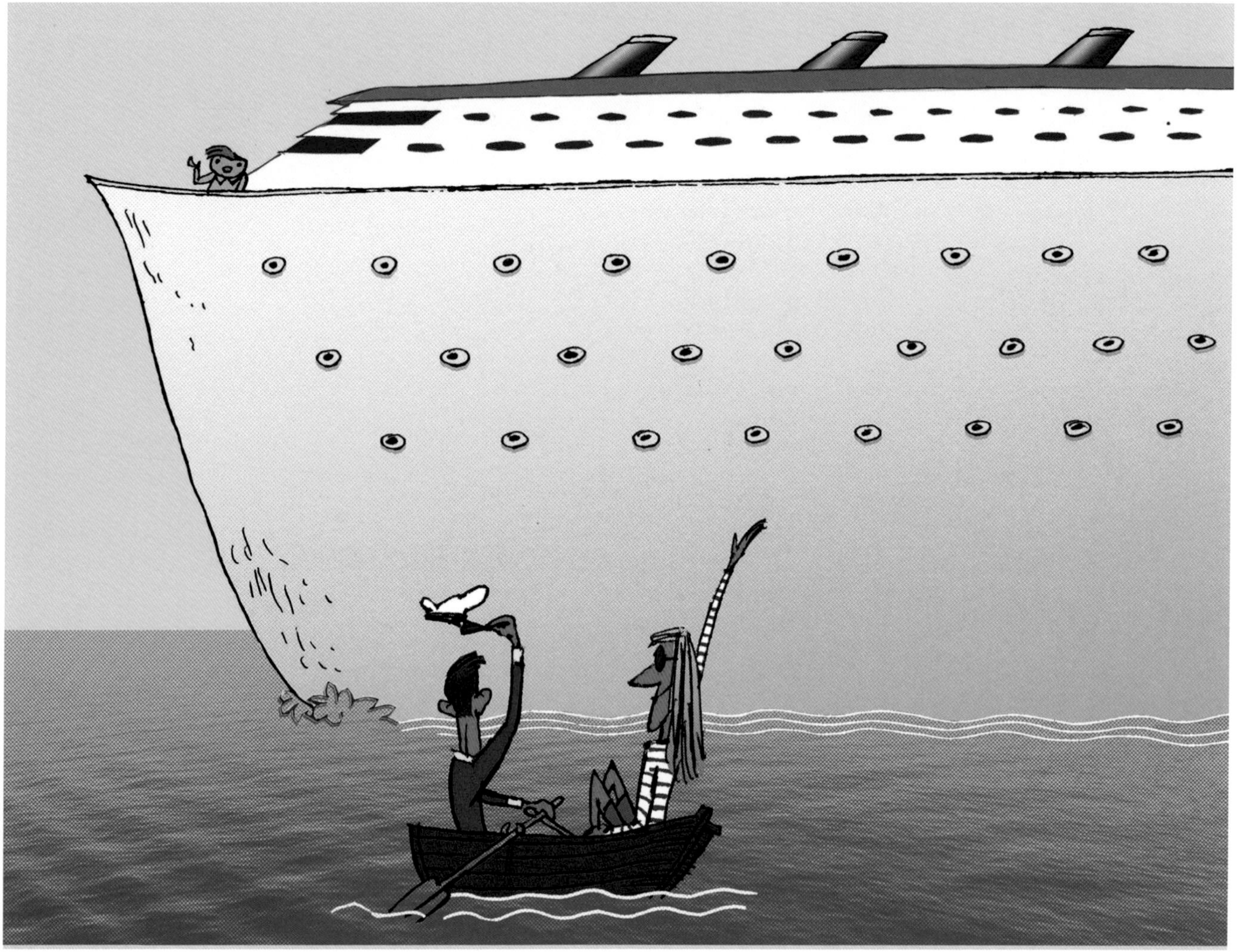

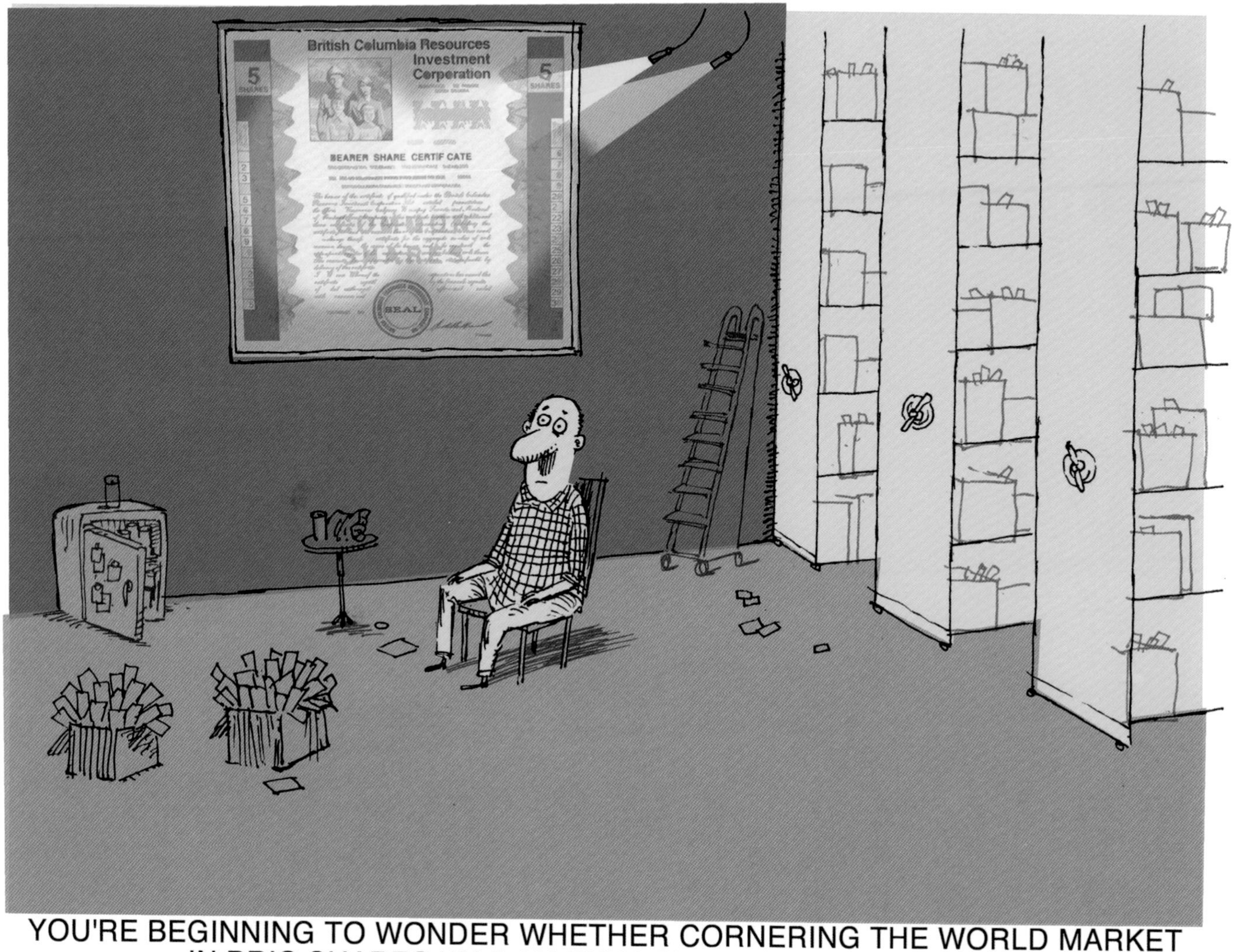
British Columbia Resources
Investment
Corporation
5
SHARES
5
SHARES
BEARER SHARE CERTIF CATE
COMMON
SHARES
SEAL

YOU'RE BEGINNING TO WONDER WHETHER CORNERING THE WORLD MARKET IN BRIC SHARES WAS AN IRON-CLAD RETIREMENT PLAN

YOU KNOW YOUR BEER

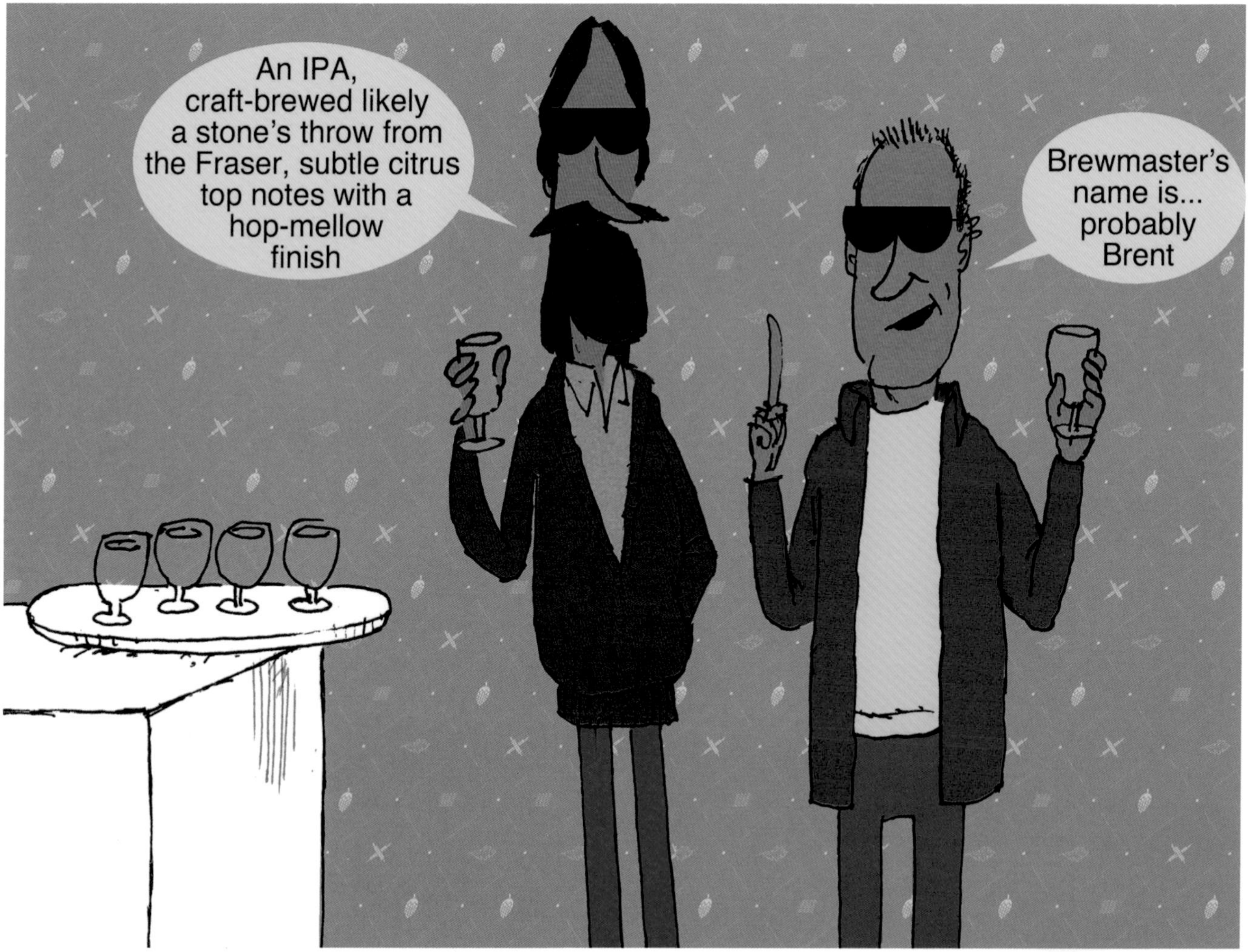
An IPA, craft-brewed likely a stone's throw from the Fraser, subtle citrus top notes with a hop-mellow finish
Brewmaster's name is... probably Brent

YOU'VE LIT A CANDLE TO THE PATRON SAINT OF PORT HARDY

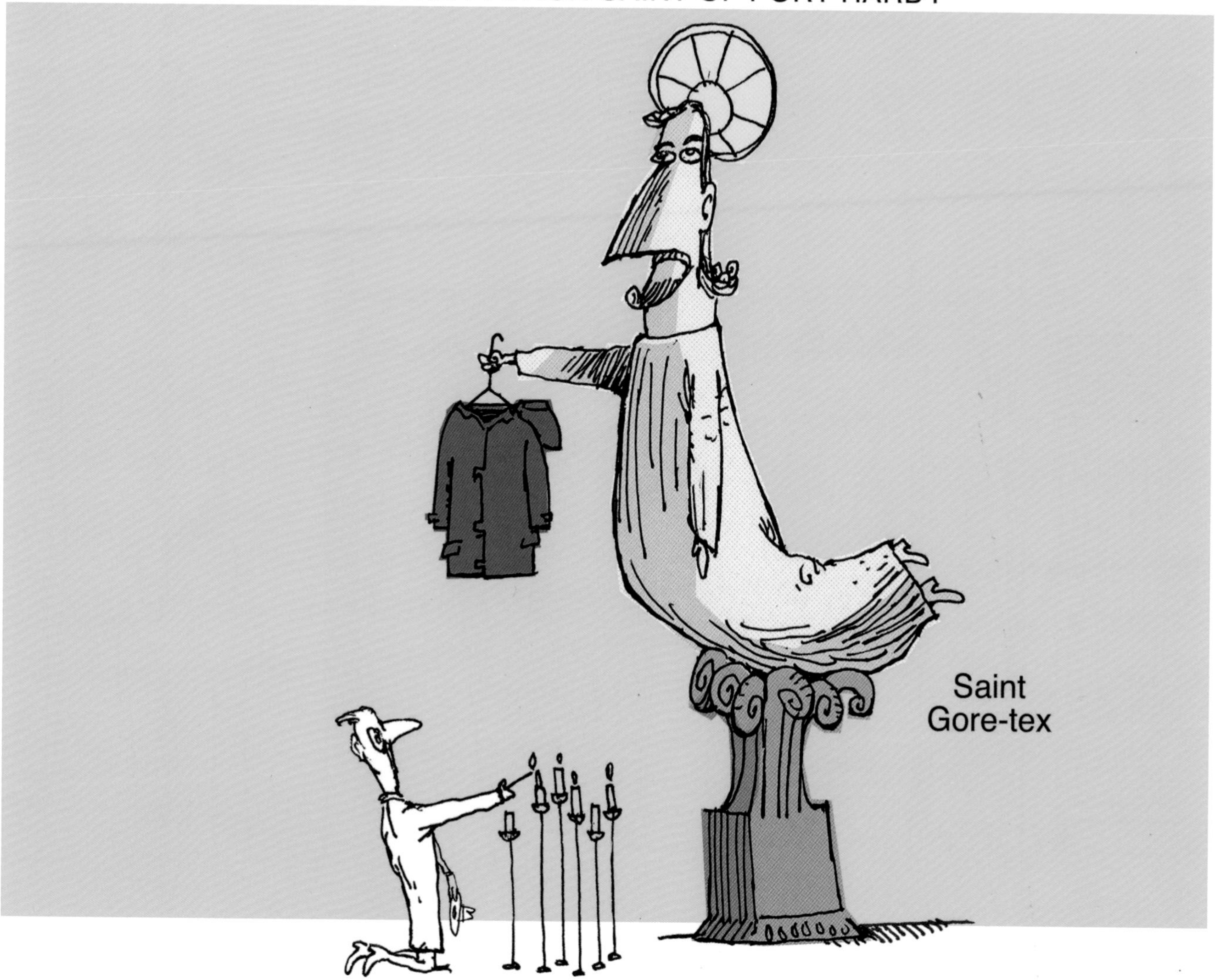
Saint
Gore-tex

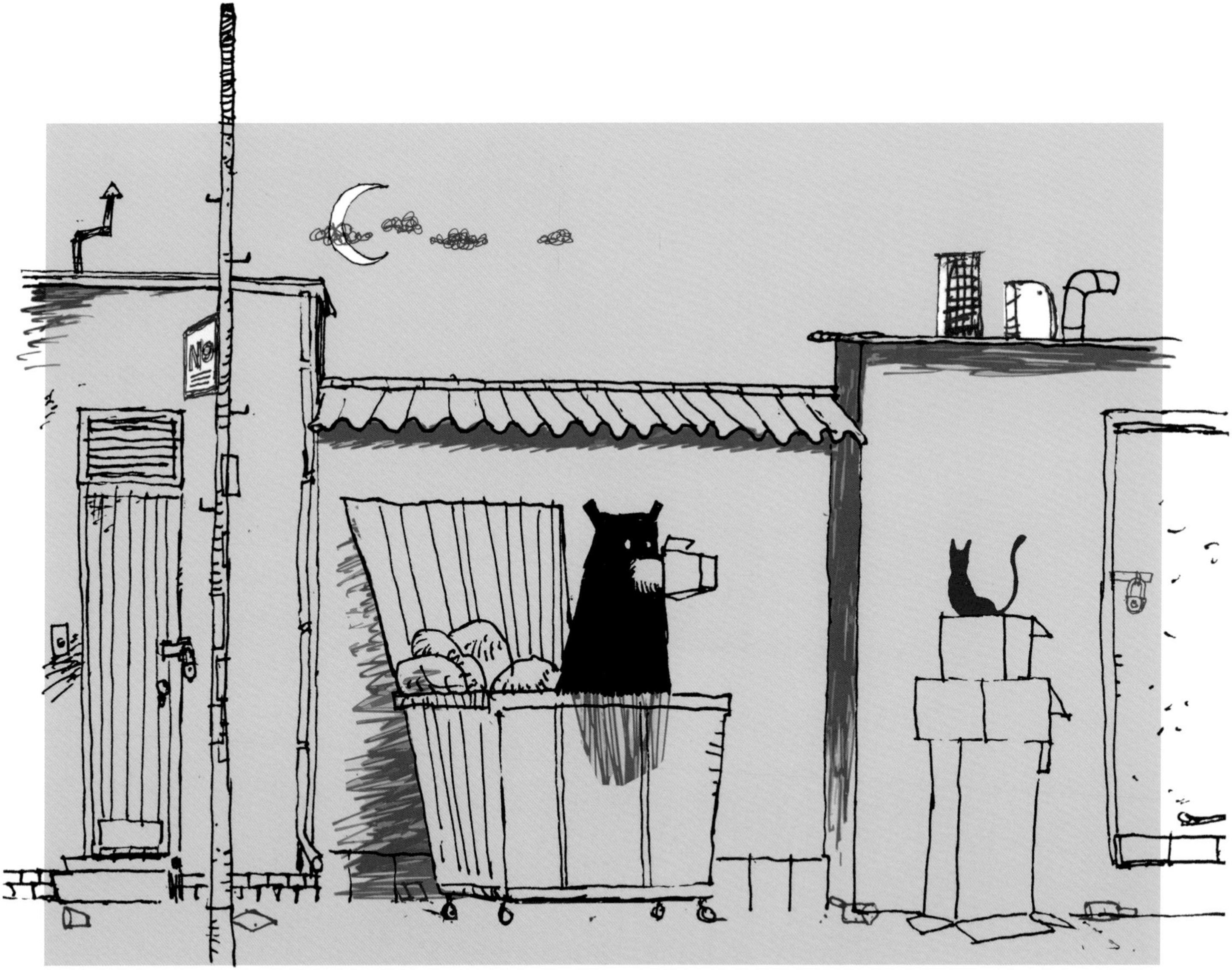
No

YOUR NEIGHBOURHOOD BINNER IS A BEAR

YOUR CHAKRAS RAN OFF WITH YOUR LIFE COACH

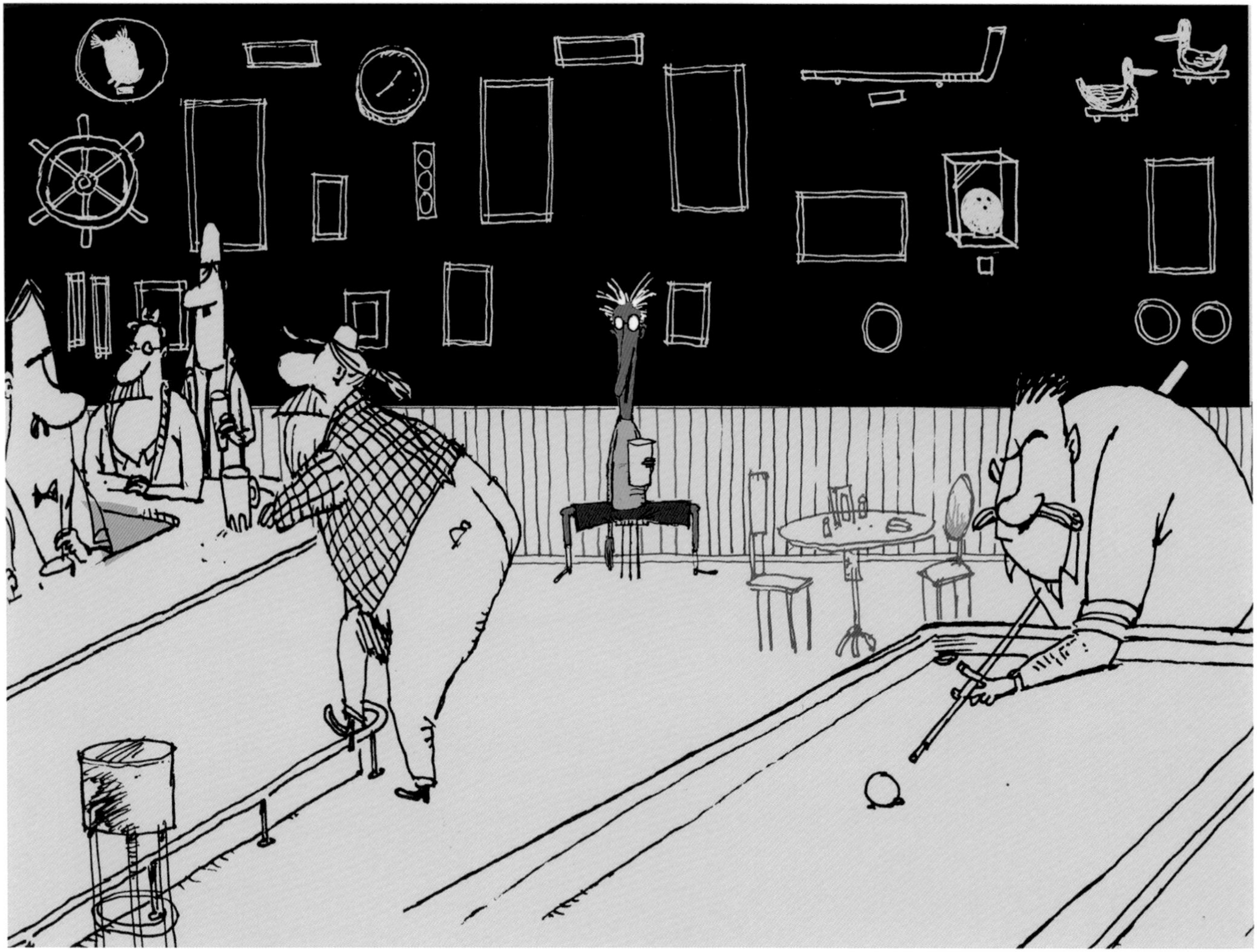

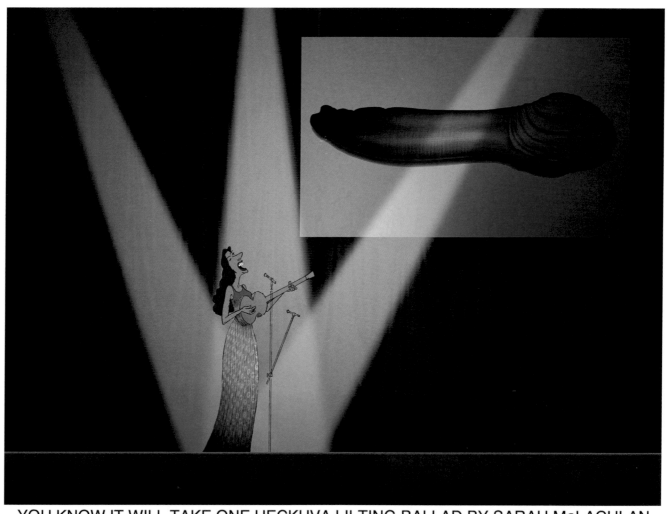

YOU KNOW IT WILL TAKE ONE HECKUVA LILTING BALLAD BY SARAH McLACHLAN
FOR B.C.'S NOBLE GEODUCK TO GET THE RESPECT IT DESERVES

YOU'VE BEEN LATE FOR A FEST BECAUSE YOU HAD TO DETOUR AROUND SEVEN FESTS

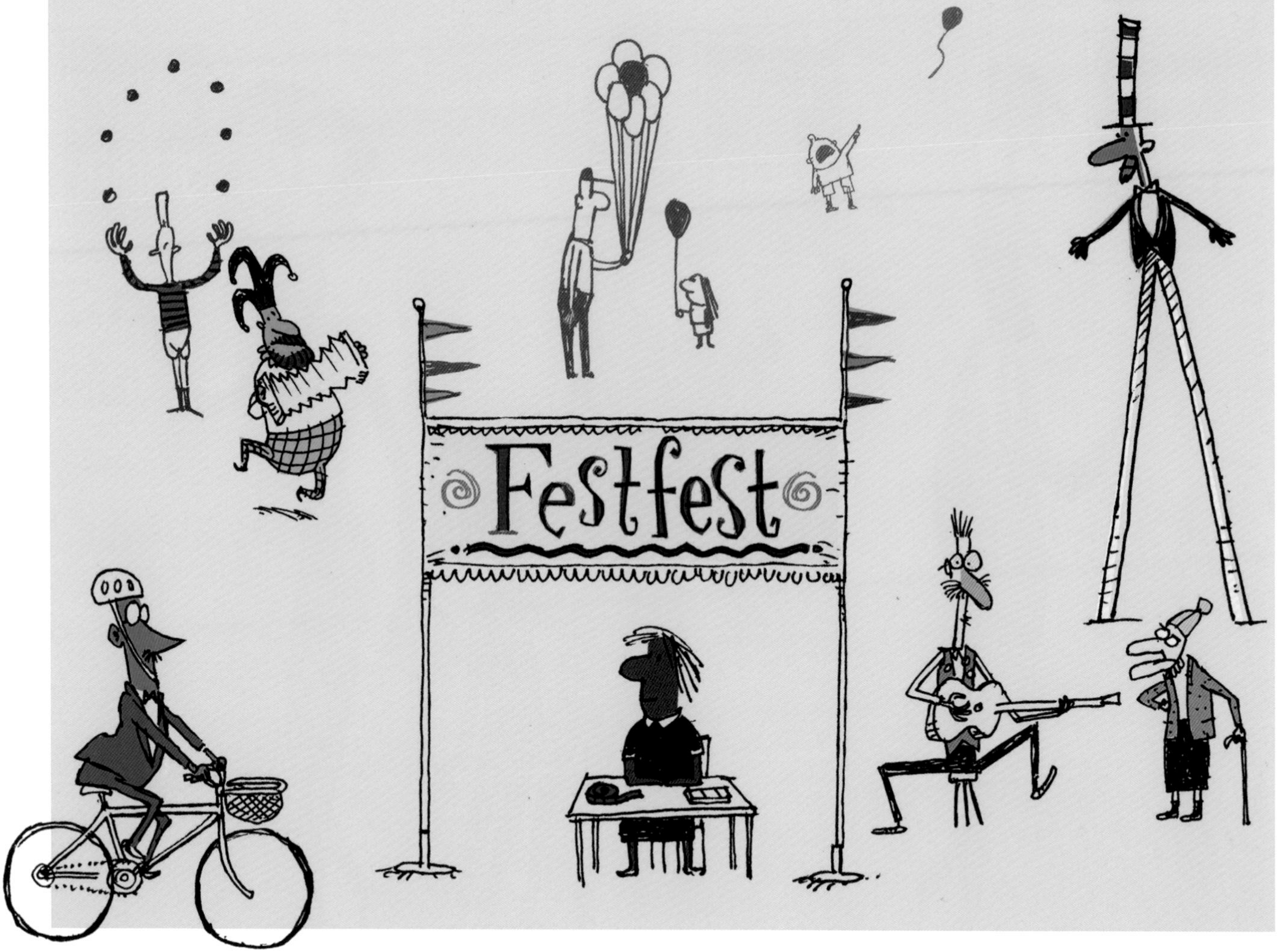
Festfest

YOUR STRIKE SIGN IS A HAND-ME-DOWN

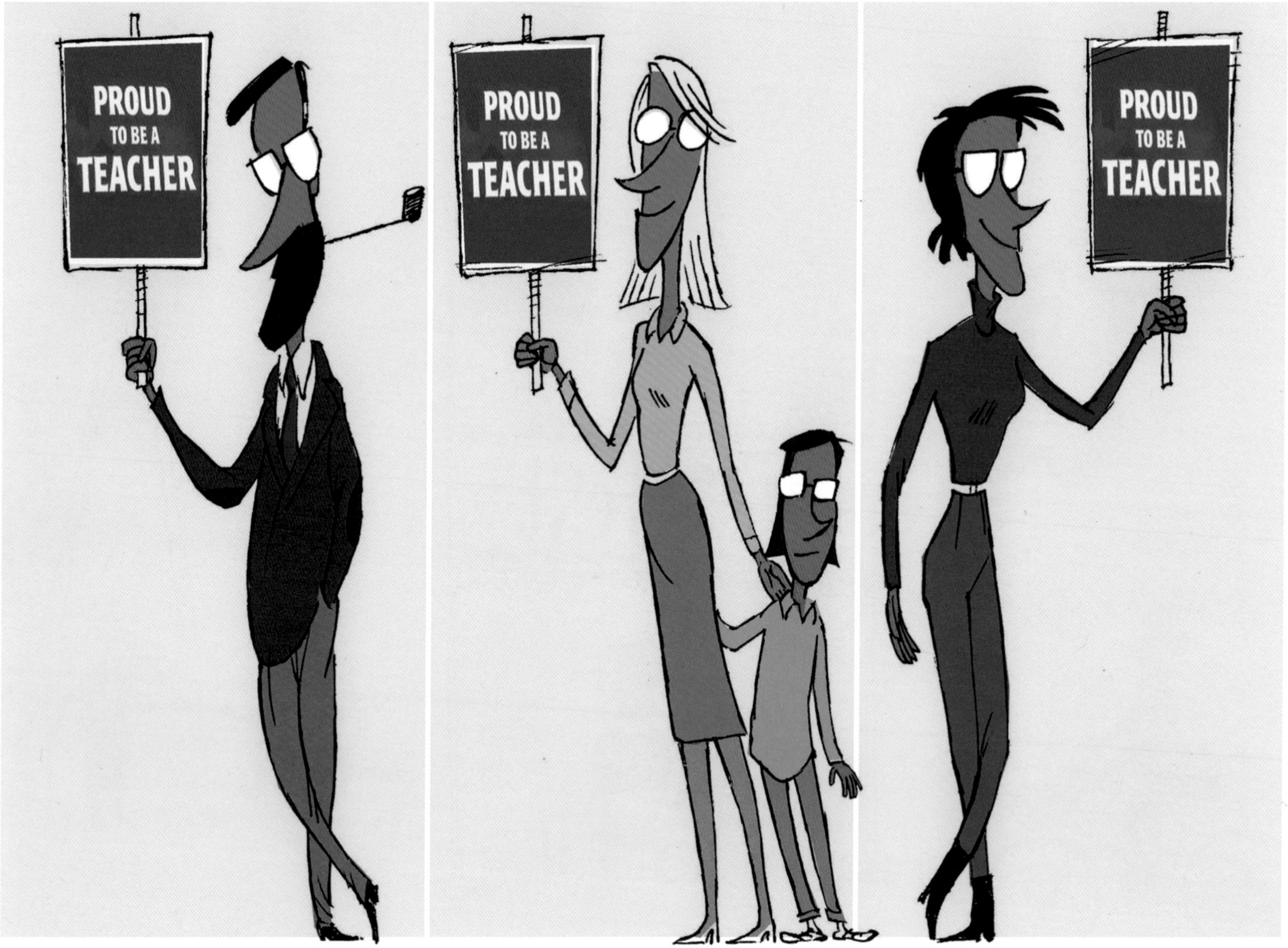
PROUD
TO BE A
TEACHER
PROUD
TO BE A
TEACHER
PROUD
TO BE A
TEACHER

YOUR OFFICE HAS A PRETTY NICE VIEW

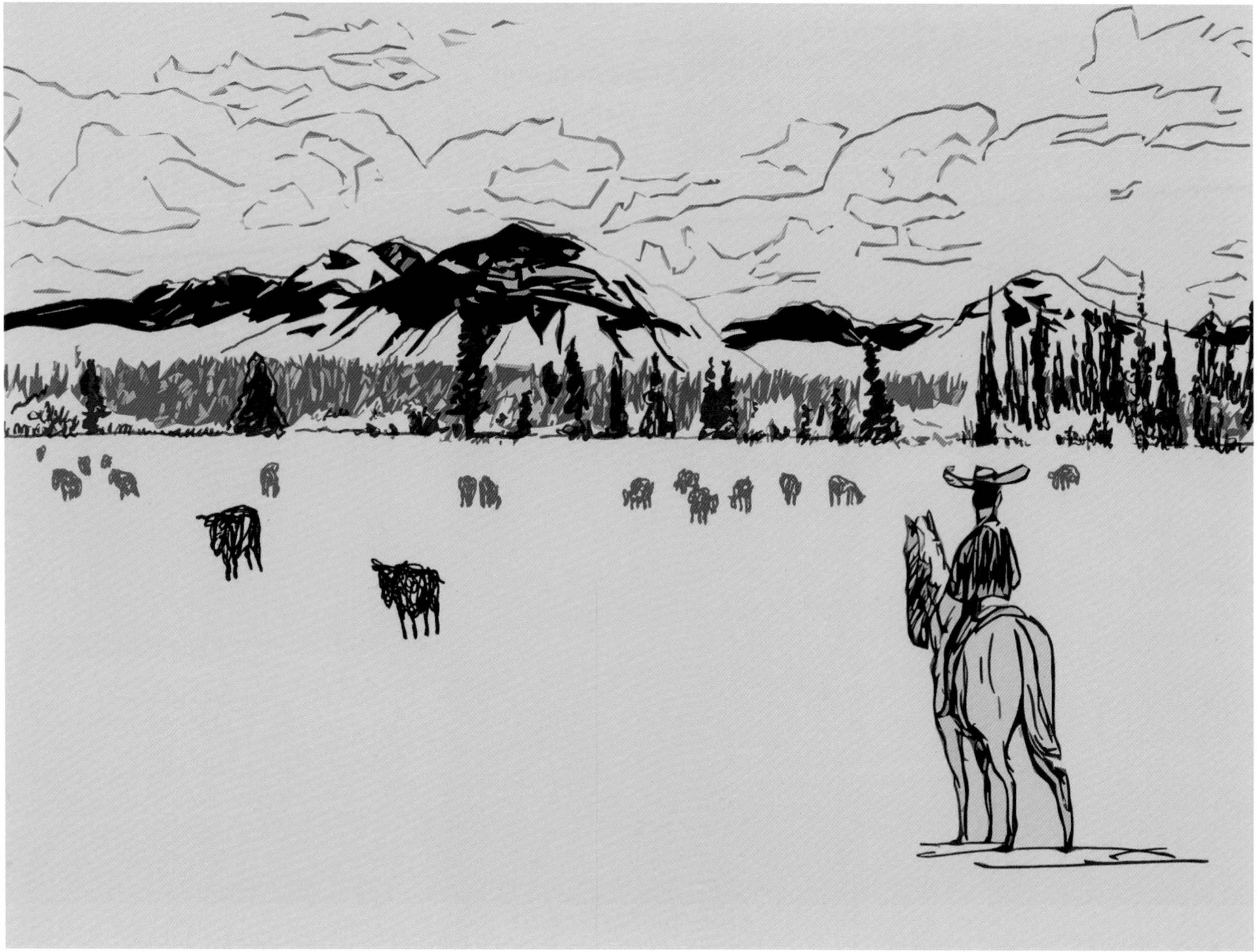

YOU'RE ON A FIRST-NAME BASIS WITH THE LOCAL CRYPTOZOOLOGY

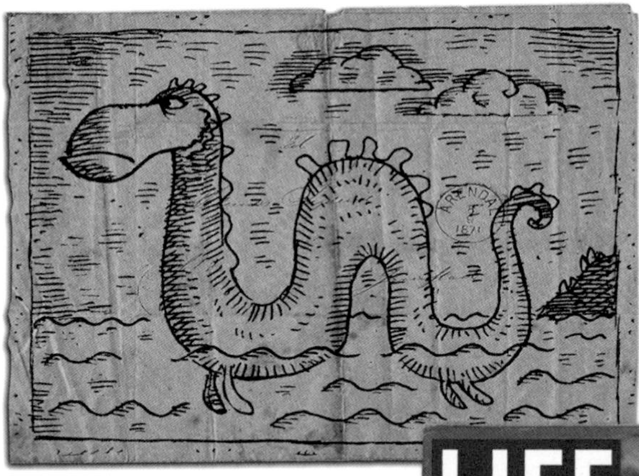

Cadbosaurus
(*Caddy*)

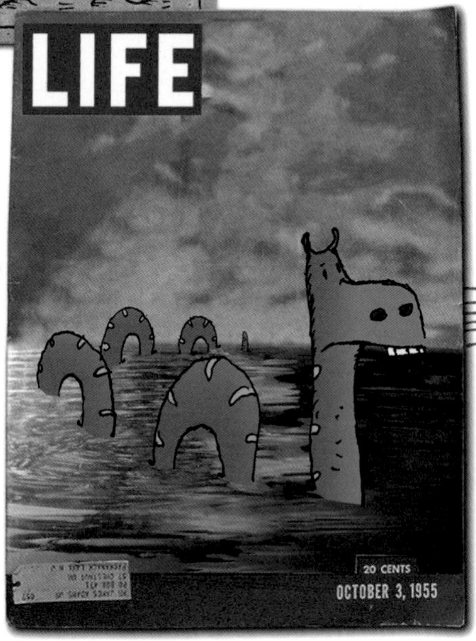
LIFE
20 CENTS
OCTOBER 3, 1955

Ogopogo
(*Poggie*)

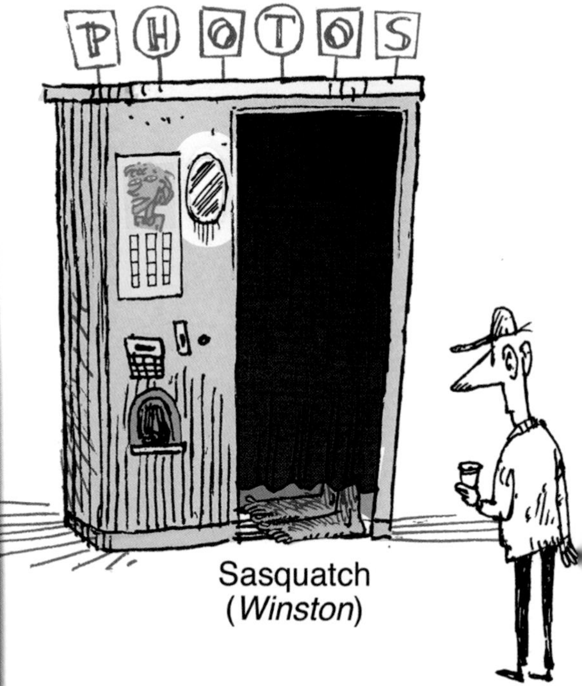
PHOTOS

Sasquatch
(*Winston*)

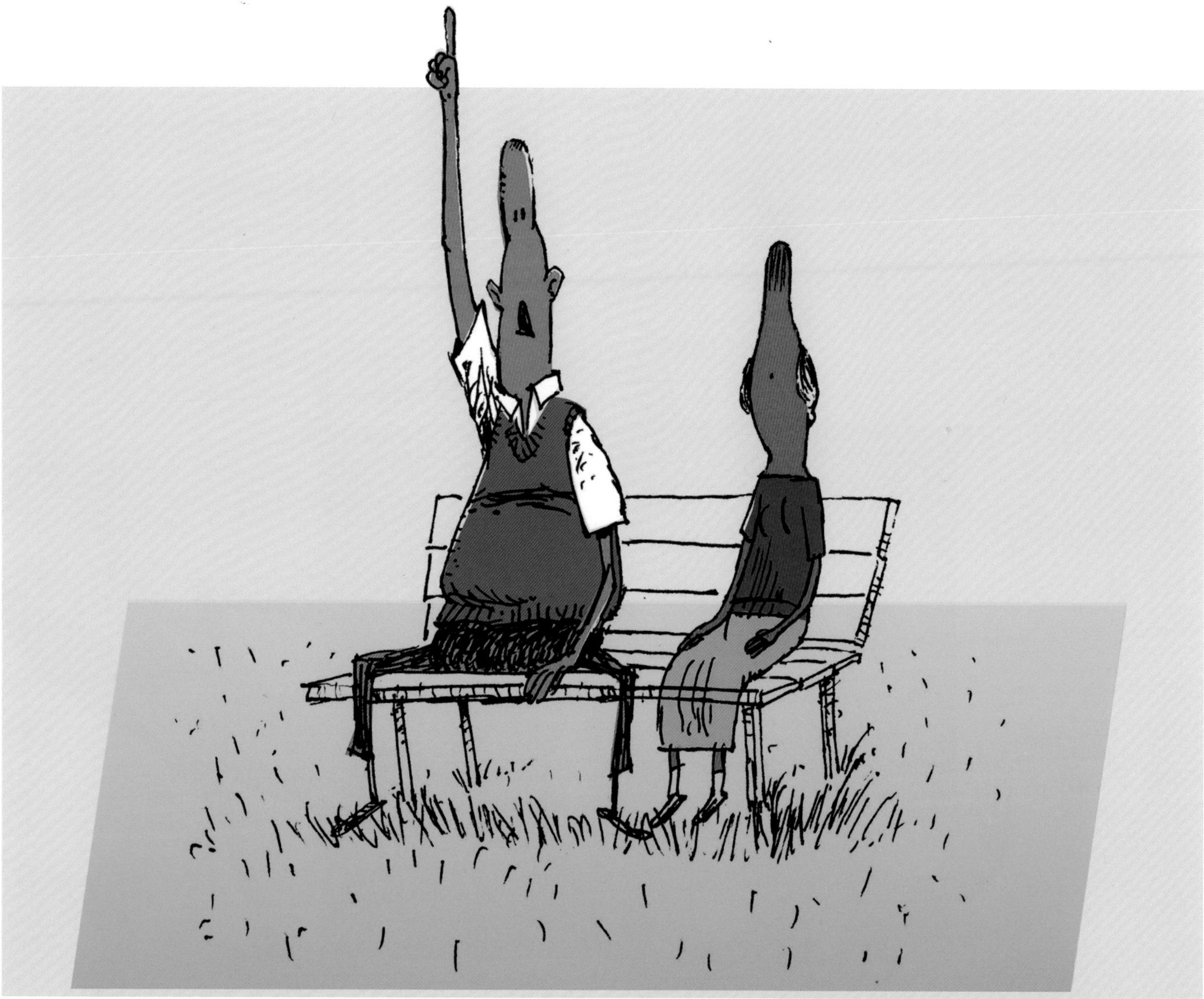

YOU'VE EVER SAID "THAT CLOUD LOOKS LIKE HARCOURT RESIGNING."

THE DIVORCE HIT A SNAG OVER CUSTODY OF THE KAYAK

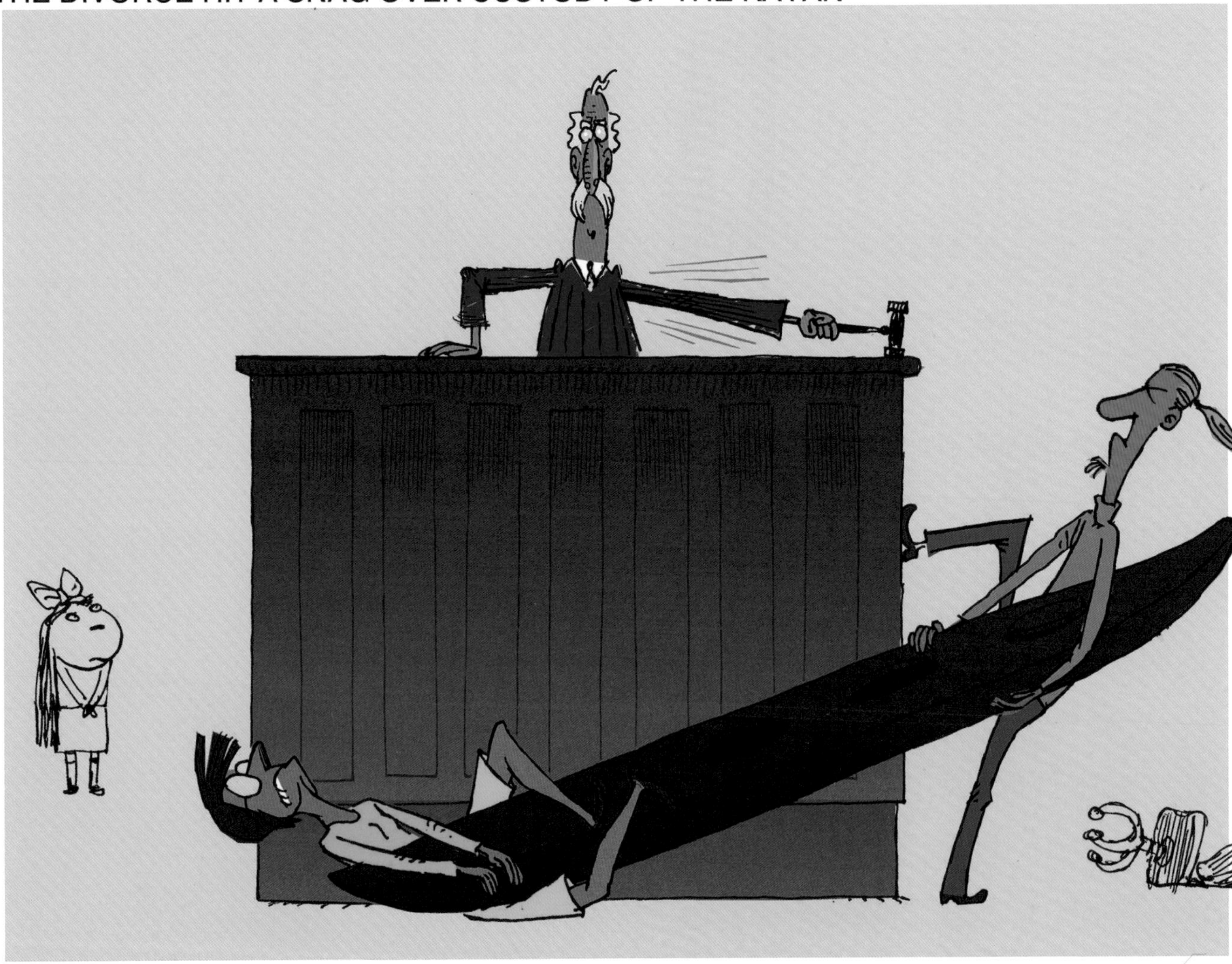

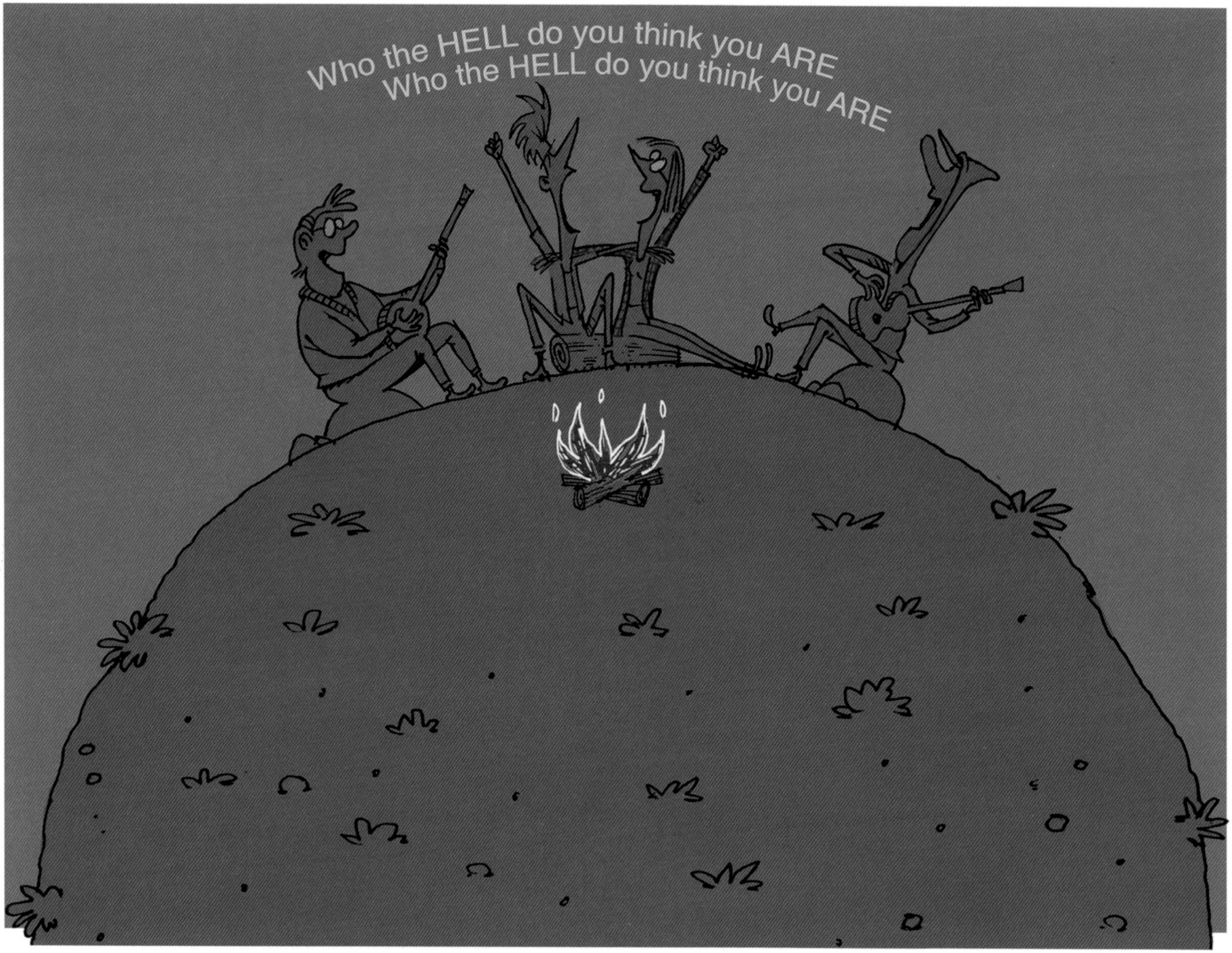
Who the HELL do you think you ARE
Who the HELL do you think you ARE

YOU'VE BEEN TO AN ALL-D.O.A. CAMPFIRE SINGALONG

YOU DON'T HAVE A PIGEON PROBLEM

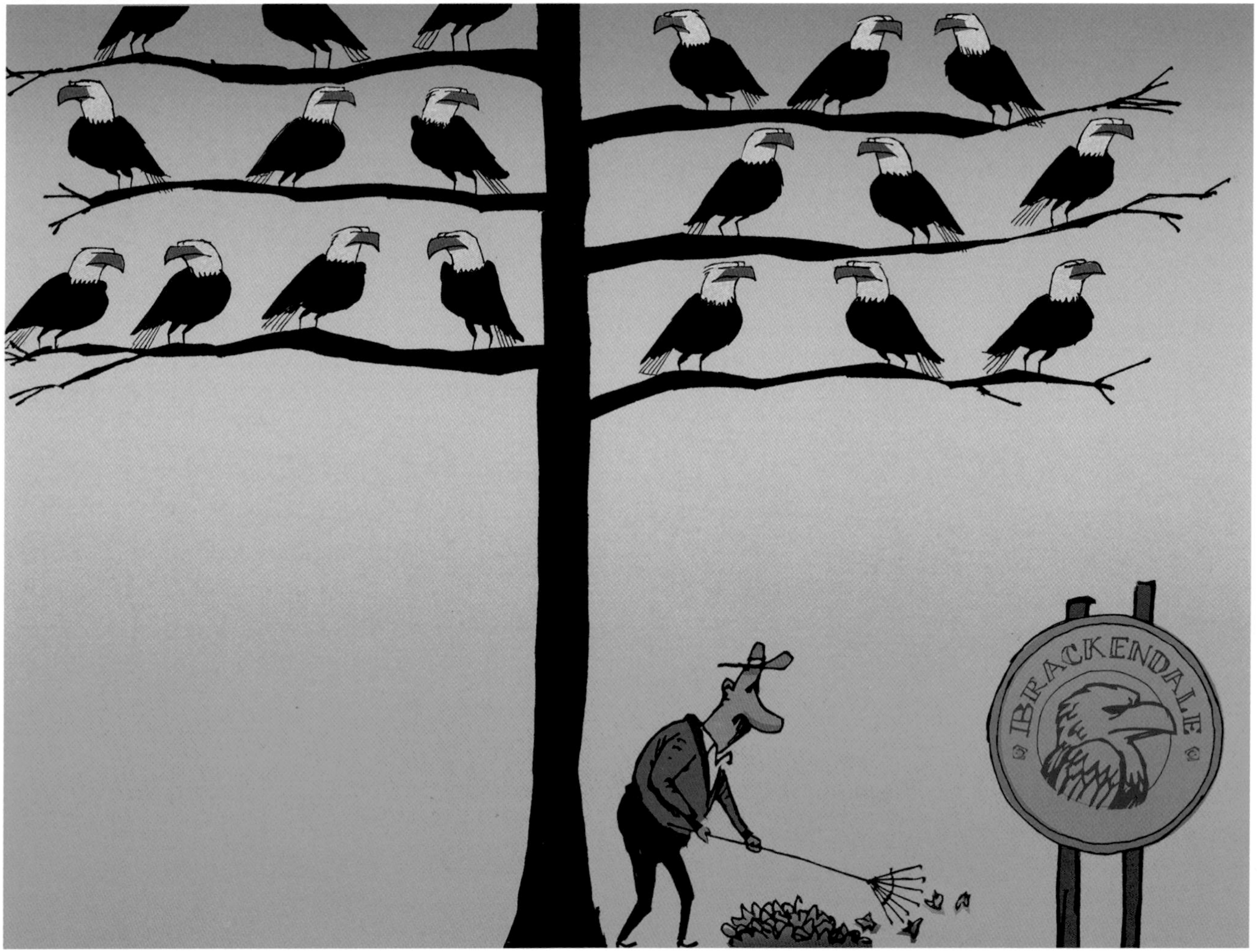
BRACKENDALE

YOU HAVE EXPERIENCED THE FIVE STAGES OF FEBRUARY

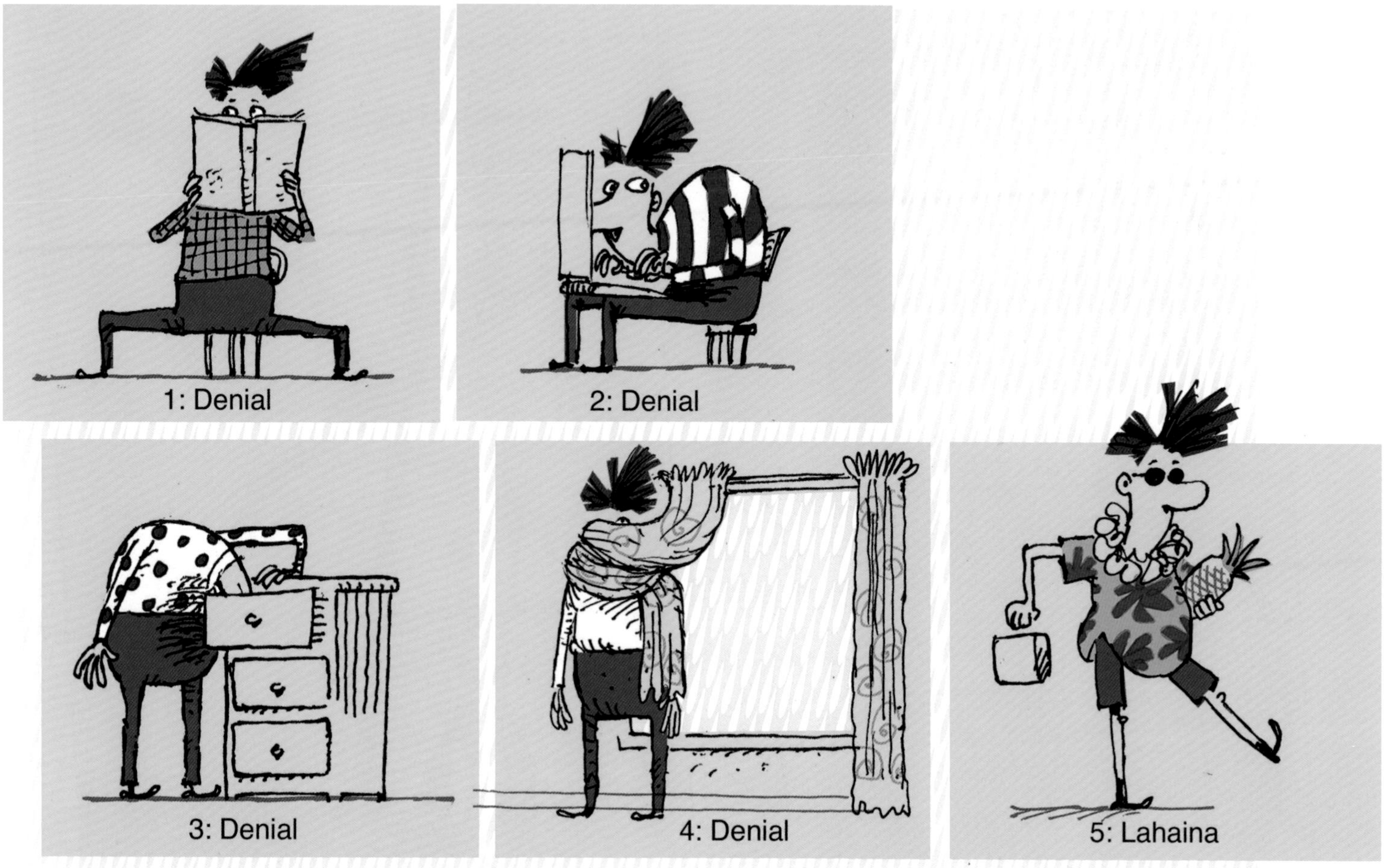
1: Denial
2: Denial
3: Denial
4: Denial
5: Lahaina

YOU ARE FAMILIAR WITH THE “FULL NANAIMO”

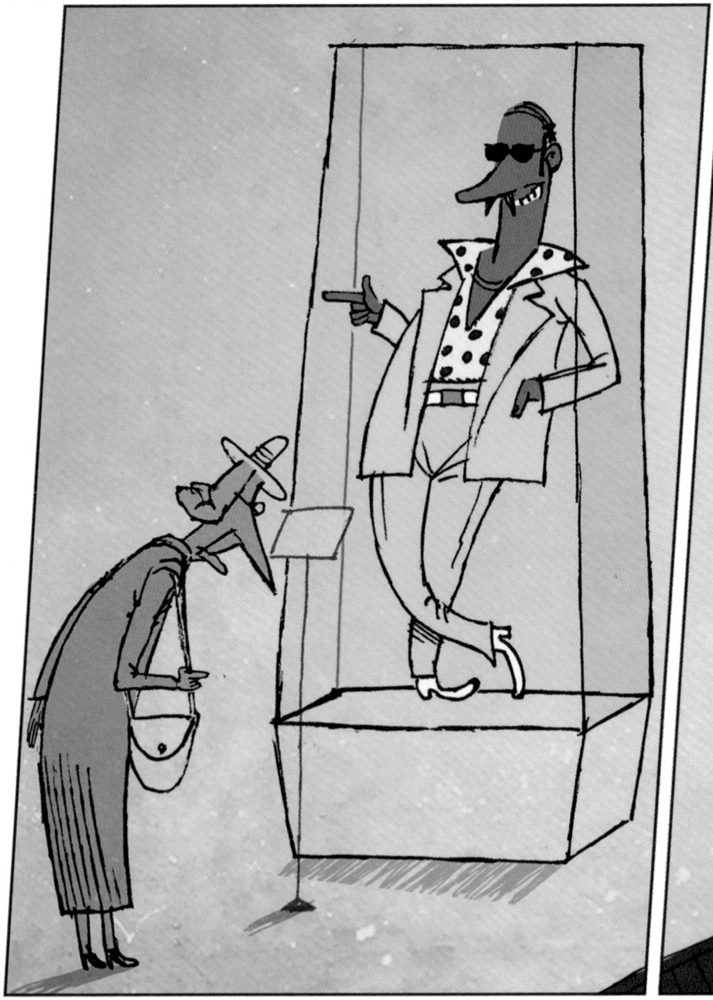

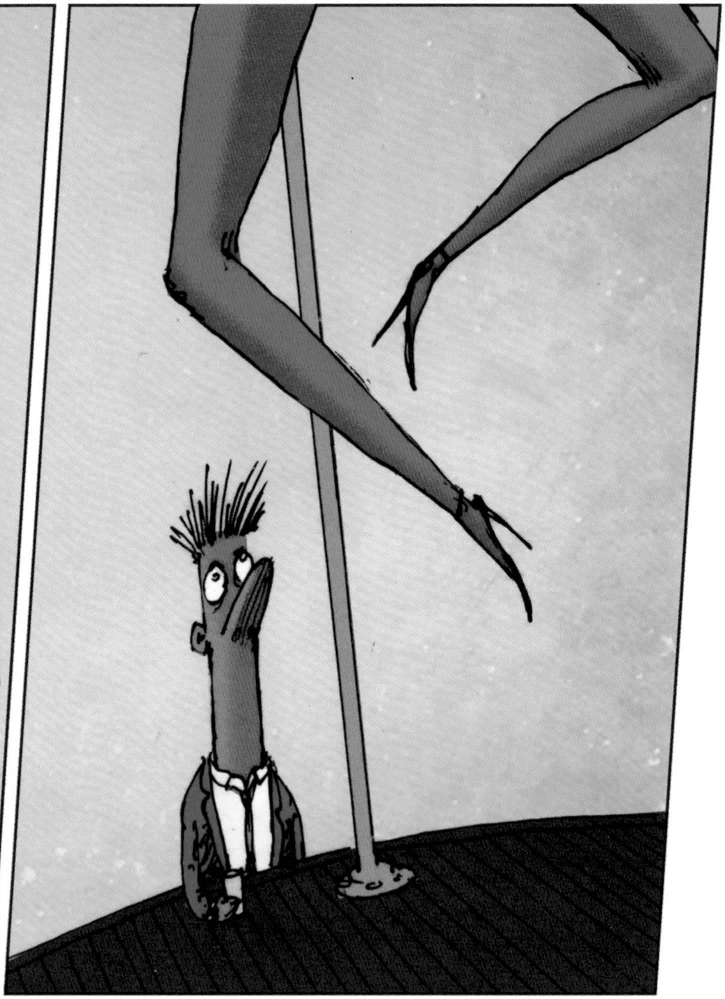

ALSO THE “FULL CECIL”

YOU KNOW THAT
THE FLAG LOOKS
LIKE THIS →

AND YOU KNOW
IT WOULD MAKE A
LOT MORE SENSE
LOOKING LIKE →

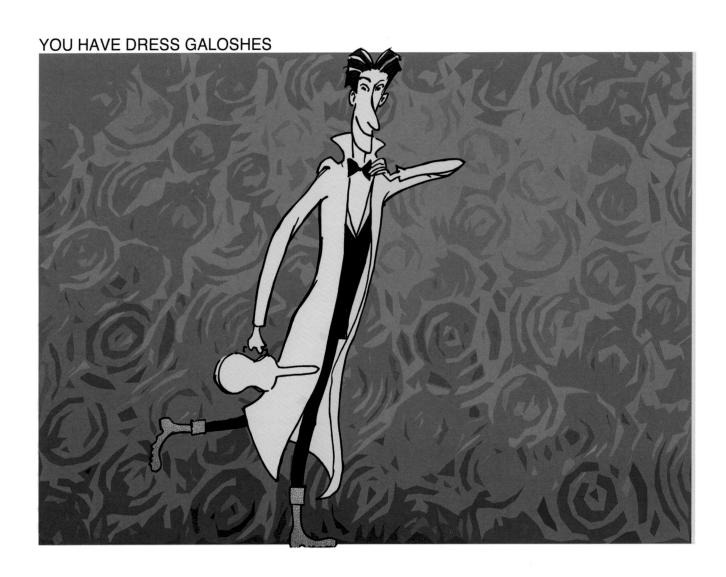

YOU HAVE DRESS GALOSHES

YOU'VE GIVEN DIRECTIONS BY MEANS OF DEMONSTRATIONS

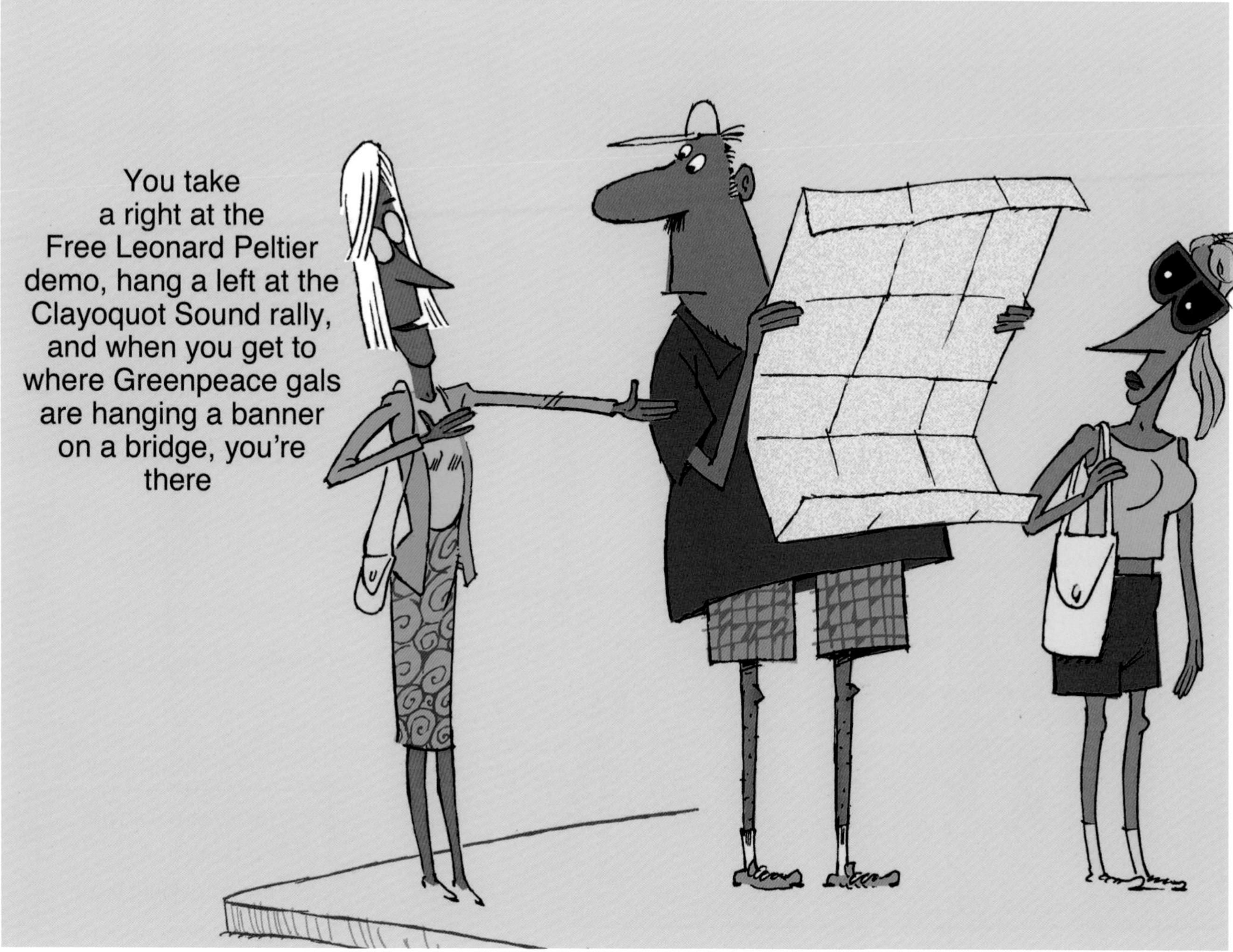
You take a right at the Free Leonard Peltier demo, hang a left at the Clayoquot Sound rally, and when you get to where Greenpeace gals are hanging a banner on a bridge, you're there

YOU RECOGNIZE THREE OUT OF FOUR OF THESE PROVINCIAL NATURAL WONDERS

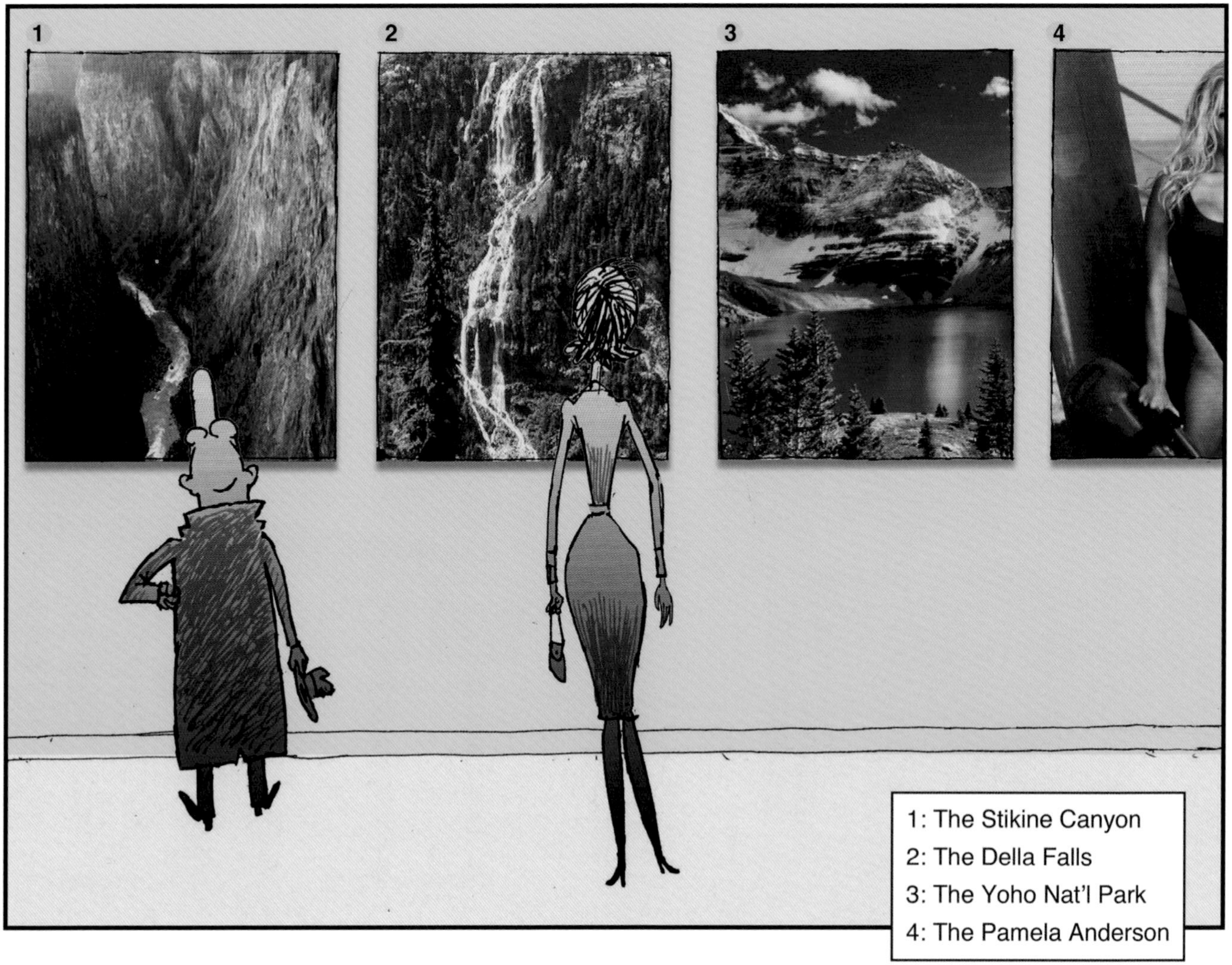
1
2
3
4
1: The Stikine Canyon
2: The Della Falls
3: The Yoho Nat'l Park
4: The Pamela Anderson

THE REPUBLIC OF EAST VAN IS ONE OF YOUR FAVOURITE REPUBLICS

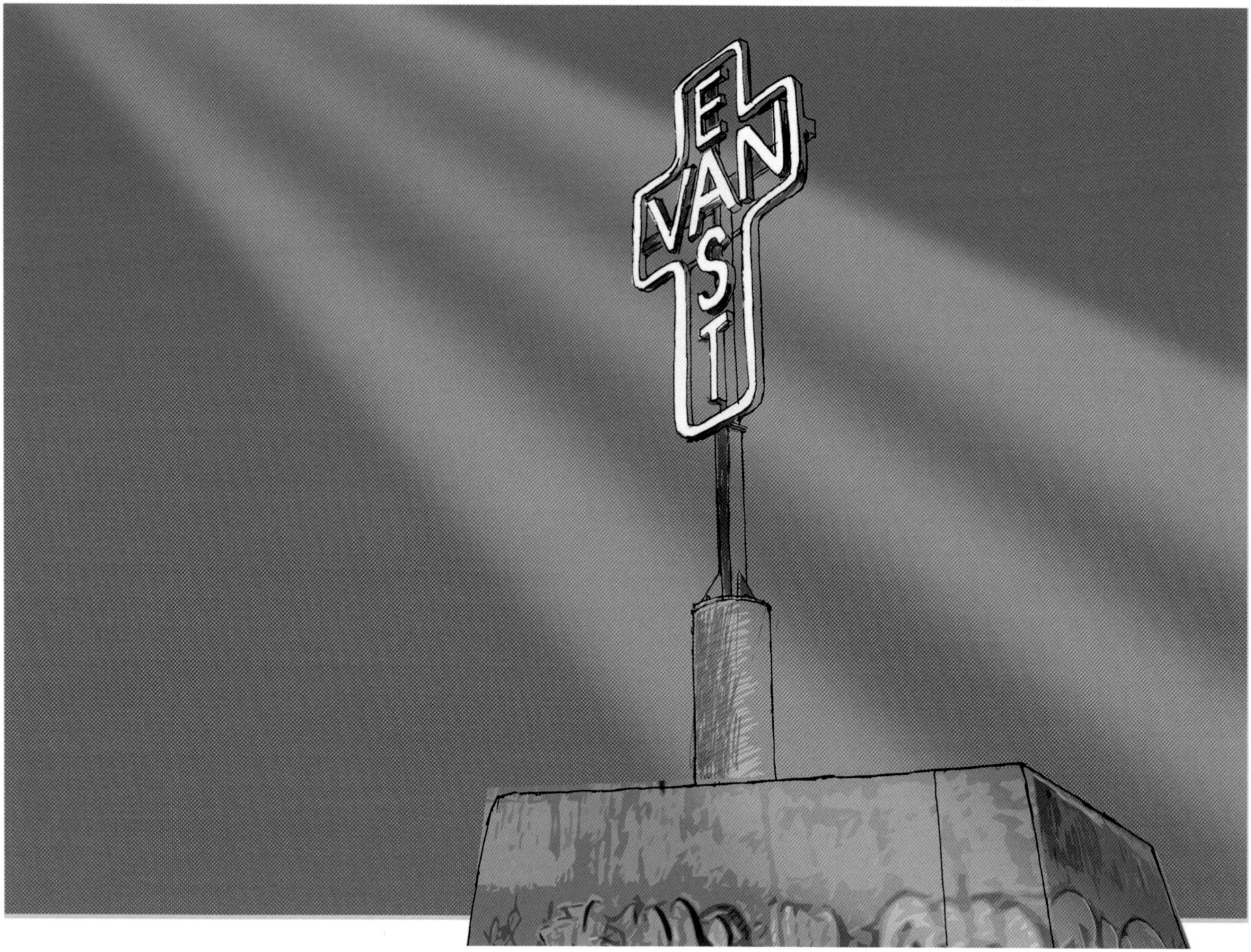
EAST
VAN

YOU RECKON IT'S ALL GONE DOWNHILL SINCE THEY CANCELLED *THE BEACHCOMBERS*

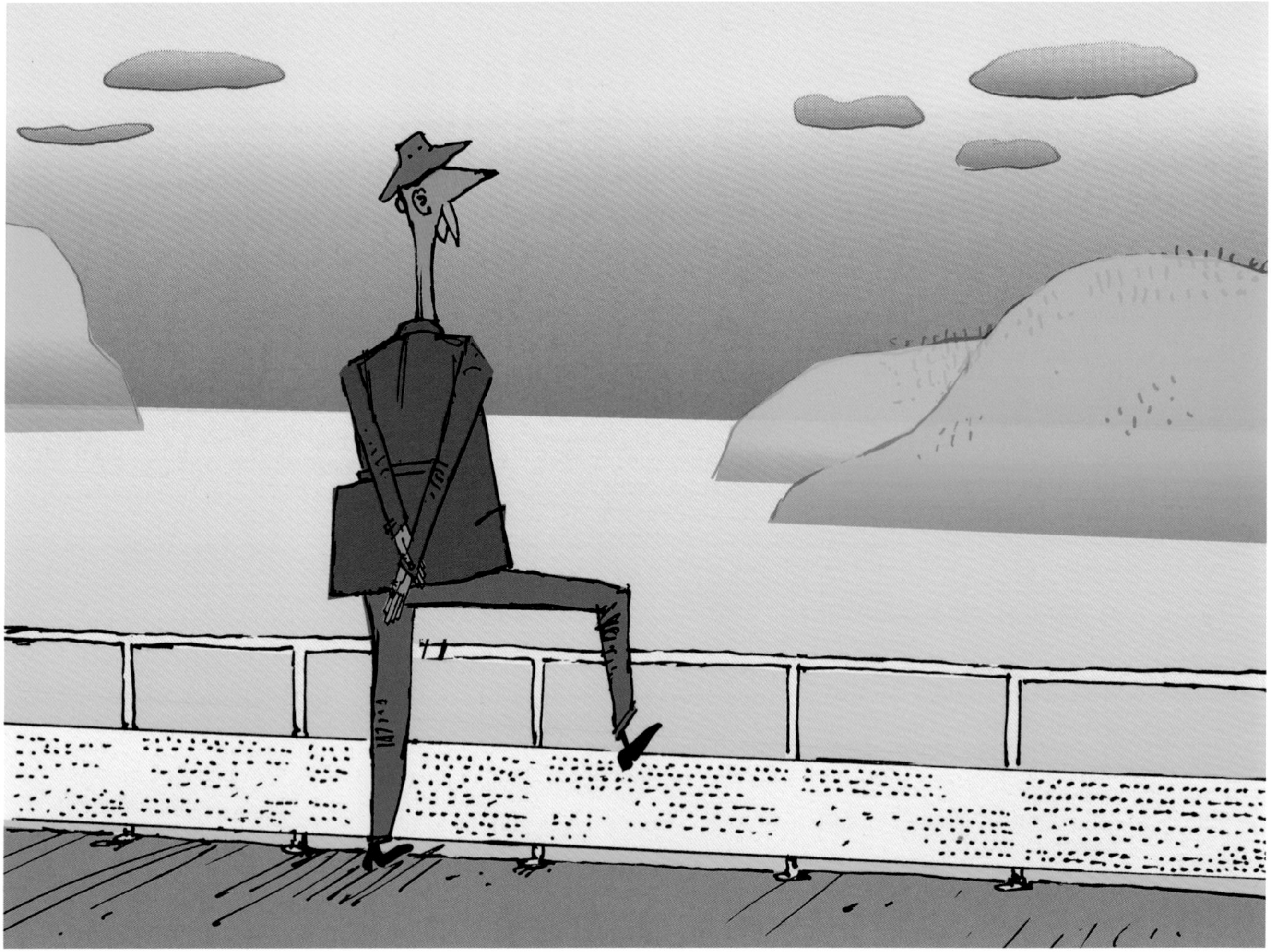

YOU KNOW THE PROVINCE'S FIRST NAME

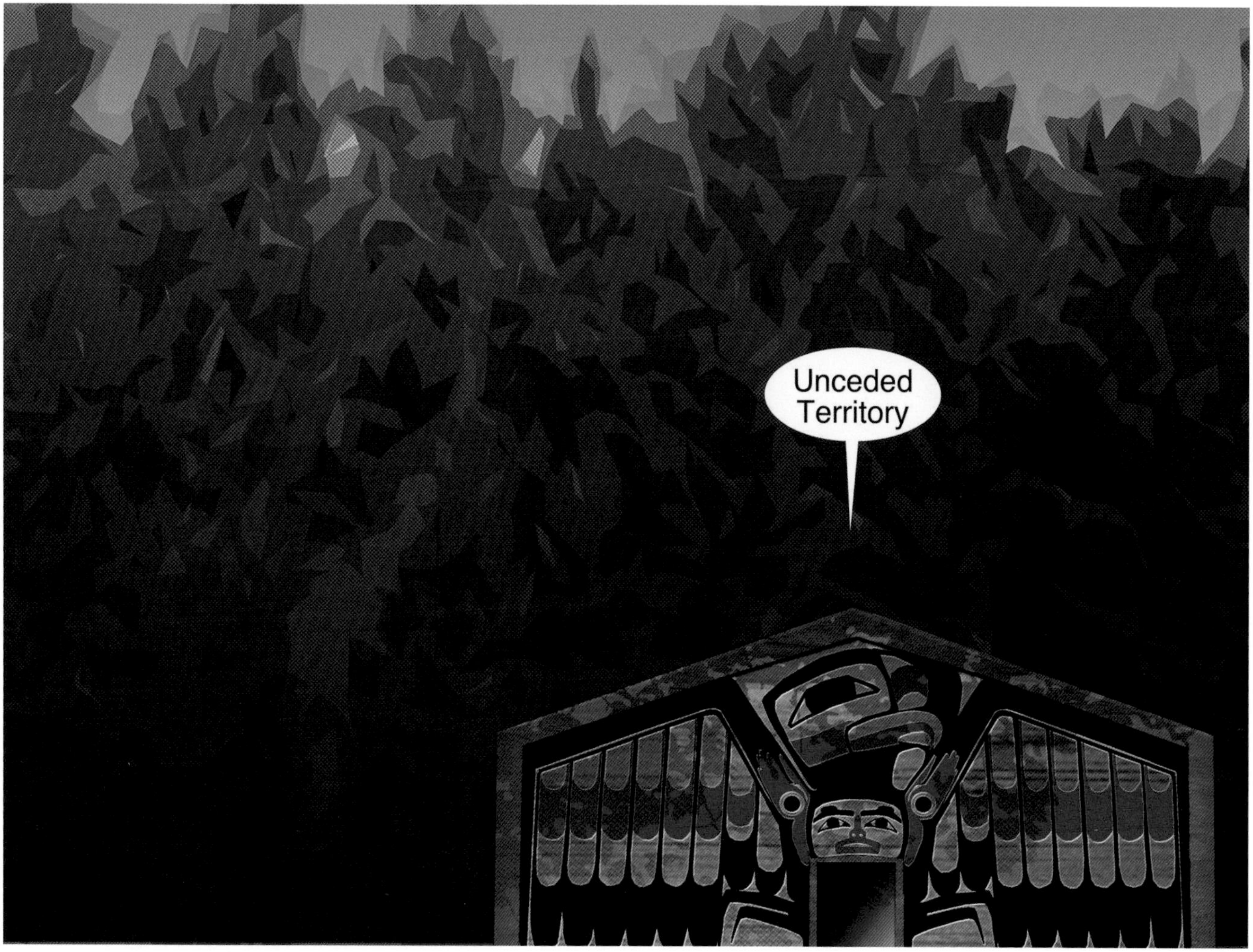
Unceded Territory

YOU'RE PRETTY SURE YOU INVENTED THE ENTIRE GRUNGE ROCK ESTHETE --
WHEN IT WAS CALLED "LIVING IN PORT ALICE"

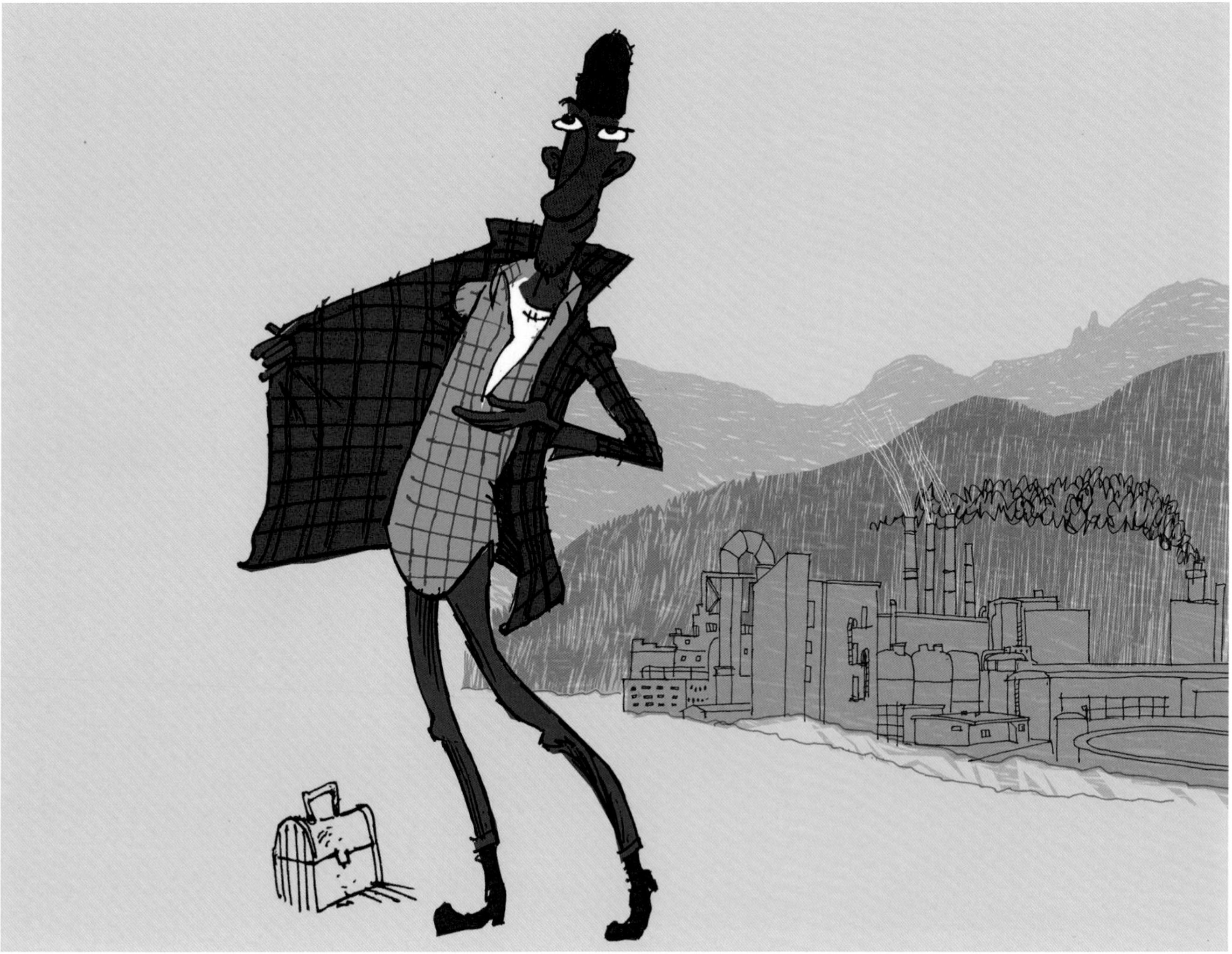

YOU'VE WATCHED CAT VIDEOS IN SPECTACULAR SURROUNDINGS

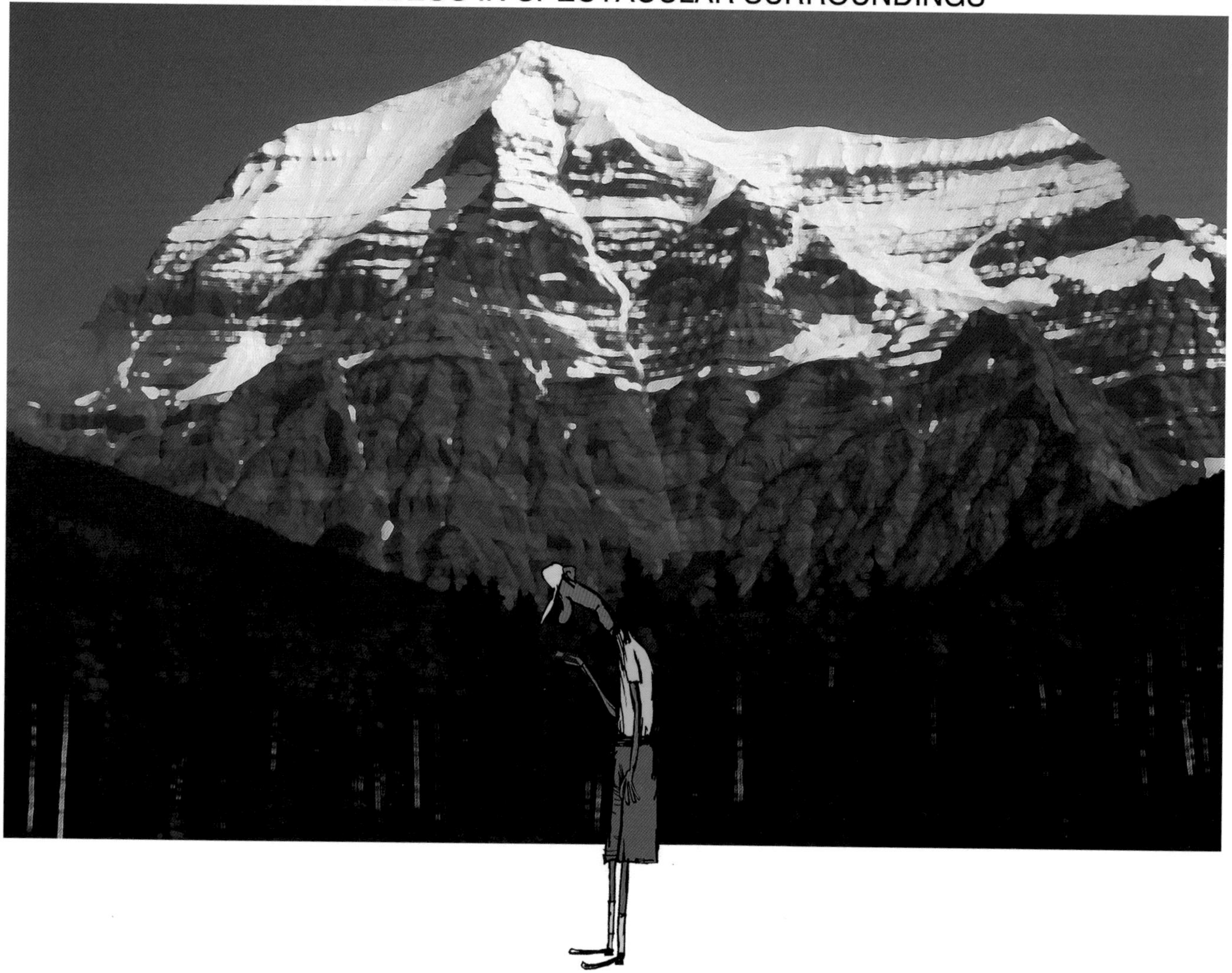

YOU WOULD BE UNFAZED BY A WEATHER FORECAST LIKE THIS

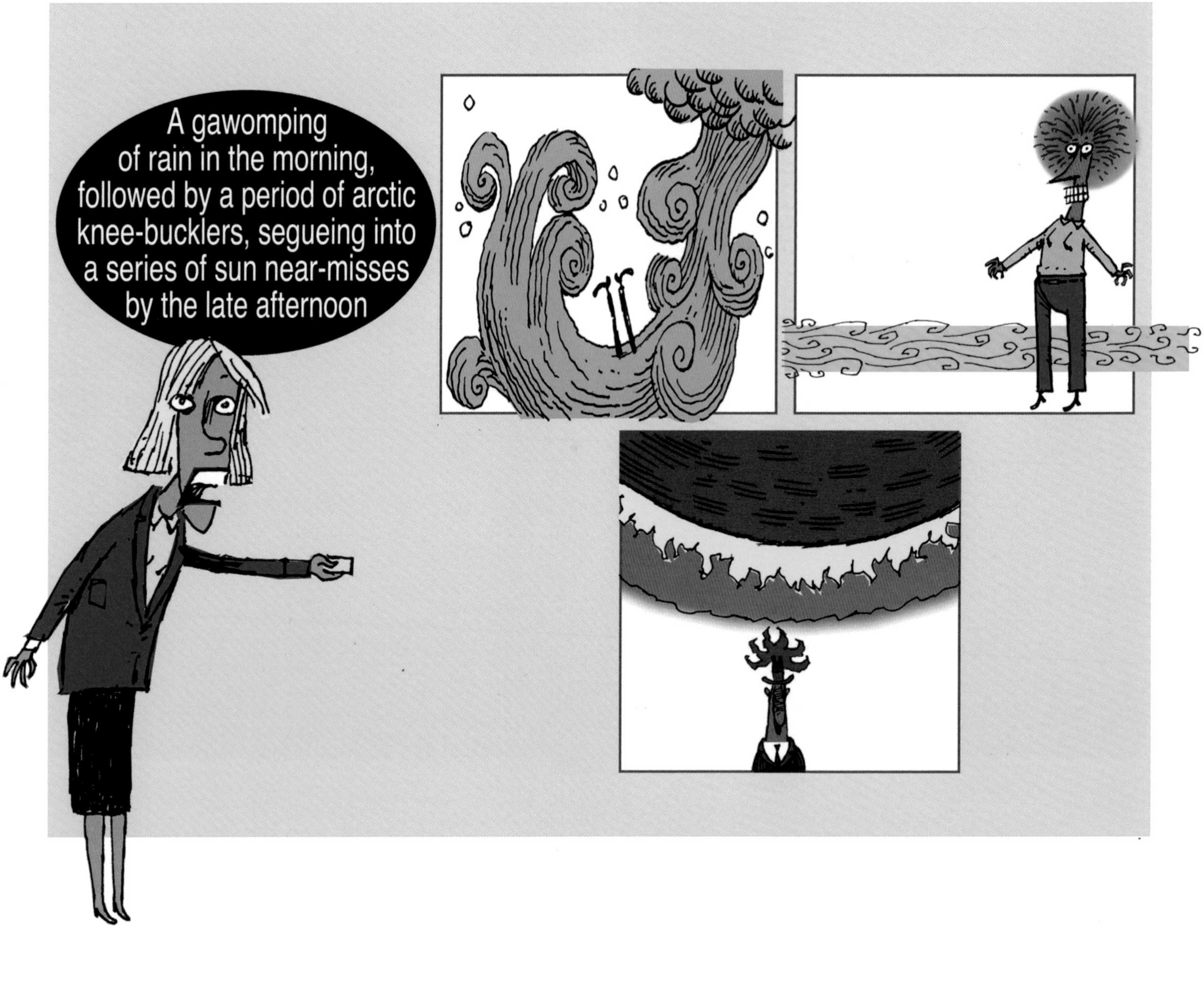
A gawomping of rain in the morning, followed by a period of arctic knee-bucklers, segueing into a series of sun near-misses by the late afternoon

YOU'VE CELEBRATED ROBBIE BURNS DAY AND CHINESE NEW YEARS SIMULTANEOUSLY — AT TODDISH McWONG'S "GUNG HAGGIS FAT CHOY"

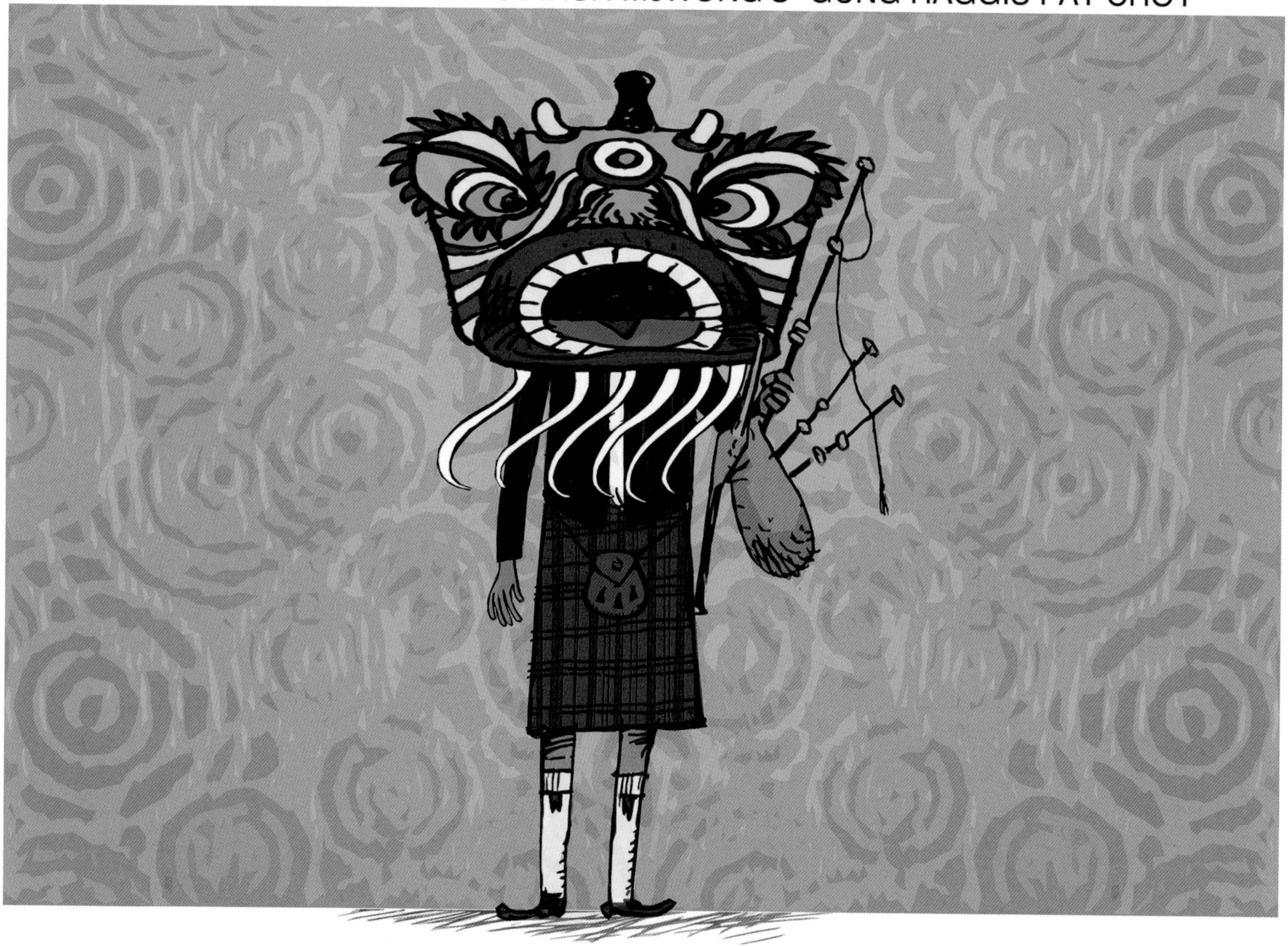

YOU HAD A "STICK IT IN YOUR EAR, McGEER" BUMPER STICKER

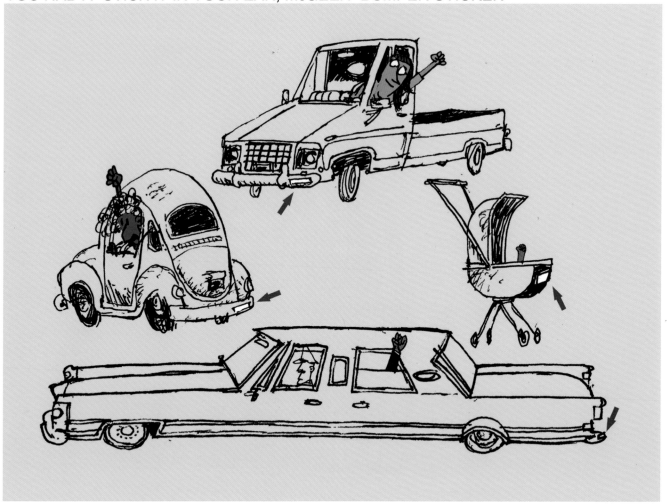

YOU'VE EXPERIENCED HEAVY TRAFFIC ON TCHENTLO LAKE

YOU'VE SPENT SOME TIME AT THE KOMAGATA MARU MEMORIAL

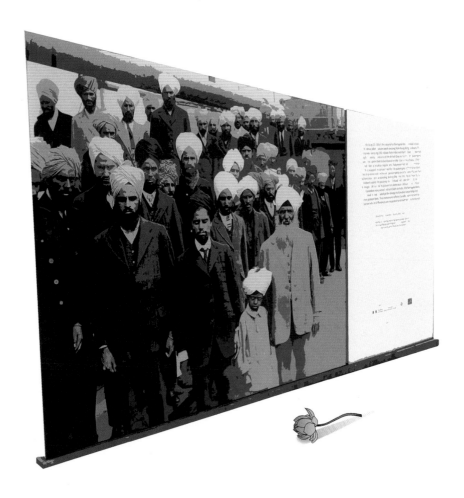

YOU HOPE NELSON WILL ONE DAY GET THE MONUMENT TO DRAFT DODGERS IT DESERVES

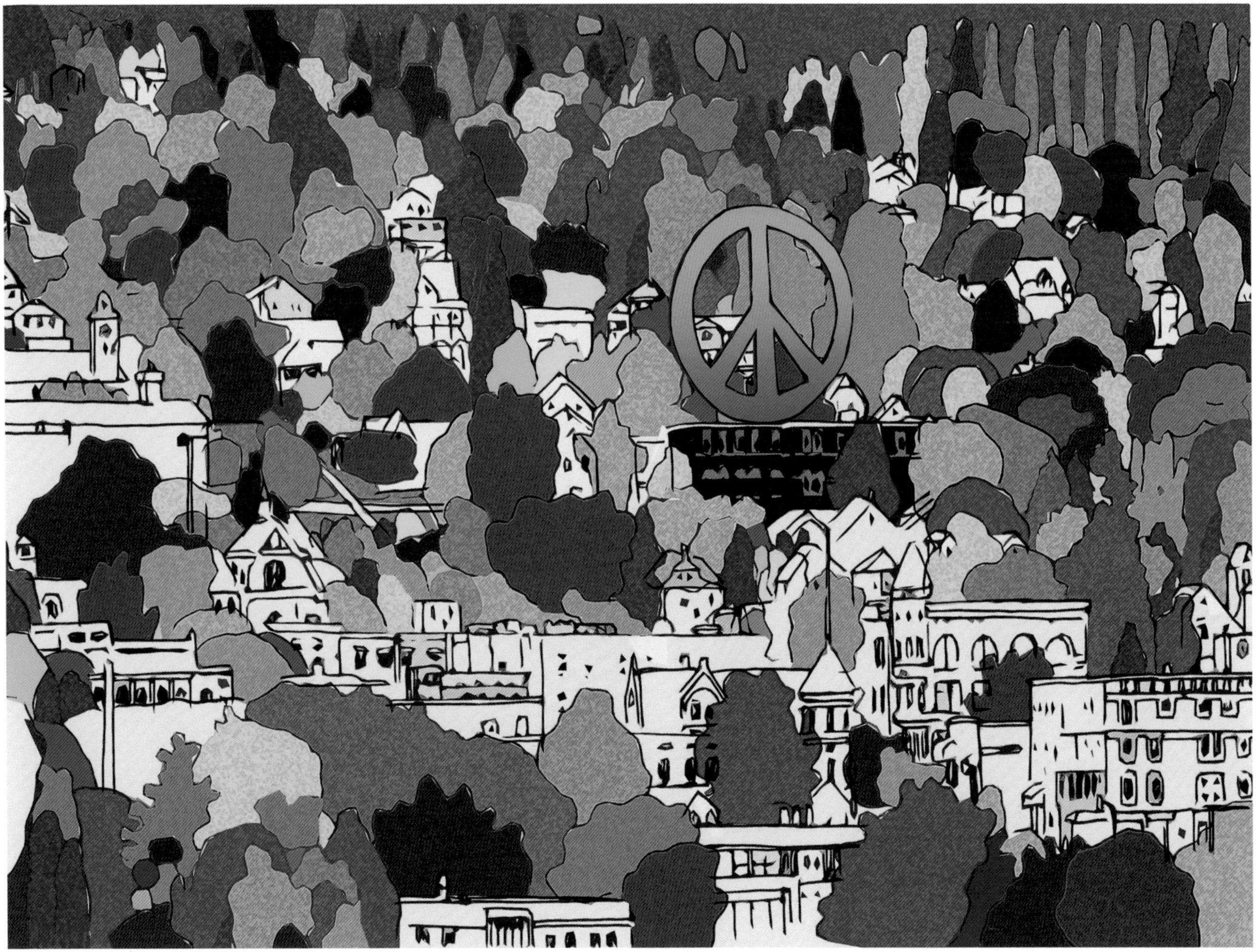

YOU HAVE A COUSIN
WHO LOVES MARMOTS

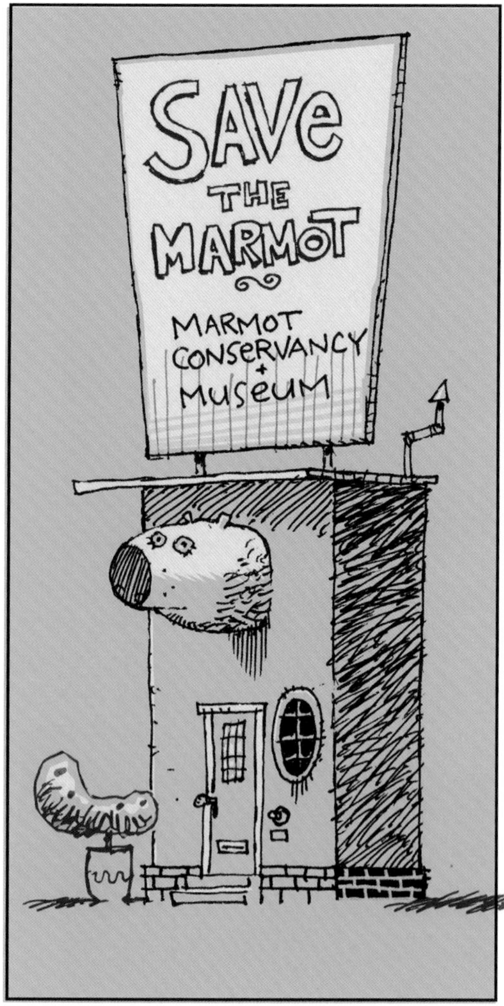
SAVE THE MARMOT
MARMOT CONSERVANCY + MUSEUM

AND ANOTHER COUSIN WHO REALLY LOVES MARMOTS

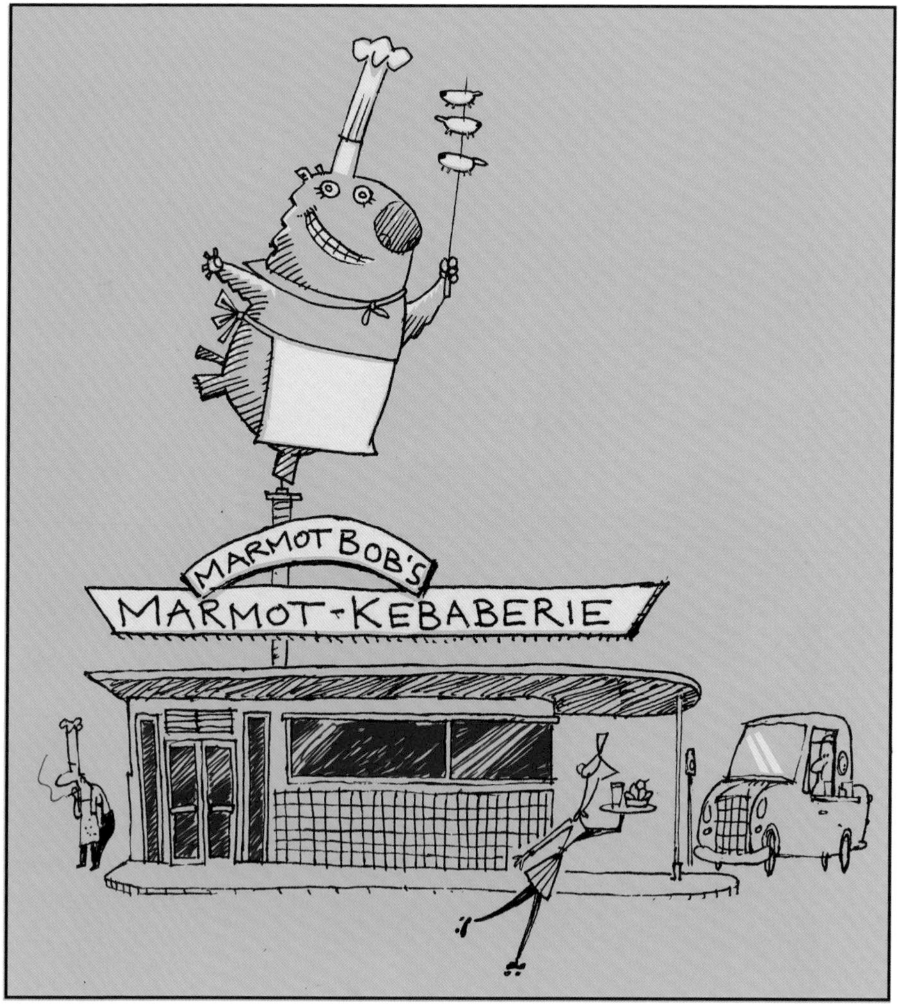
MARMOT BOB'S
MARMOT-KEBABERIE

YOU'VE MADE FRIENDS DOING THIS

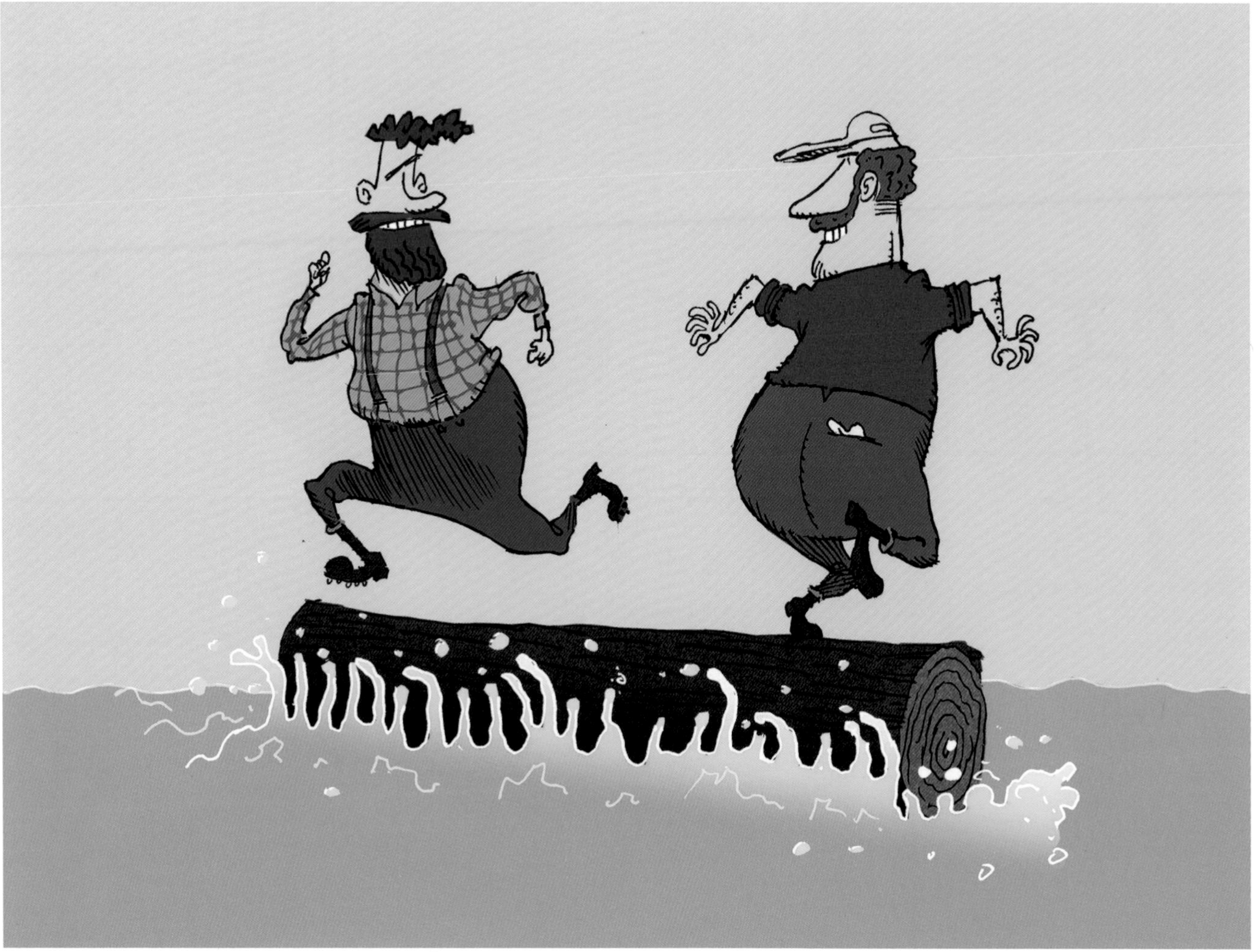

YOU PROPOSED ON A GLACIER

YOU PROPOSED IN PIGEON PARK

THERE ARE DAYS IN MARCH WHEN YOU'RE THINKING THE SAME THING AS A NANAIMO PALM TREE

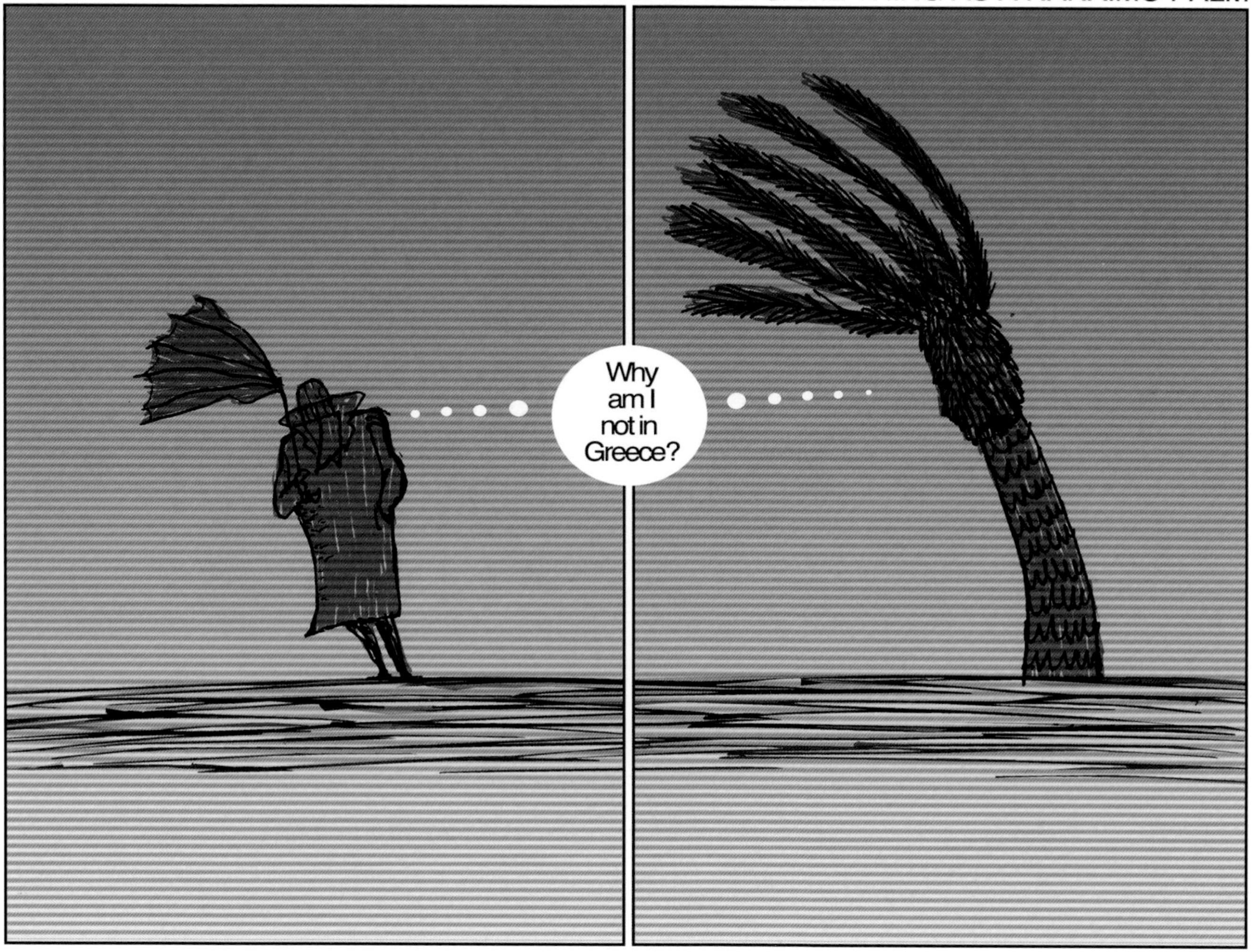
Why am I not in Greece?

YOUR COMFORT FOOD IS TRAD

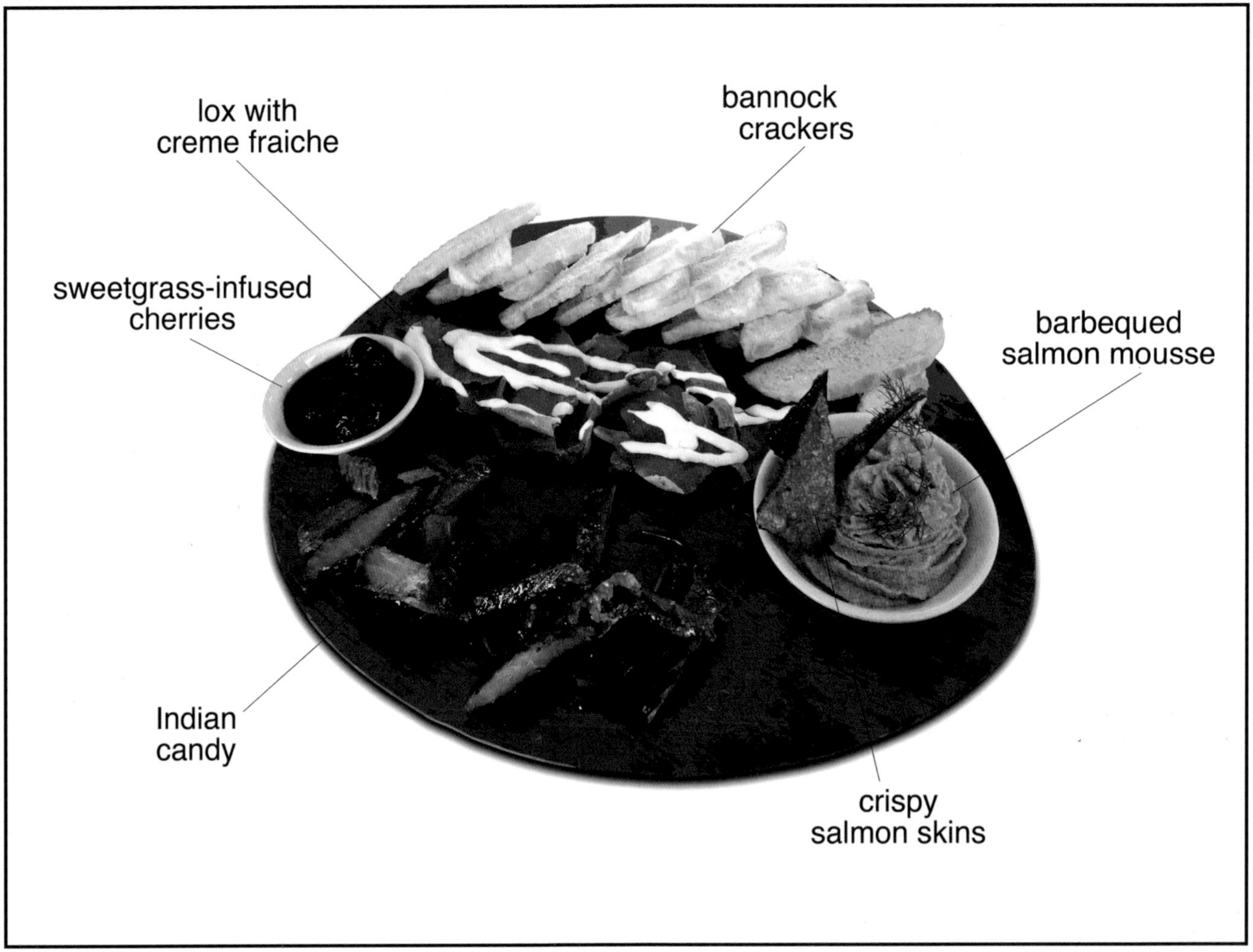
lox with
creme fraiche
bannock
crackers
sweetgrass-infused
cherries
barbequed
salmon mousse
Indian
candy
crispy
salmon skins

YOU THINK YOUR NEIGHBOURHOOD BORDERS BOTH SAN FRANCISCO AND 1962

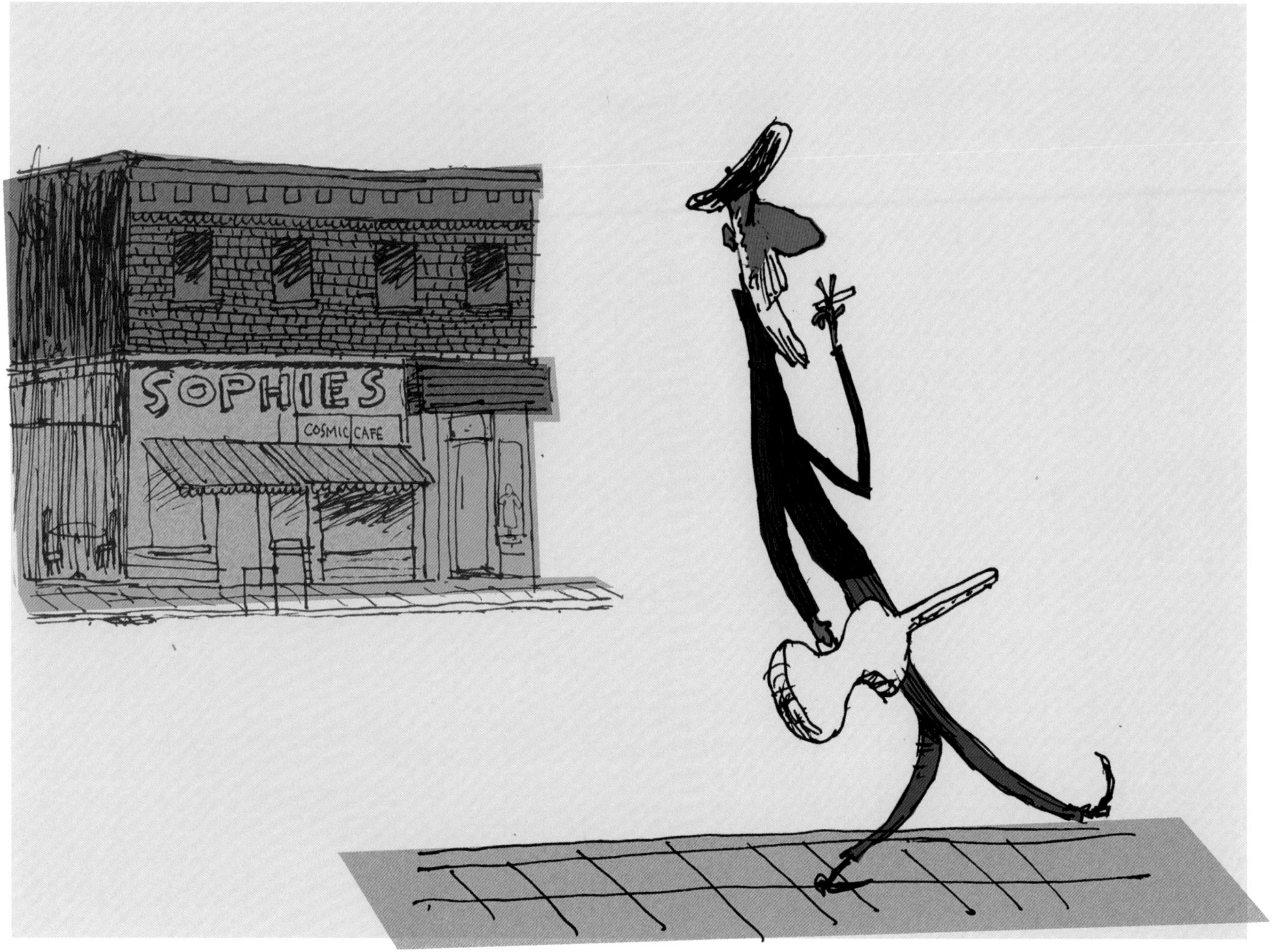
SOPHIES
COSMIC CAFE

YOU HAVE RECURRING NIGHTMARES OF FINDING AN INTRUDER IN YOUR HOT TUB

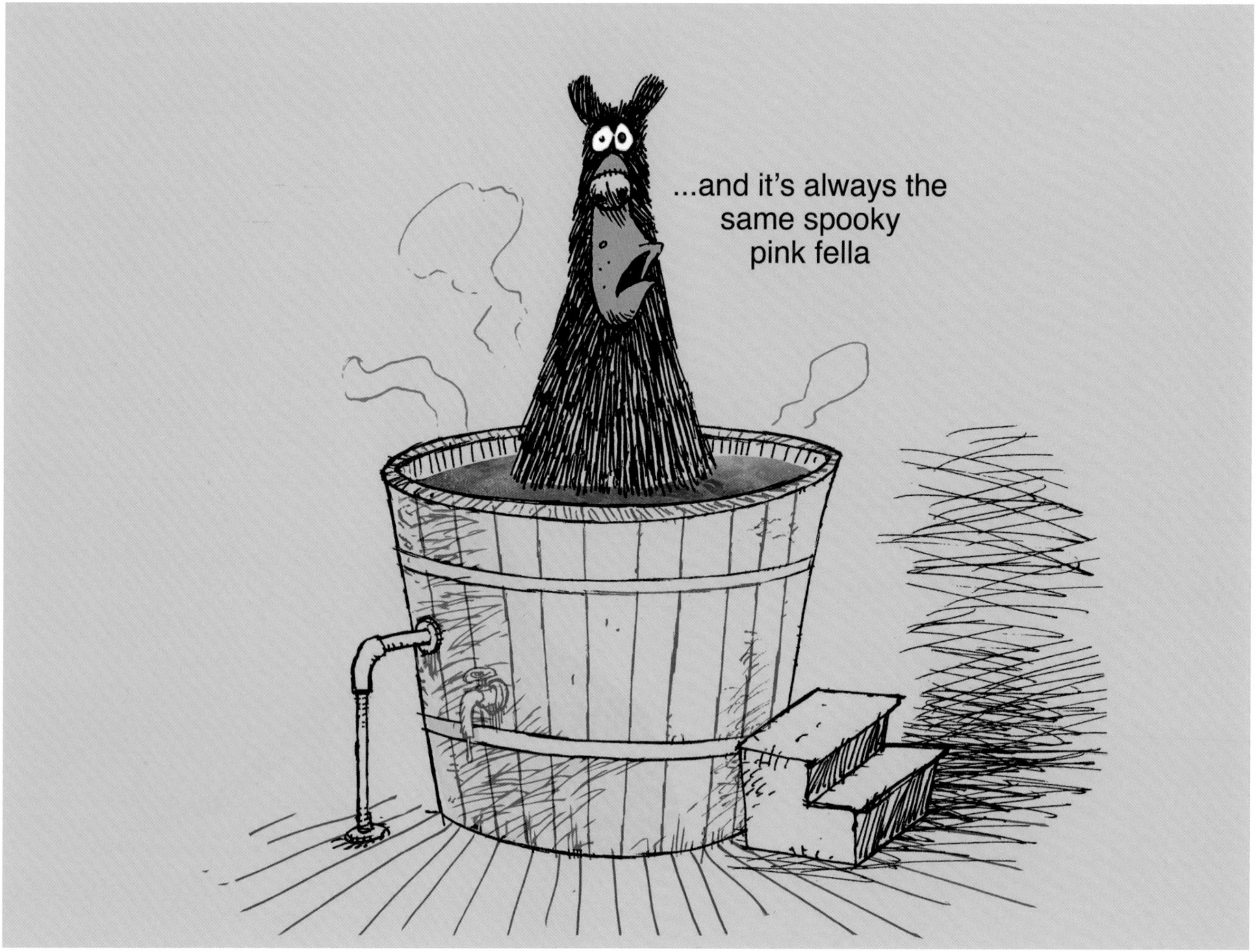
...and it's always the
same spooky
pink fella

YOU CAN GET AN IDEA OF FOLKS' POLITICAL LEANINGS FROM THEIR KIDS' NAMES

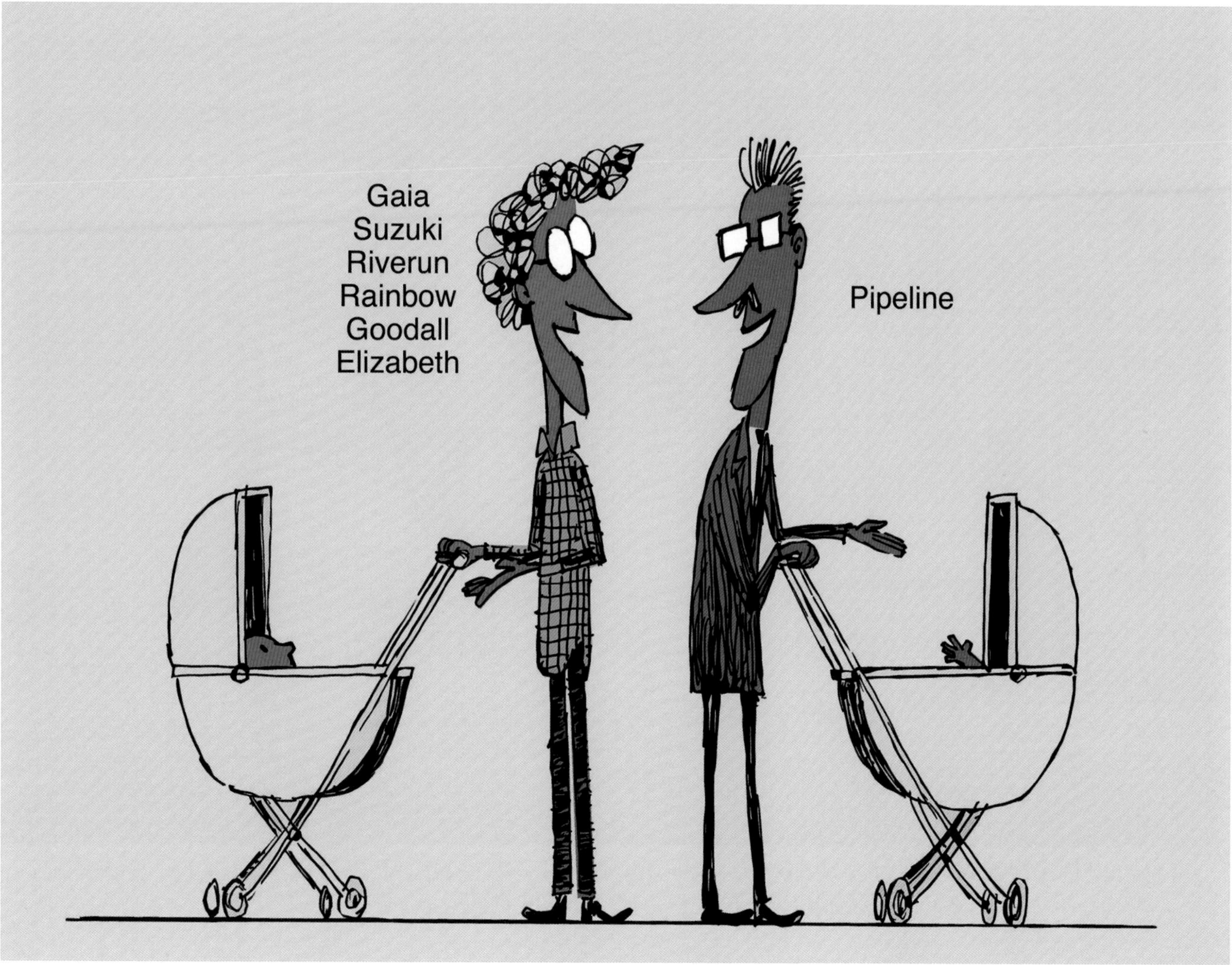
Gaia
Suzuki
Riverun
Rainbow
Goodall
Elizabeth
Pipeline

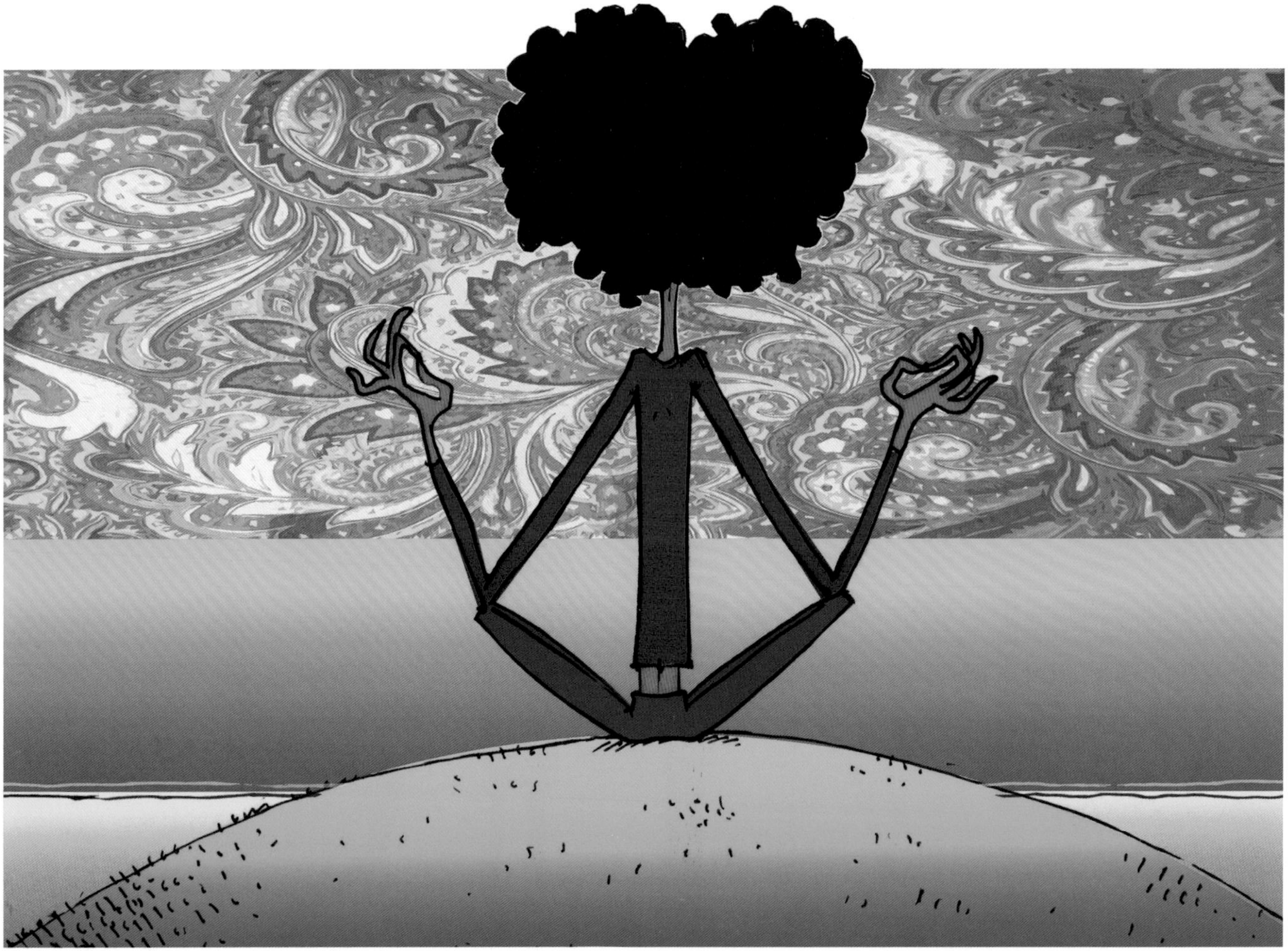

THANKS TO A STANLEY PARK LOVE-IN, YOU EXPERIENCED A PAISLEY SUNSET AT SECOND BEACH . . . WHICH REPLAYED TWICE

BASED ON PROVINCIAL POLITICIANS' COLLECTIVE TRACK RECORD, YOU WONDER IF IT WOULDN'T BE BETTER JUST TO LET THE RACCOONS RUN THE PLACE

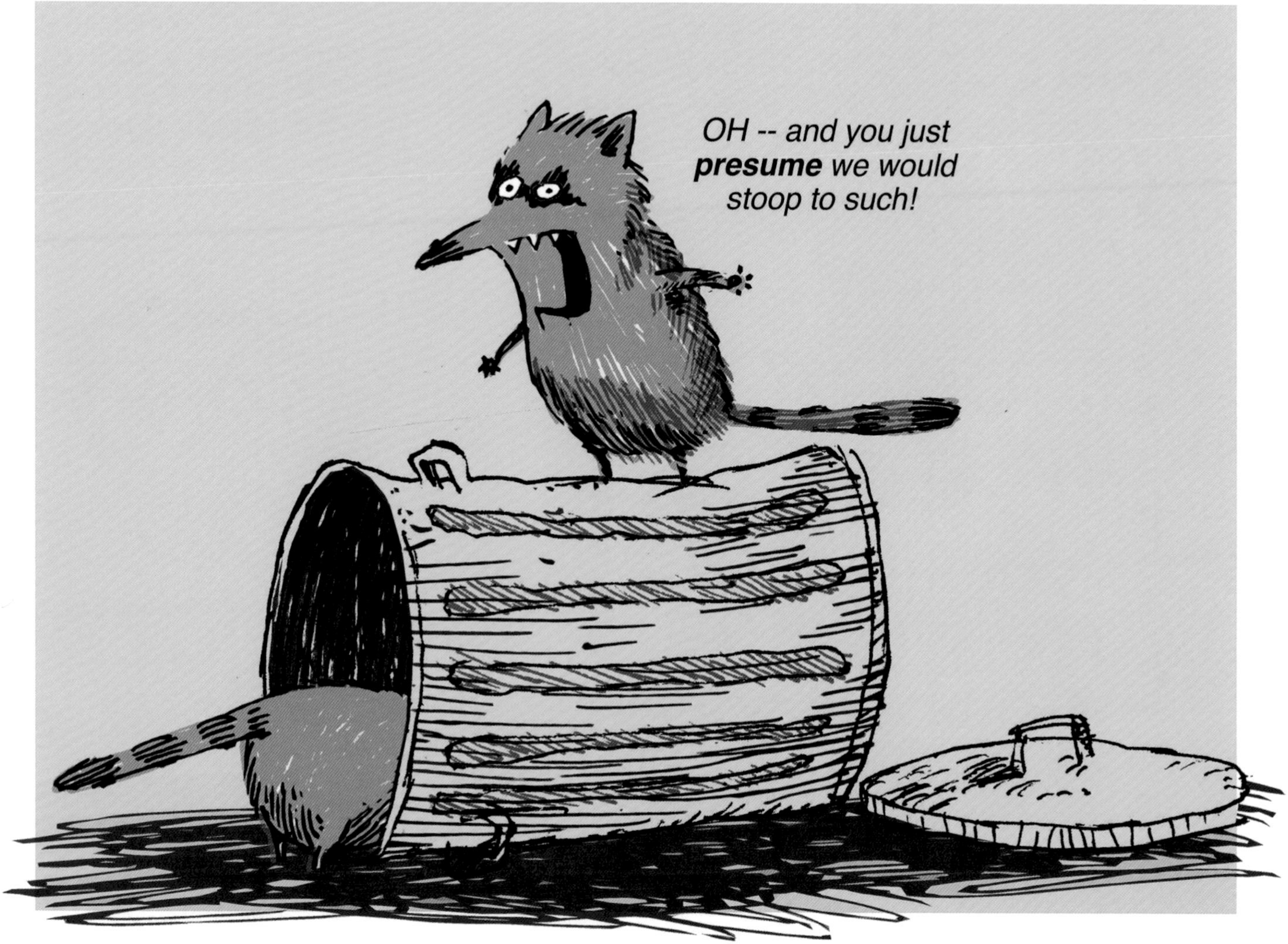
OH -- and you just **presume** we would stoop to such!

YOU BELIEVE THEY SHOULD PUT TOMMY CHONG ON A STAMP. . . AND IT SHOULD TASTE LIKE BROWNIE

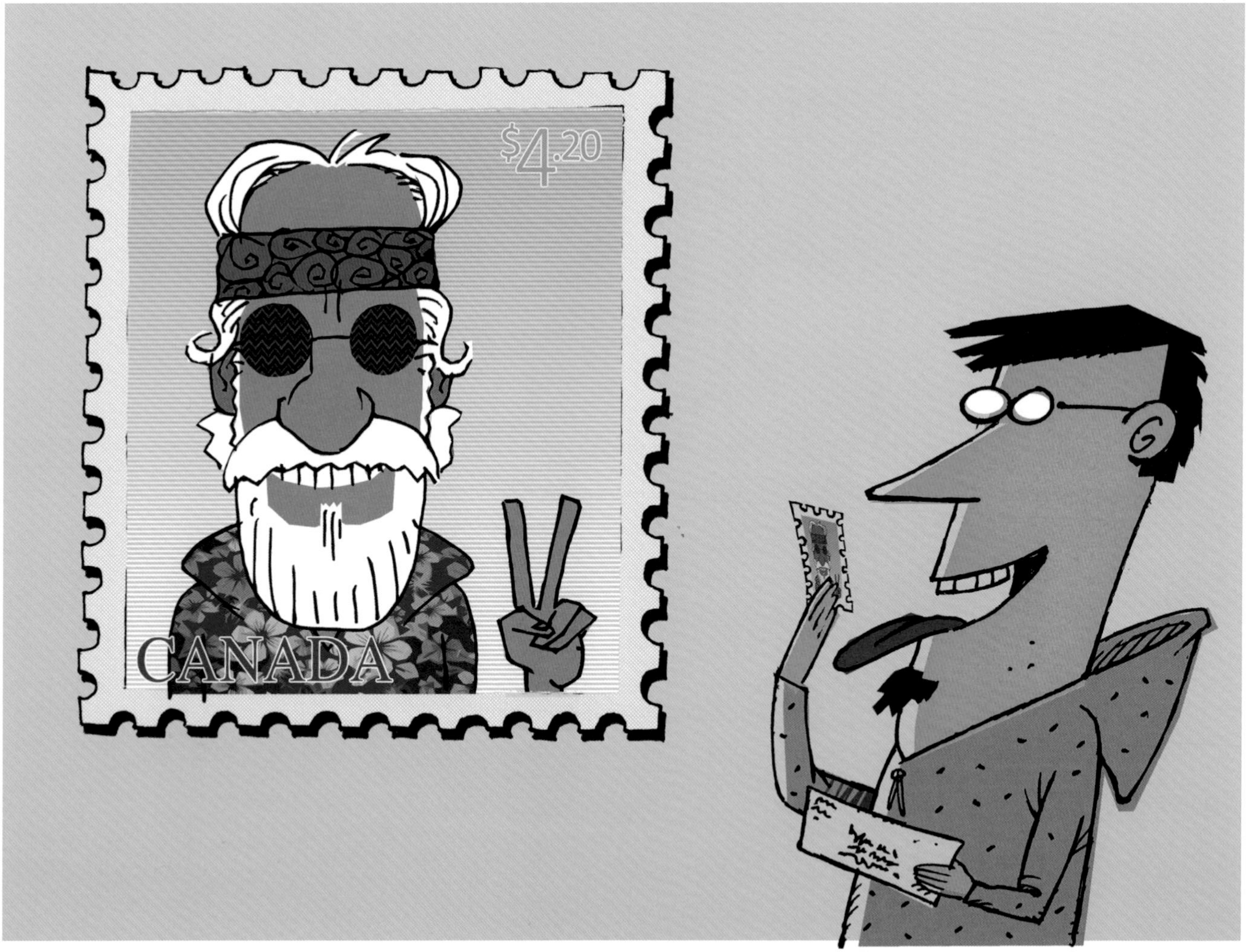
$4.20
CANADA

YOU HAVE 417 RECYCLING BINS

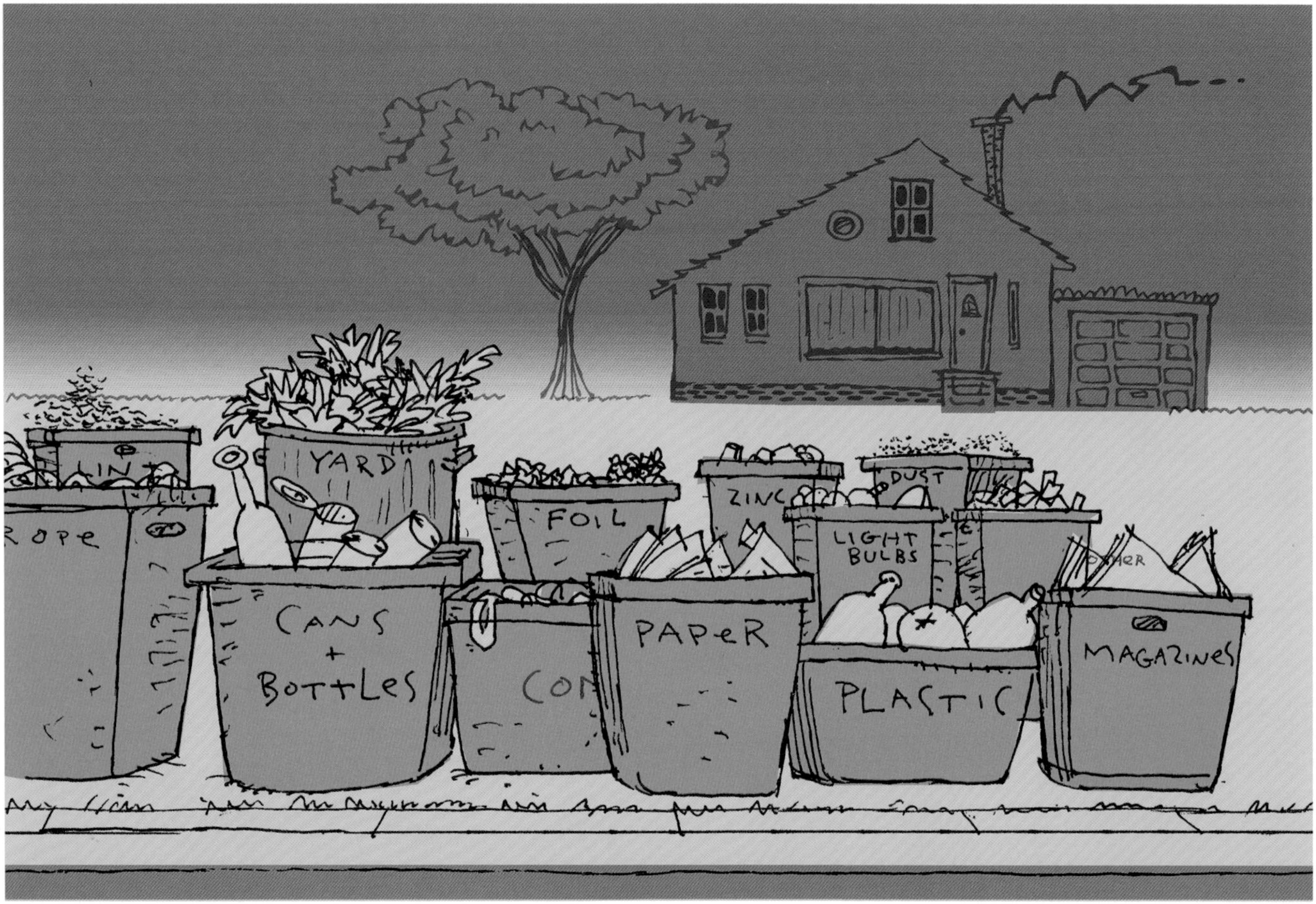
YARD
FOIL
ZINC
DUST
LIGHT BULBS
CANS + BOTTLES
PAPER
PLASTIC
MAGAZINES

YOU HAVE DISTINCT REACTIONS TO MOST OF THE 200 TYPES OF RAIN KNOWN TO THE PROVINCE

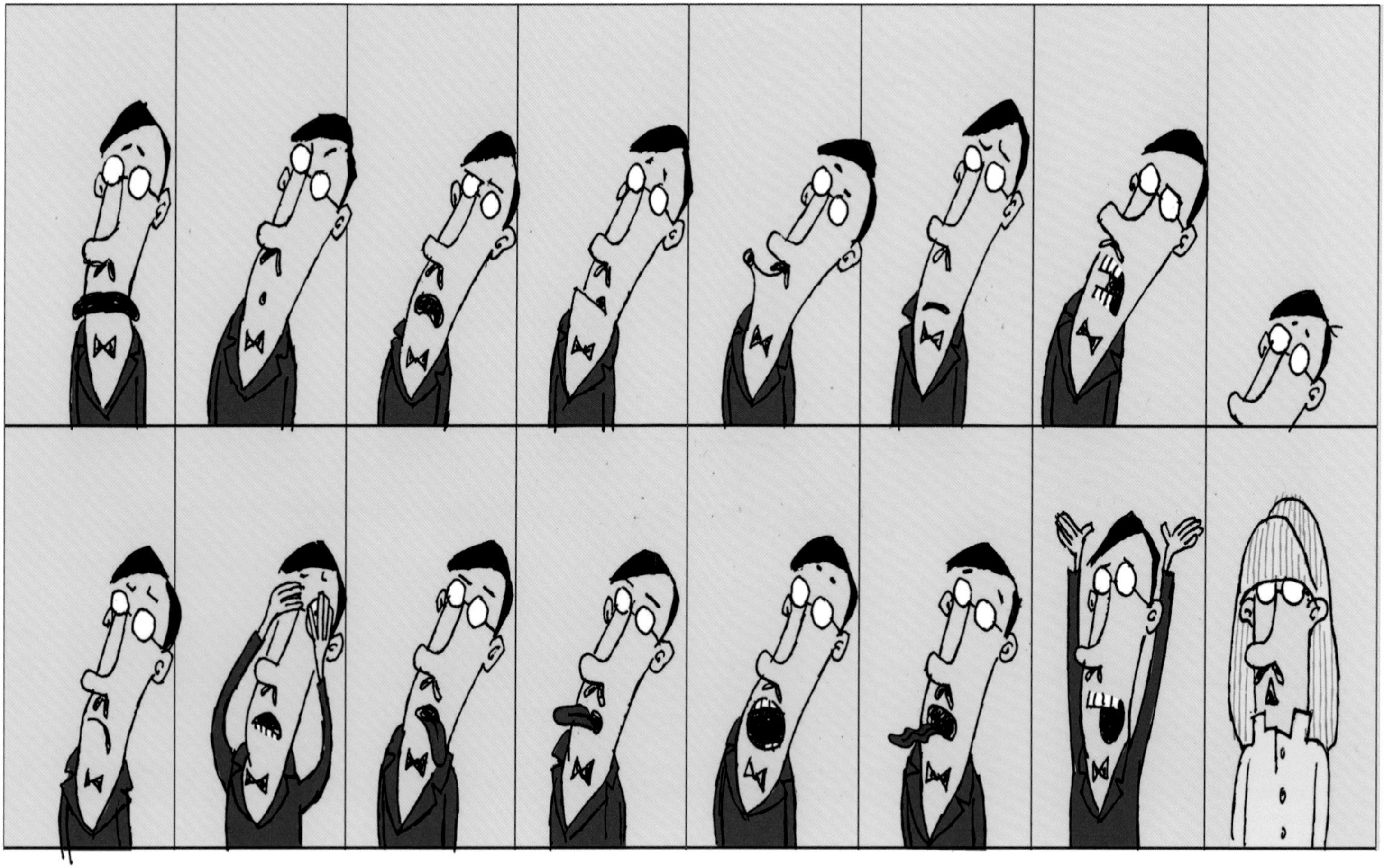

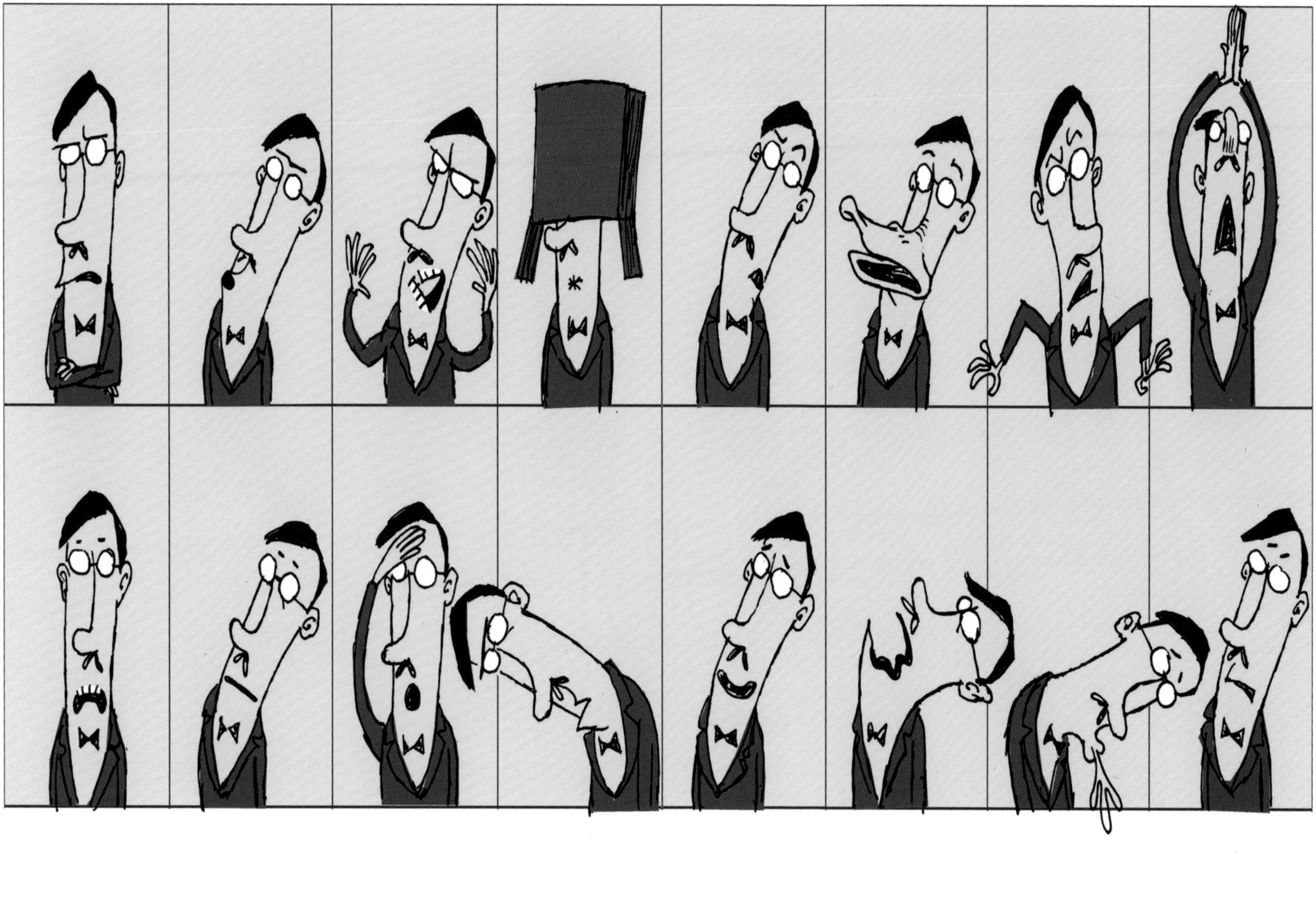

YOU FIND NEWS OF LOWER MAINLANDERS' RAIN WOES QUAINT

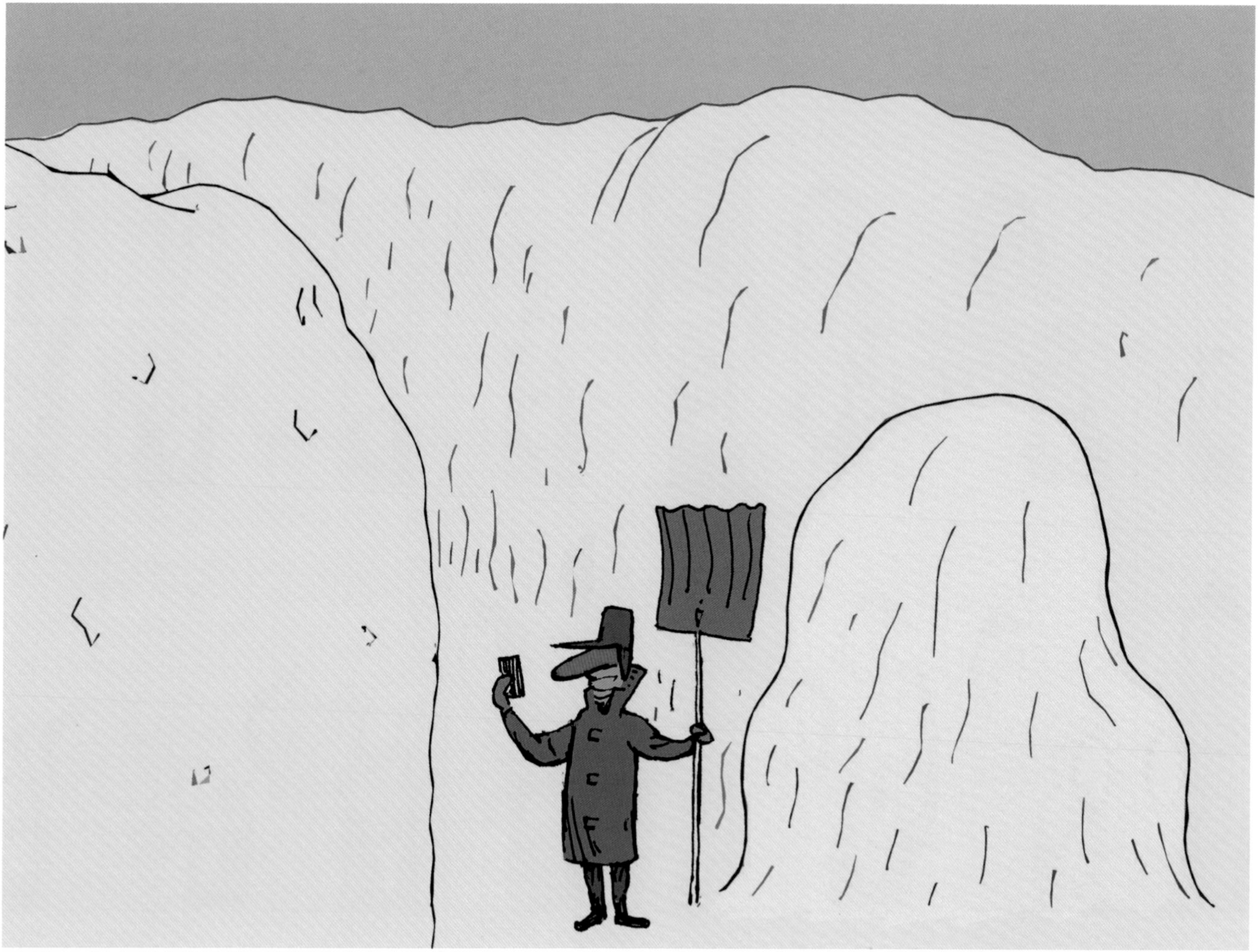

YOU REJOICE AT THE YEARLY RETURN OF THE SNOW GEESE

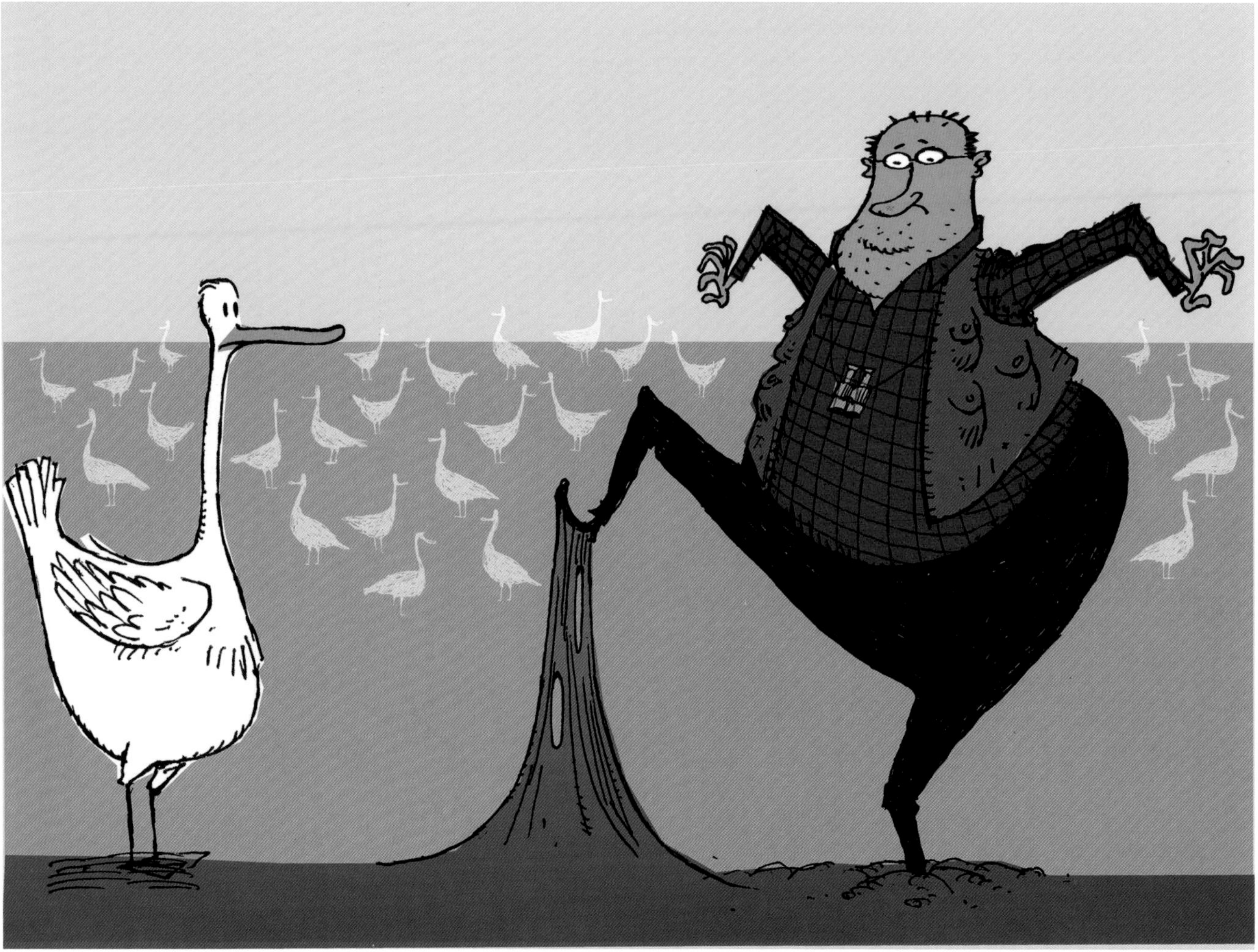

WHEN SOMEONE SAYS “VANCOUVER STANLEY CUP RIOT,” YOU SAY:

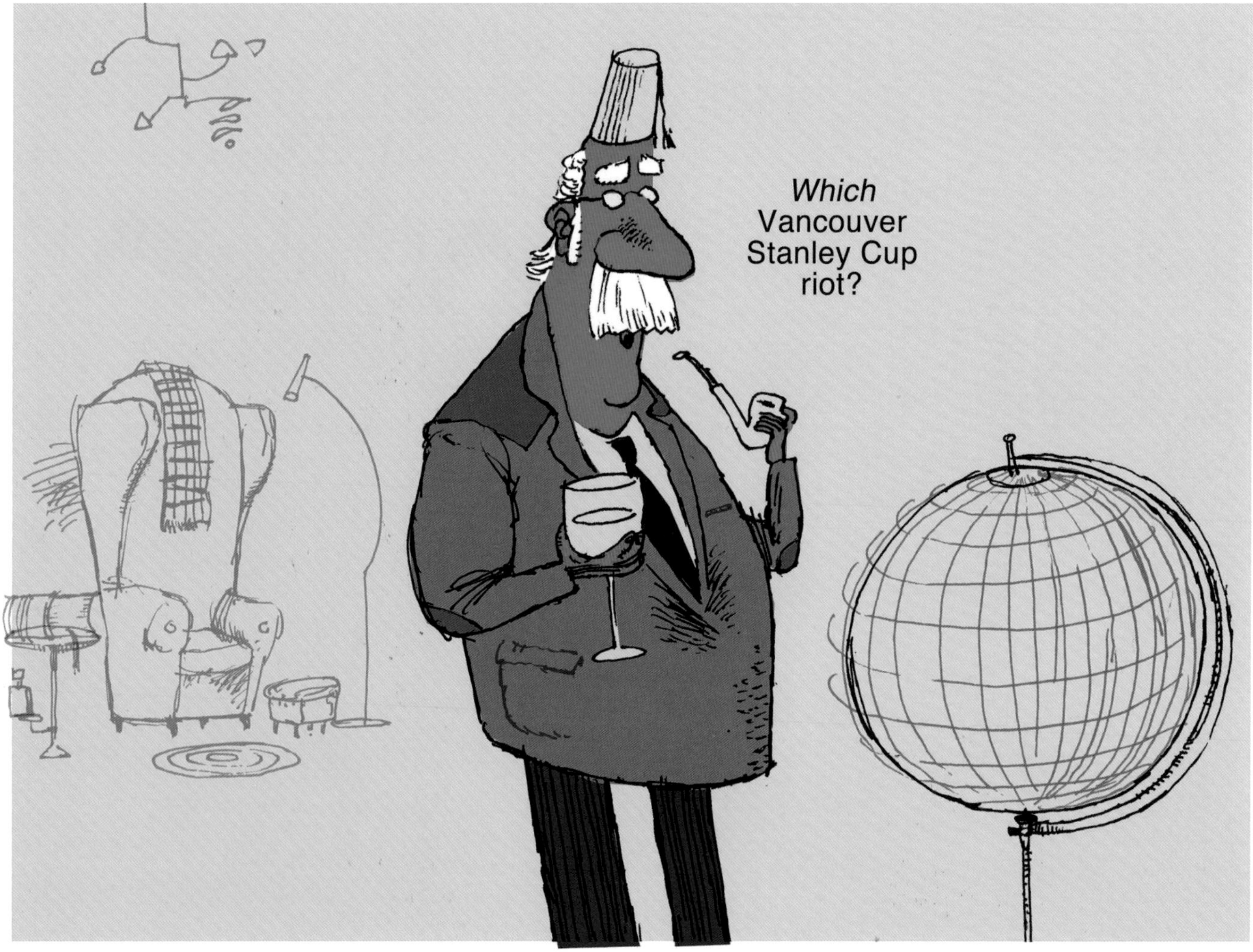
Which Vancouver Stanley Cup riot?

YOU'VE EXPERIENCED YACHT RAGE, ROAD RAGE AND SLOPE RAGE ON THE SAME DAY

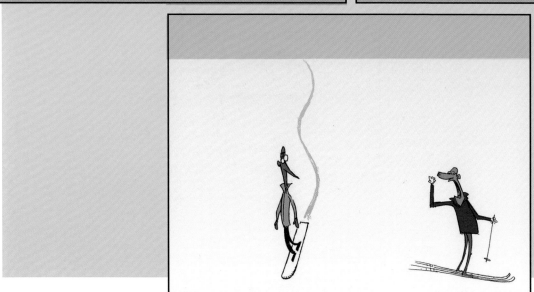

YOU HAVE NO IDEA WHY THEY CALL IT BRITISH COLUMBIA

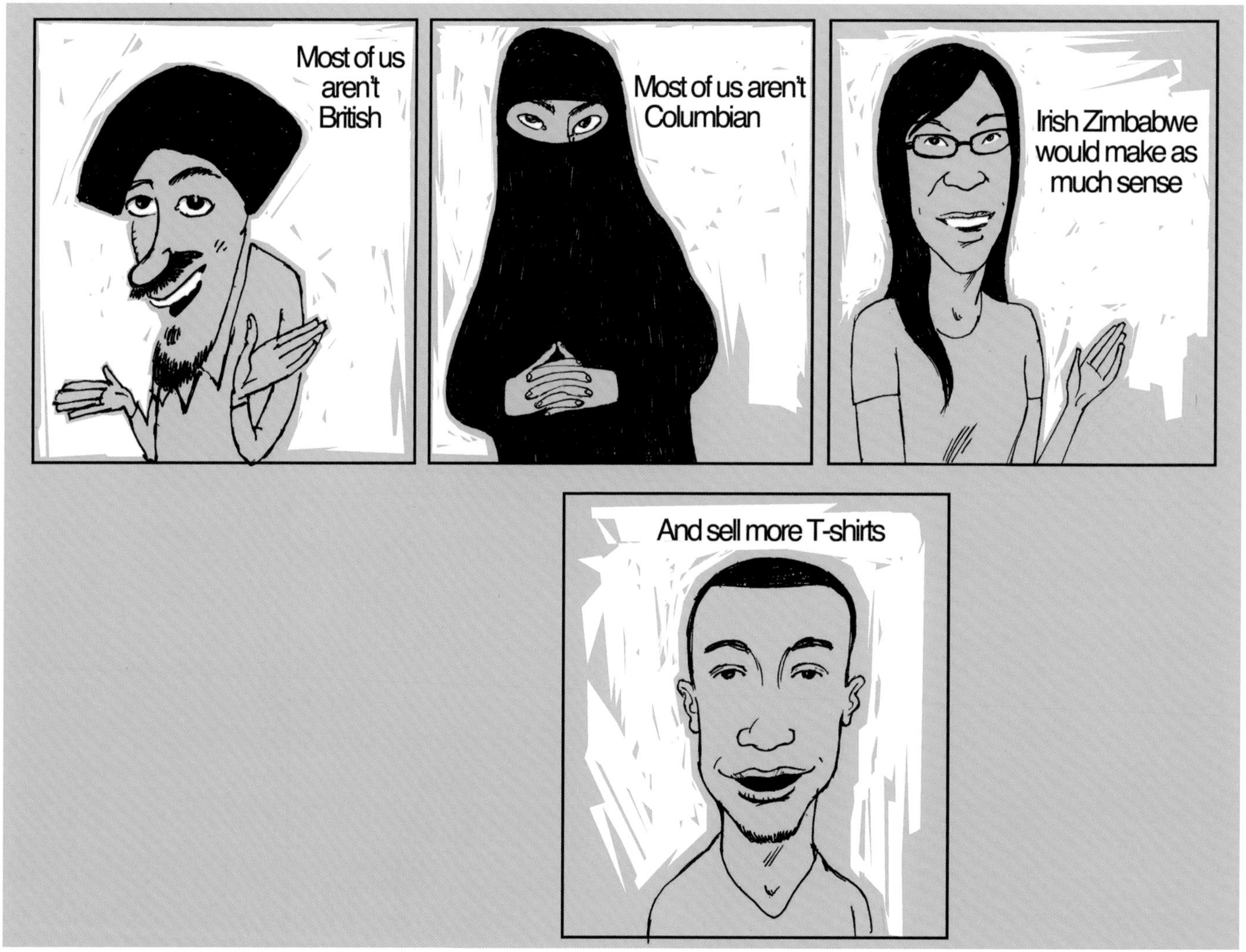
Most of us aren't British
Most of us aren't Columbian
Irish Zimbabwe would make as much sense
And sell more T-shirts

YOU'VE GONE TO OSOYOOS AND KNOW WHAT A CANADIAN CACTUS LOOKS LIKE

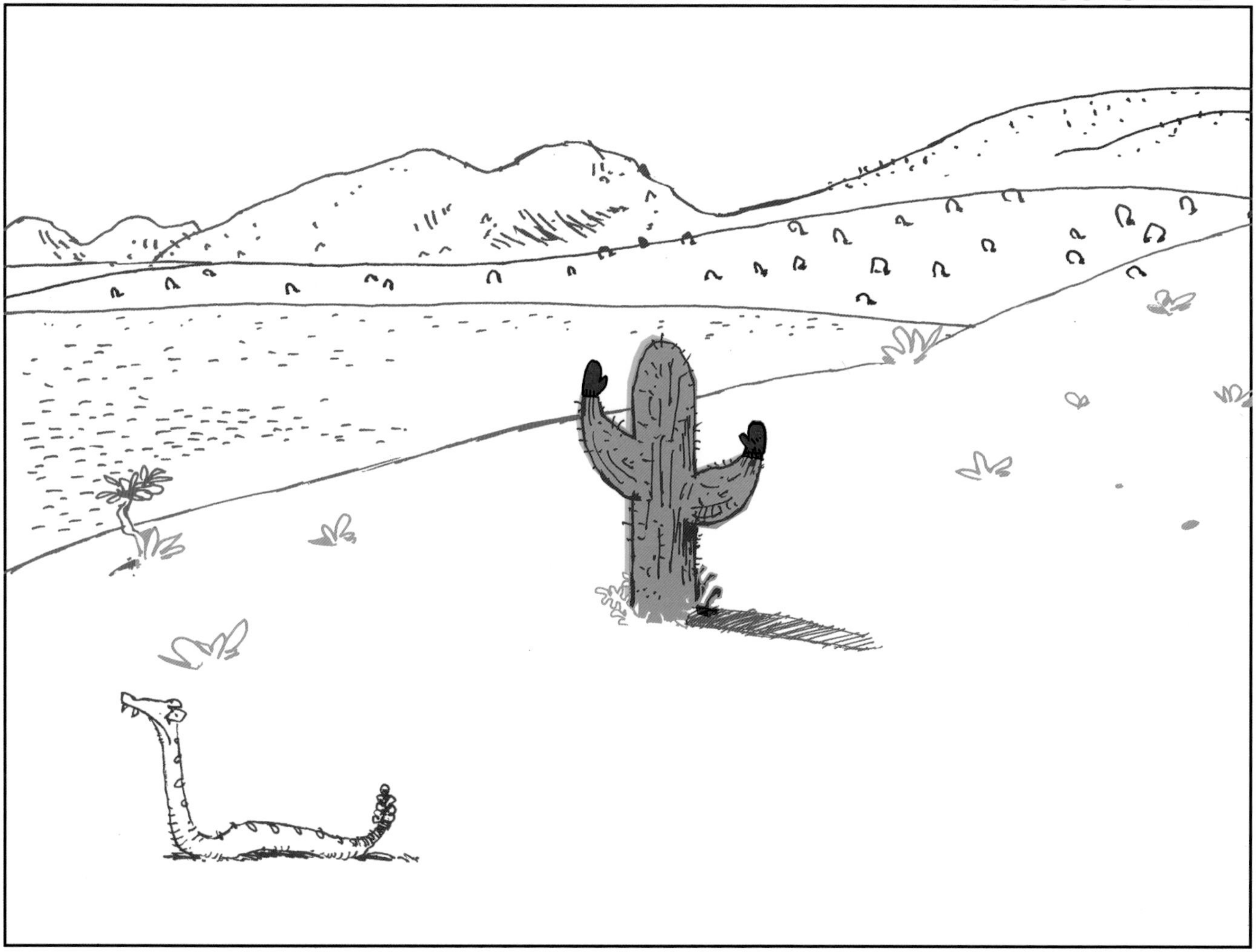

YOUR TRUCK OCCASSIONALLY SUFFERS FEELINGS OF INADEQUACY

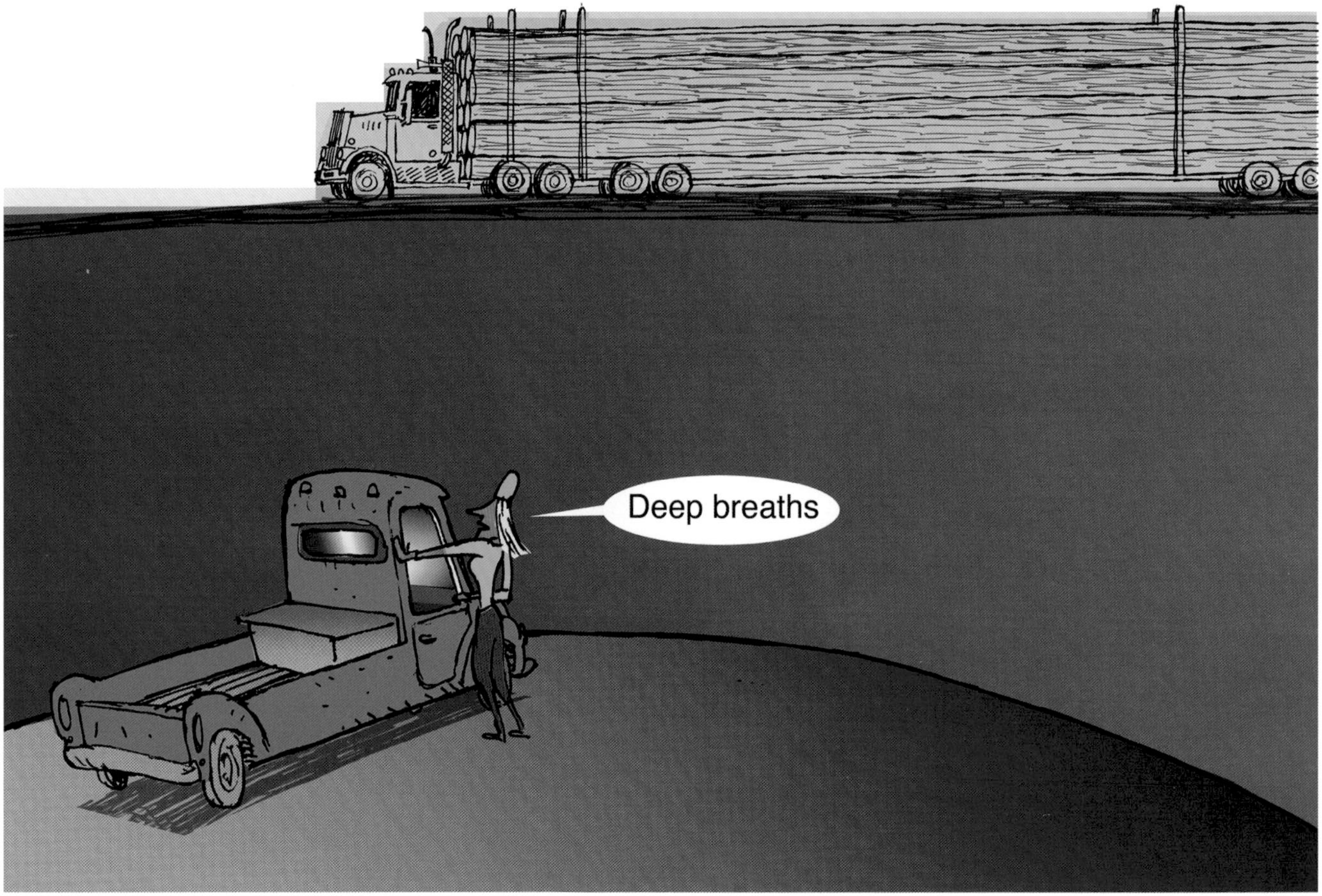
Deep breaths

YOU ARE ALL FOR GRIZZLY TROPHY HUNTING

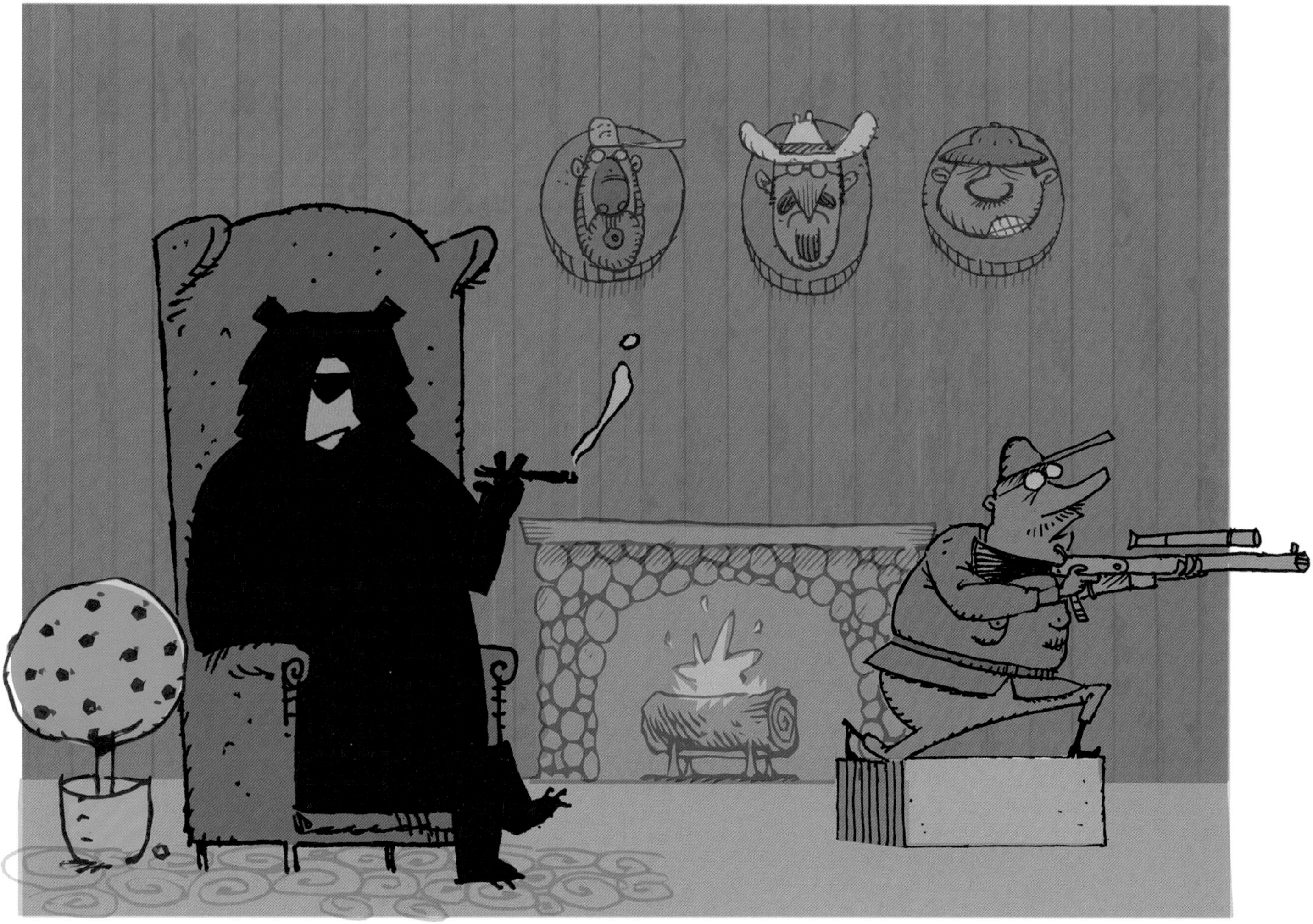

YOUR WEDDING SONG WAS BY TROOPER

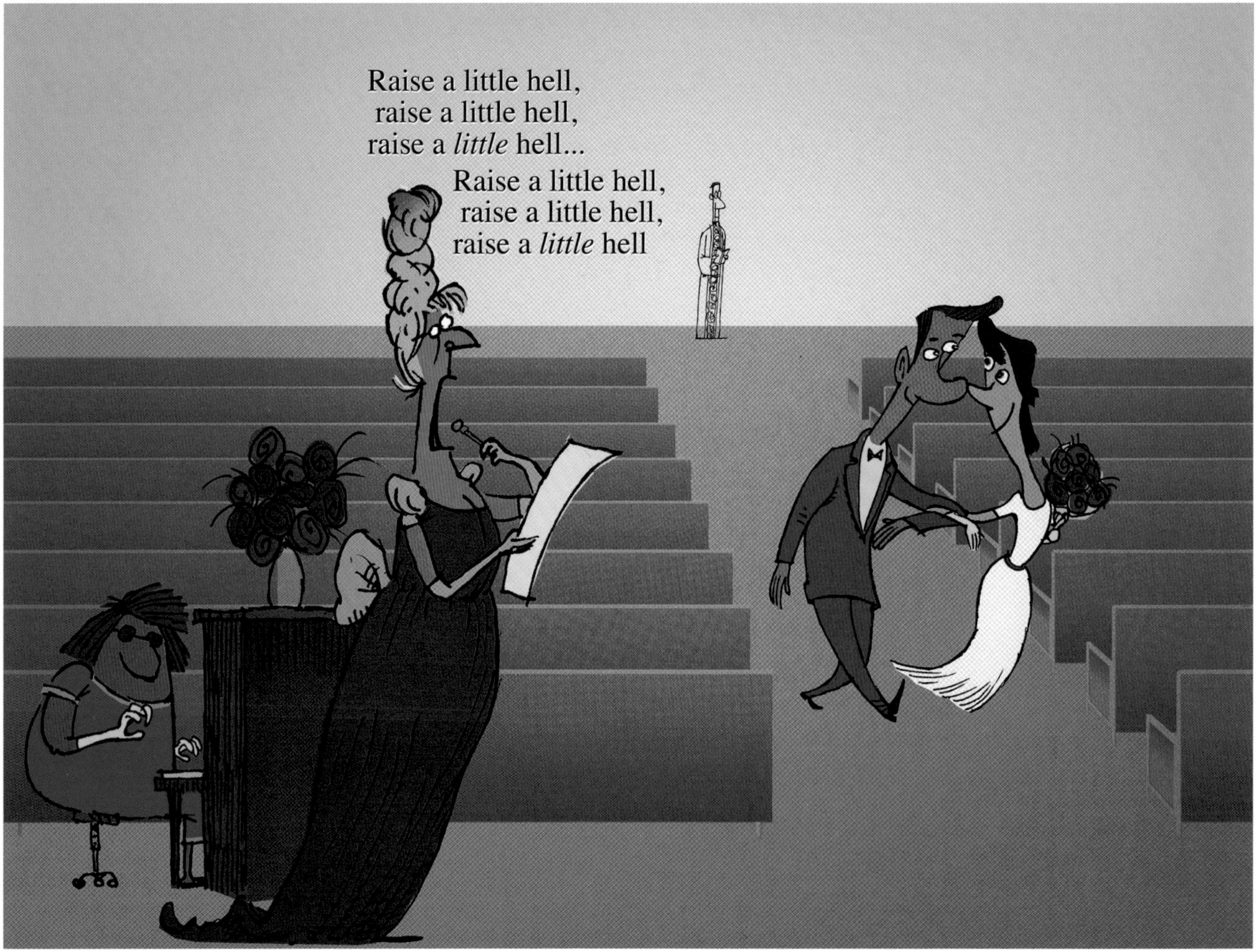
Raise a little hell,
raise a little hell,
raise a *little* hell...
Raise a little hell,
raise a little hell,
raise a *little* hell

YOU KNOW YOUR PROVINCIAL SIGNS

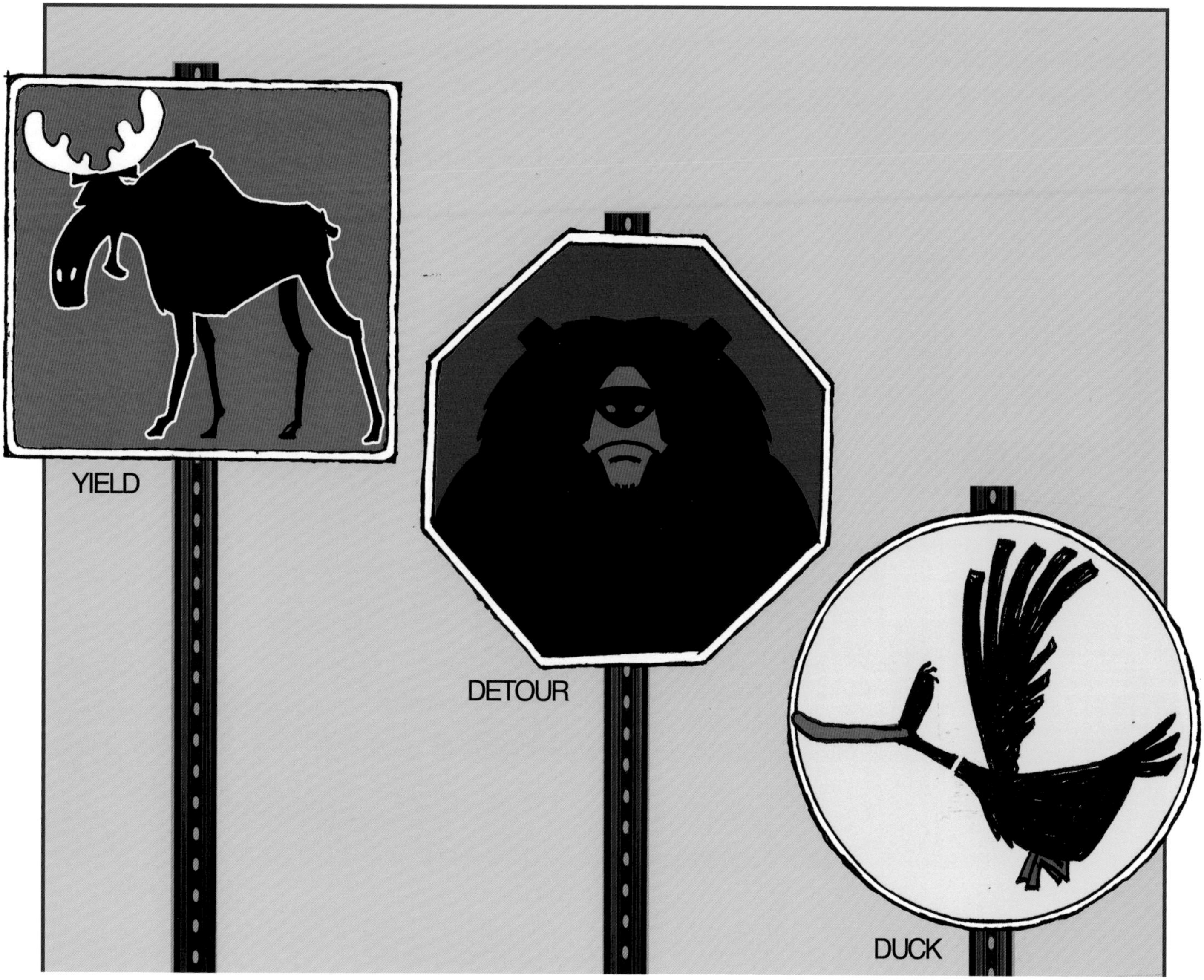
YIELD
DETOUR
DUCK

YOU KNOW YOUR SALMON

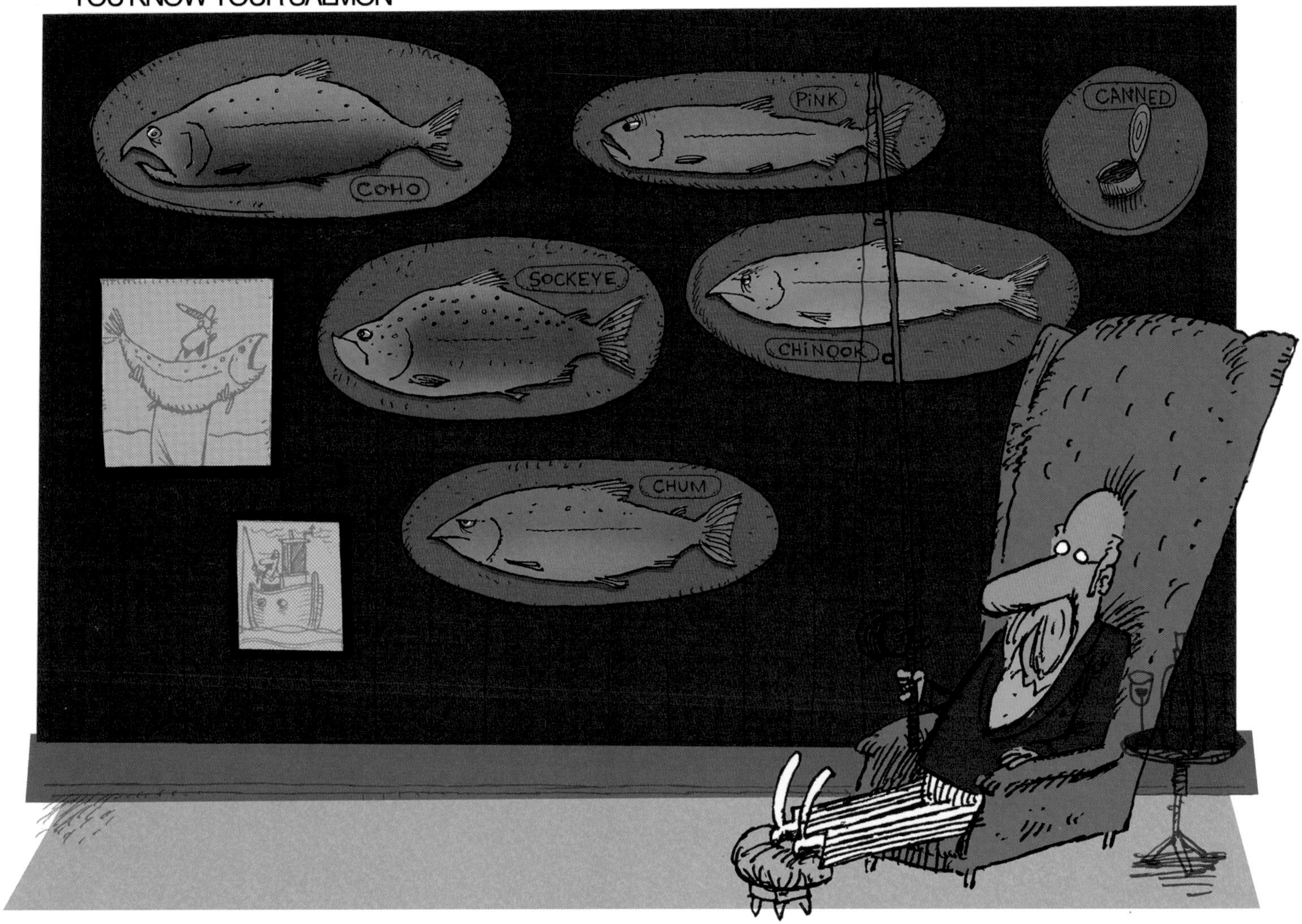
COHO
PINK
CANNED
SOCKEYE
CHINOOK
CHUM

YOU TAKE YOUR THERAPY SESSIONS IN TOFINO

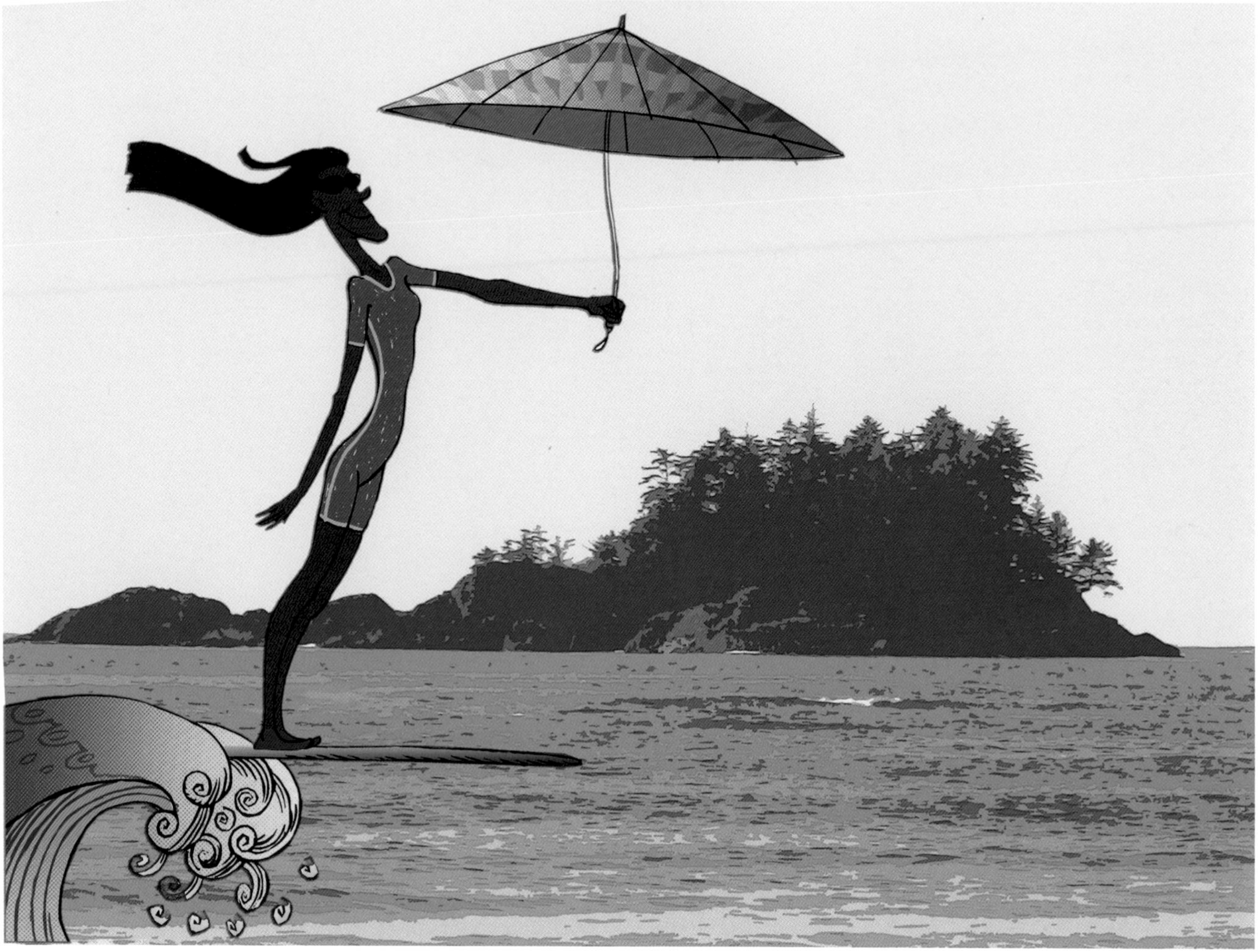

YOU'VE CONCLUDED THAT THE OATH OF OFFICE
FOR A PREMIER CONSISTS OF A SINGLE WORD:

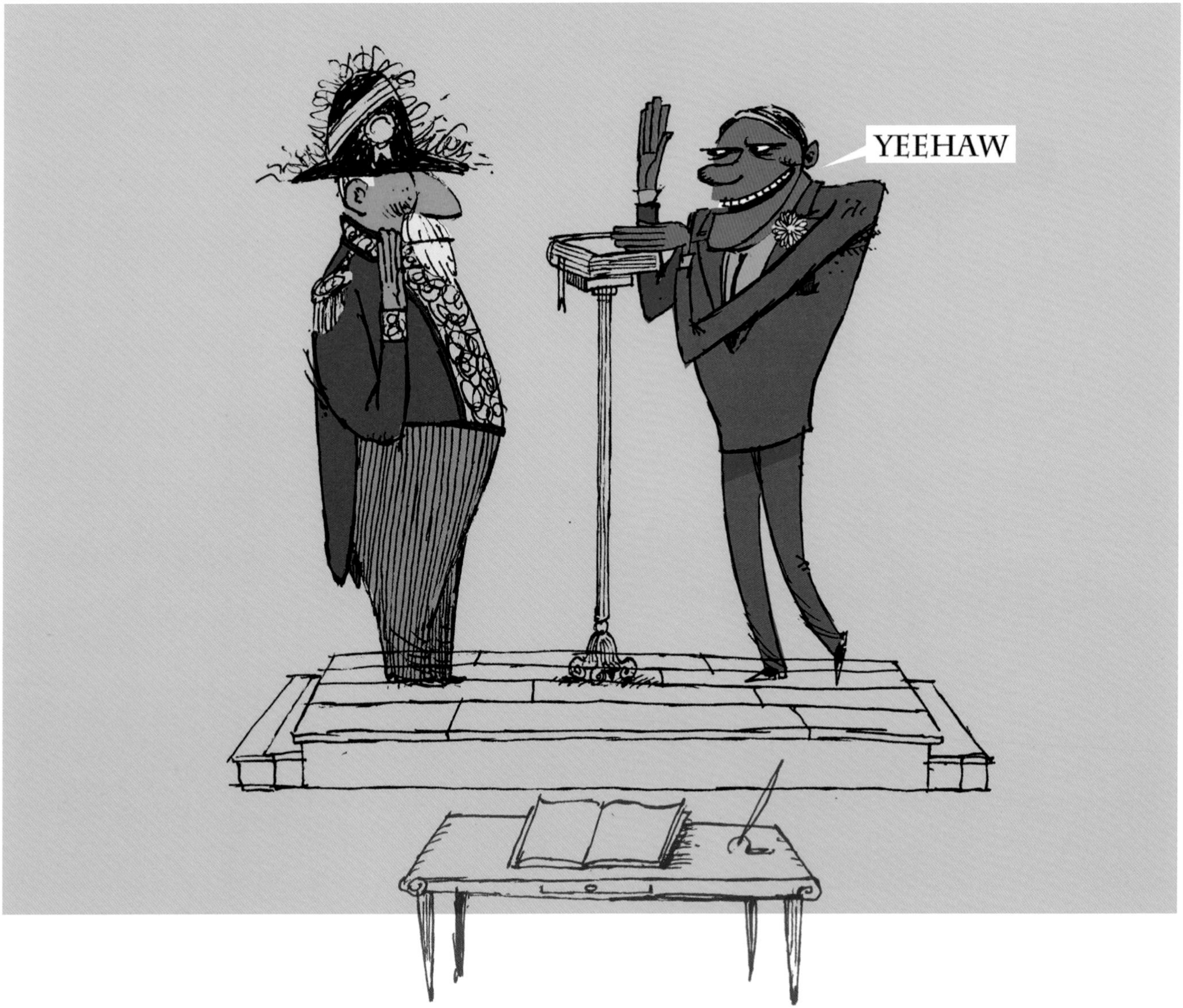
YEEHAW

AMONG YOUR KEEPSAKES OF THINGS NO LONGER AROUND: A GRIZZLIES T-SHIRT, SOCRED PARTY BUTTONS, AND FROM THE MERRITT MOUNTAIN MUSIC FESTIVAL...

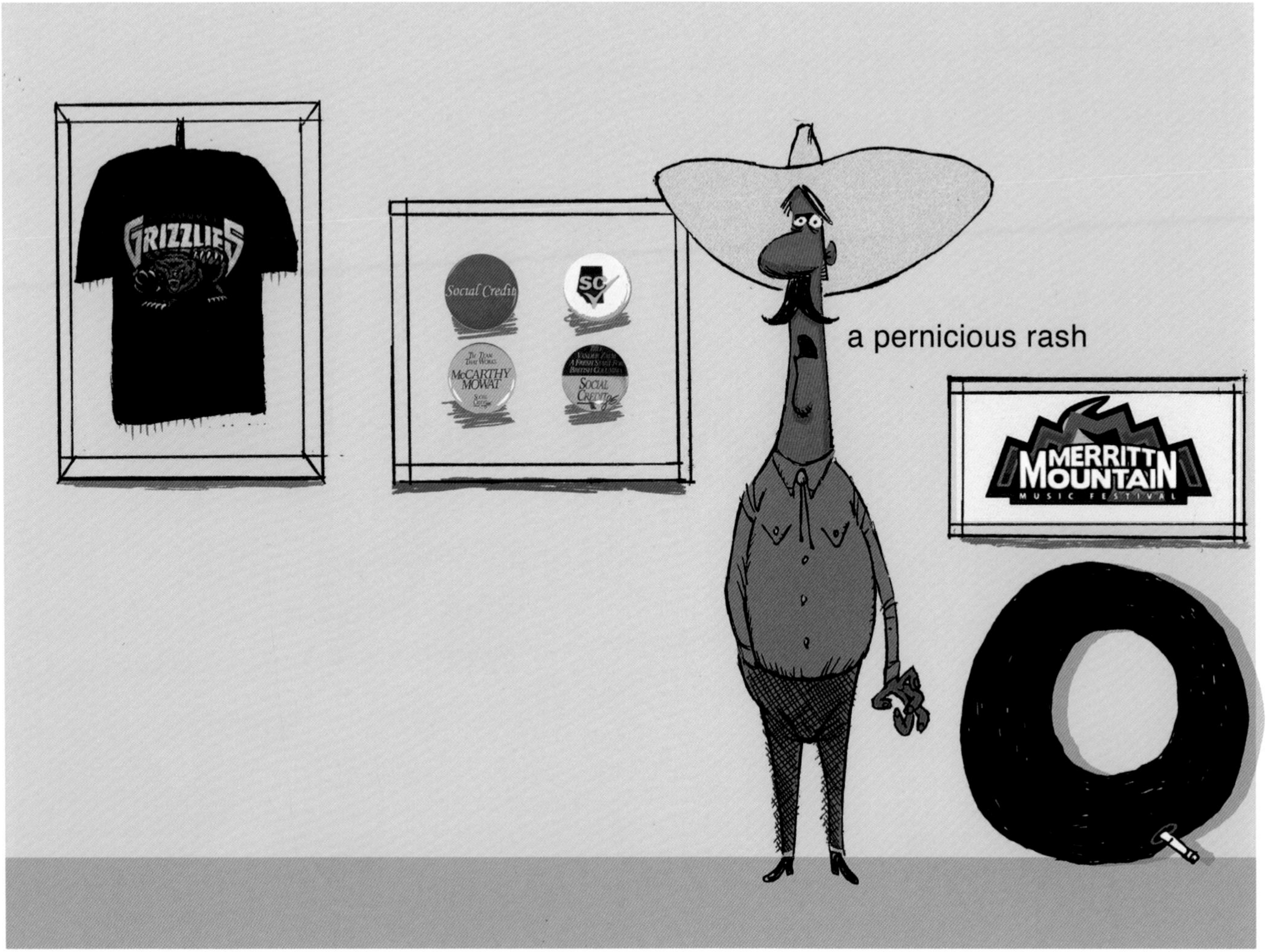
GRIZZLIES
Social Credit
SC
McCARTHY MOWAT
SOCIAL CREDIT
a pernicious rash
MERRITT MOUNTAIN
MUSIC FESTIVAL

YOUR COMPANY HAS AN EXECUTIVE NEW-AGE DRUM CIRCLE

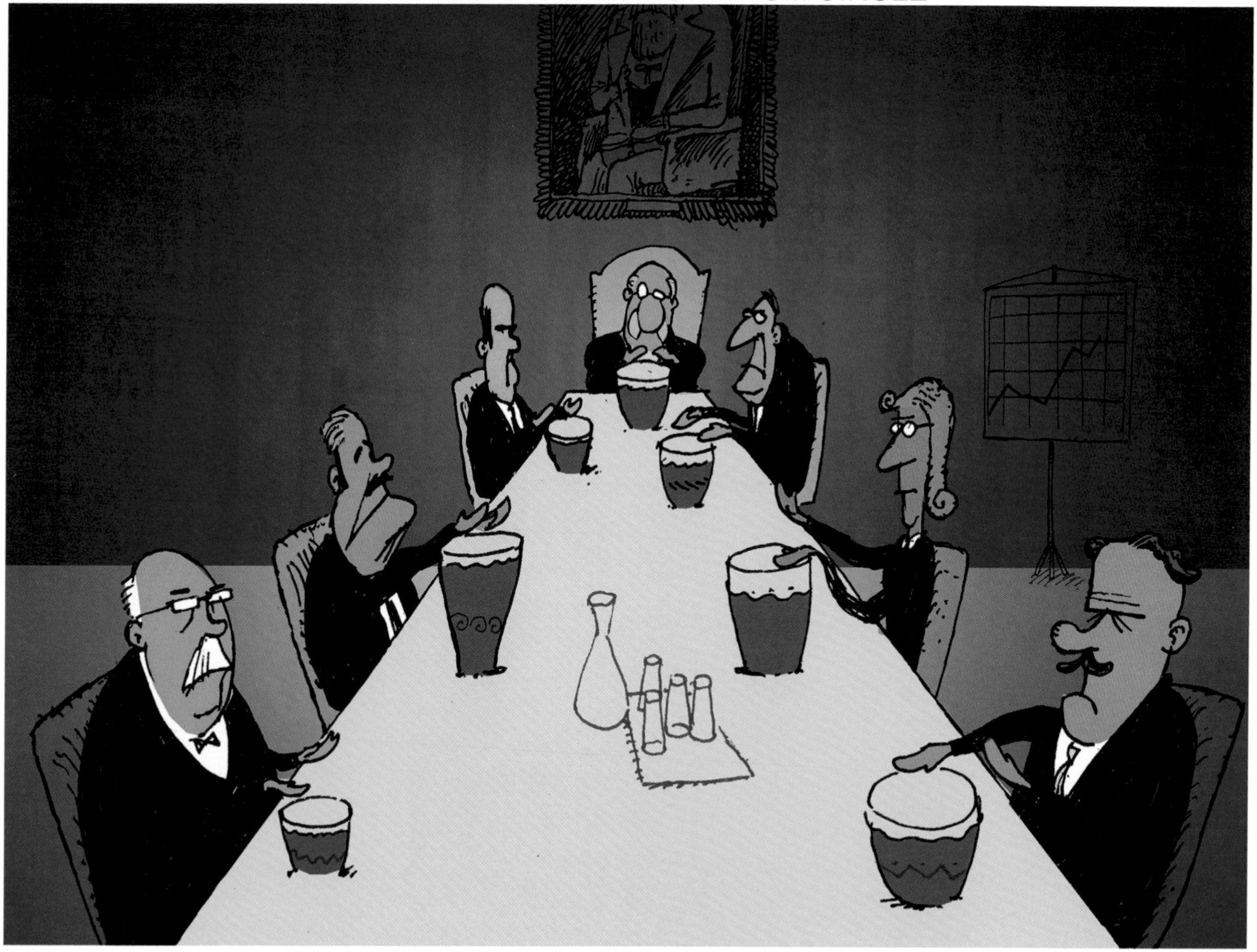

YOU KNOW WHICH TOQUE GOES WITH GIVENCHY

YOU GOT THIS BOOK FROM A HIKER IN BELLA COOLA

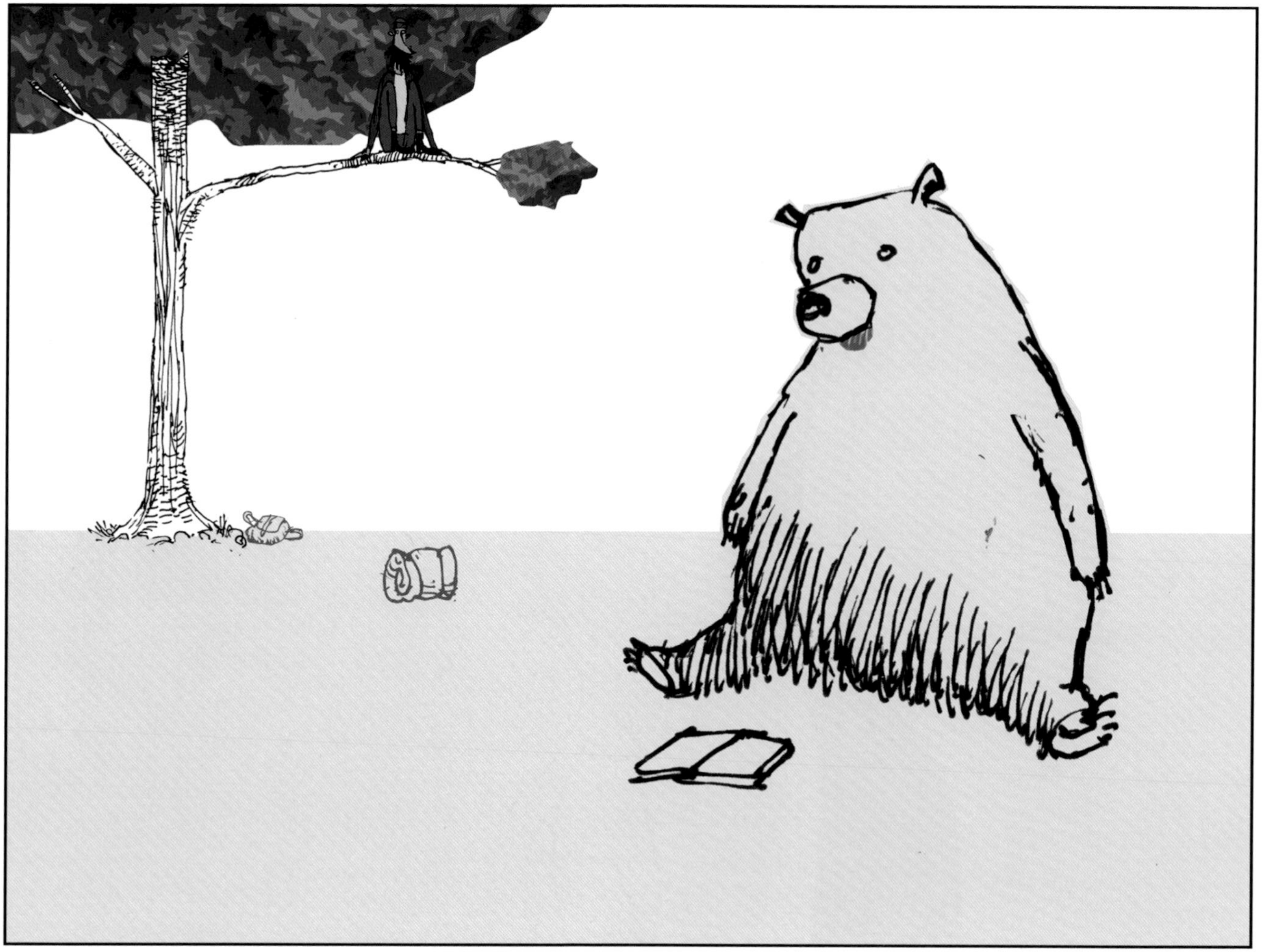

YOU HAVE, MORE OR LESS, PARTAKEN IN HIGH TEA AT THE EMPRESS

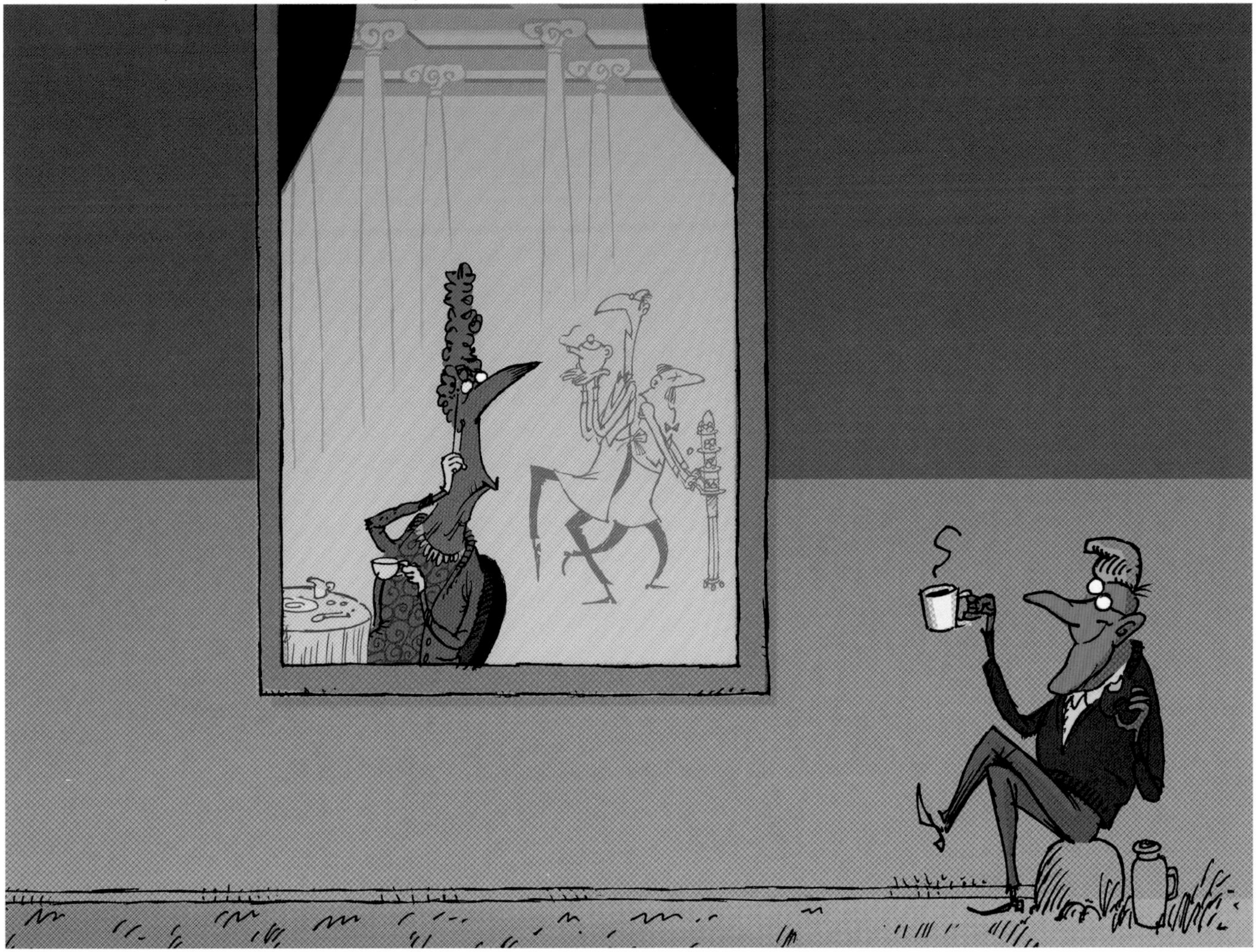

YOU LOVE B.C.

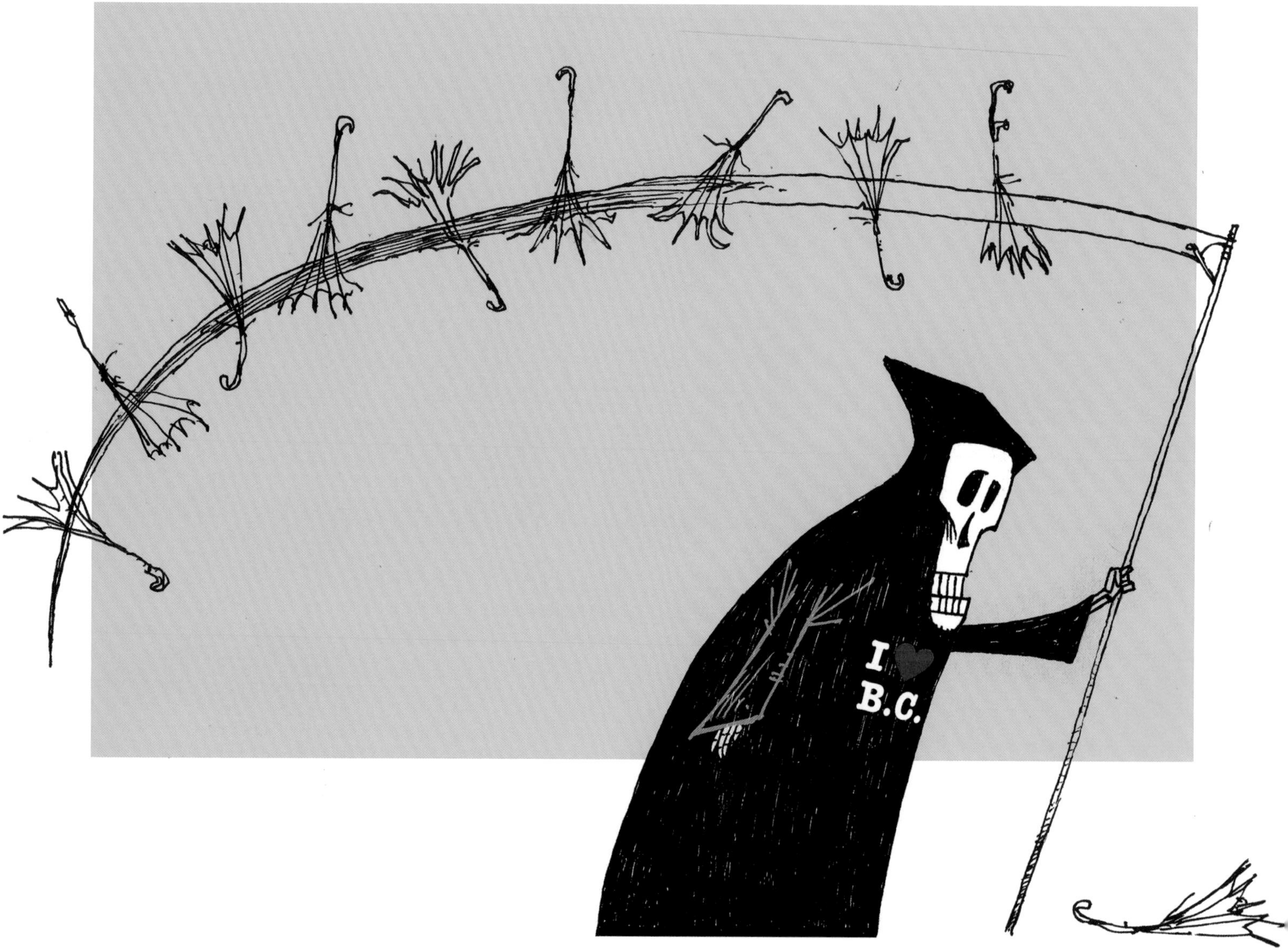

I ♥
B.C.